Tafelberg,
an imprint of NB Publishers,
a division of Media24 Boeke (Pty) Ltd
40 Heerengracht, Cape Town, South Africa
© Marita van der Vyver 2021
All rights reserved

Translated by Annelize Visser
Cover design by Michiel Botha
Set in 11.5 on 17 pt Sabon by Susan Bloemhof

Printed by **novus print**, a division of Novus Holdings

First edition 2021

ISBN 978-0-624-09004-5
ISBN 978-0-624-09005-2 (epub)

a long
letter to
my daughter
Marita van
der Vyver

TAFELBERG

In memory of Harry Kalmer and Ryk Hattingh,
whose untimely departure reminded me
that there are still things I need to say
before it is too late.

What's past is prologue.

– William Shakespeare, *The Tempest*

1

MY DARLING DAUGHTER

I should really be writing this letter in French, but a second or third language will always be a language of the head rather than the heart. And when a mother wants to tell her own story to her daughter, she has to do so in the language of her heart.

It's a dilemma, this business of living between languages, that is certainly shared these days by many Afrikaans parents who have been blown to faraway lands like the poet Van Wyk Louw's plumed grass seeds. (And the fact that our children no longer even know who NP van Wyk Louw was, is part of the dilemma.) So many of us have children who write and read and dream in other languages. Even Afrikaans parents still living in South Africa have in recent decades raised children who speak other languages.

When I was your age, towards the end of the seventies, twenty years old and on the brink of my adult life, I never dreamt that forty years later I would be living in France and have a French daughter. Although it is true that I had silly daydreams about an attic in Paris – I even wrote about it in one of my early novels, *Childish Things*, in which a teenaged main character explains why she would want to live in such an alluring attic one day:

To read lots of books while eating long loaves of French bread, drinking cheap French wine and smoking strong French cigarettes. And when I wasn't reading, I would write romantic Afrikaans poetry which I would declaim with great feeling to madly attractive Frenchmen with black eyes and sunken cheeks who naturally wouldn't be able to understand a word . . .

I never did get that attic in Paris, but a stone house in Provence instead. Nor a Frenchman with black eyes and hollow cheeks, but one with blue eyes and a dimpled chin. Who still doesn't understand a word of anything I write in my mother tongue. I may have stopped dreaming about writing poetry long ago, but in the past forty years I've written just about everything else that it is possible to write in Afrikaans, from children's books and books about food and newspaper columns and short stories to radio dramas and novels.

What I did manage to do was eat lots of French bread and drink cheap wine and smoke strong cigarettes.

That's something, at least.

The dreams of our youth never really come true, at least not when and where and how we wanted them to, and for that we should probably be grateful. But sometimes we are fortunate enough that small fragments of our dreams become our everyday reality in all kinds of twisted ways. This is what happened to me – although a French daughter was never part of even my wildest dreams.

Oh, I had wanted a daughter for as long as I could remember. It had just never occurred to me that she would live in a different language.

It's not that I didn't want a son too. In my misguided youth I thought it would be lovely to have as many as half a dozen children, girls and boys. Of course, that was when I thought I would raise them in South Africa, with family around to look after them and a domestic helper to clean up the chaos that so many children were bound to cause, while I reclined on a chaise longue like a well-to-do Victorian lady scribbling away at my next book.

And then in the second half of my life I ended up in France, with a patchwork family of four children and no Afrikaans or French family living close enough to me to help look after them. And domestic help was simply unaffordable in this new life. That was when I became grateful that the daydreams of youth don't always come true. Four children were already more than I could handle at times, trying to write in a rowdy, messy house. Another two would've driven me to despair.

Or that was what I thought. When you were small, I taught you the Afrikaans saying about Mister Thought, who planted a feather and thought a chicken would grow. You found it very funny, and even funnier when I translated it into French, because the French have no equivalent saying. Perhaps your Afrikaans ancestors were just more inclined to wishful thinking than the rational French, who account for the other half of your genes.

Now that all four children have left home and I can write in complete silence and solitude for the first time in decades (in a house that, alas, will never be tidy, as I now know, and which I can no longer even blame on the children), I hanker a little after the chaos of so many souls together under one roof. And if there had been two more, we would somehow have made room for them, too. That's something else I now know.

But I am grateful, nonetheless, that making room wasn't necessary.

My lifelong yearning for a daughter probably has something to do with an instinctive kind of feminism, because long before I'd heard that f-word for the first time I knew there was something wrong with a world in which half of humanity was held to be inferior. It had troubled me since my childhood that so many parents everywhere on earth wanted sons rather than daughters, that historically queens literally lost their heads if they couldn't bear sons, that in my own lifetime baby girls were killed or given away in countries like China where having more than one child was forbidden, that even in my own small Afrikaans world I could see that fathers were generally prouder and happier when a son was born than when it was 'just a girl'.

Perhaps it was simply that I had sided with the underdog since childhood. In any sports competition I would root for the team or competitor with the least chance of winning. In the world in which I grew up, it was evident from the start that girls were the underdogs.

I yearned for a daughter precisely because so many people didn't. As if a single person wanting a daughter with her whole heart could compensate for the contempt or disdain of millions.

Simone de Beauvoir said that one is not born a woman, but becomes a woman. That is just as true today as it was seventy years ago when she wrote *Le deuxième sexe*, or forty years ago when I read the English translation, *The Second Sex*. Being a young woman at the start of the twenty-first century is still not the same as being a young man. And in far too many countries the difference between what men and women are permitted to do remains a chasm that cannot be bridged.

That was why I wanted you, my dear daughter, and why I am writing to you now.

You arrived late in my life, when I had already stopped dreaming about a daughter. And when you've had to wait for a gift a long time, of course, you appreciate it even more.

Before you I gave birth to two sons, and for them both I cherish a love without limits. Beyond the limits of death, in the case of your eldest half-brother, Ian, who died when he was ten months old. And then your next half-brother, Daniel, came along and rescued me from the valley of the shadow of death; literally gave me the courage to carry on living after I had started to doubt whether I could.

Ian's father was an Afrikaans man with an English surname,

David Bishop; Daniel's father is an English man with a French surname, Sean Fourie; and you have a French father with a surname
that was originally Flemish, Alain Claisse. When I describe myself
as a woman who's had three children by three men, I sound like a
slutty loser from a storybook. When I add that each of these men
came from a different cultural background, each with a different
passport, I wonder whether that makes me sound wild and daring –
a fearless, liberated kind of woman like Madame de Staël, who had
five children by four men without ever ceasing to write or be a thorn
in the flesh of bombastic men.

In my younger days, long before I read this formidable French-
Swiss woman's biography, I heard something she was believed to
have said: 'To understand everything is to forgive everything.' These
seemed like magnificent words to live by, and I immediately wanted
to know more about a woman who could utter such wisdom.

I later established that the remark was attributed to Madame de
Staël, but that the exact words are not to be found anywhere in her
extensive works. What she did however write in one of her novels,
Corinne, is this:

*To understand everything makes one very tolerant, and to feel deep-
ly inspires great kindness. (Tout comprendre rend très indulgent, et
sentir profondément inspire une grande bontée.)*

Which is still an inspiring worldview, don't you think?

My admiration for Madame de Staël's political and personal daring notwithstanding, I have always viewed myself as a bit scared
and timid.

I certainly never planned to have such a multilingual and multicultural love life when I was young.

Life simply happened to me while I was dreaming of other things,
to twist John Lennon's famous phrase a little. But I did dream, from

an early age, and perhaps all courage and daring spring from the very impossibilities we dream about?

Some of my youthful dreams were so far-fetched that I couldn't even share them with my best friends or my family. For example, I dreamt that one day I would write books that would win literary prizes and make readers see the world in new ways.

This was not the sort of thing that a shy child from a middle-class Afrikaans family – that had been a working-class family barely a generation earlier – could ever say out loud without feeling ridiculous. There were no writers or artists in our family, or even among our family friends. There was no higher education. I was the eldest child and eldest grandchild, and the first on either Ma or Pa's side to go to university directly after school.

Pa had wanted to study, but his father, who was a policeman, decided that there wasn't money for university unless he wanted to become a dominee. In that event, the Lord would provide. Evidently you couldn't count on the Lord for studies in any other field. My father was a born salesman, but he never pictured himself on a pulpit, peddling God's Word to a congregation. He wanted to study business and economics, learn how to make money, how to sell houses and cars and other tangible things, not abstract ideas.

So, after matric he went to work at a bank and studied part-time for years, attending evening classes and sometimes studying right through the night, until he finally obtained a commerce degree from Stellenbosch University when he was already the father of three children. I was at the graduation ceremony in the Stellenbosch town hall, but all I remember of it are the shaky moving images on the 8-mm home movie that Pa and Ma filmed in the street outside the town hall.

Ma in a marshmallow-pink skirt suit, with this round little hat in exactly the same shade of pink stuck onto the back of her head, over a high bun. A style that was apparently considered the height of chic in the sixties, if the old photographs of Princess Grace of

Monaco are anything to go by. Me in a navy-blue dress with white socks pulled up to my skinny knees and a white hat balancing on top of my head like an enormous Easter egg. Oupa Willie, who was by then a retired policeman and hopefully still proud of his son who hadn't wanted to become a dominee, in his church suit, and Ouma Hannah in a Crimplene church dress. Pa looking delighted and swanky in the black gown he'd hired (the closest he would ever come to dressing like a dominee), holding his precious rolled-up degree certificate in one hand and tapping the palm of the other with it. Purely, perhaps, because he had no idea what to do with his hands at so big a moment, like most of us back then when we were being photographed. That was before we started living our entire lives in front of camera lenses and on cellphone screens.

What strikes me when I watch this little movie today is that all the women are wearing hats, and that all the smiling people in the background, all the new graduates and their families, are white. And although Pa's old-fashioned home movie has no sound, just this buzzing noise that sounds to me like what we mean when we say that time flies, I can see the people's lips move. I am convinced they are all speaking Afrikaans. This was Stellenbosch in the mid-sixties. As white as sin, as Afrikaans as could be.

How will I ever be able to explain that time and that place to you, my French daughter?

You live in the era of Black Lives Matter, and although many white people still insist on retorting with slogans like 'All Lives Matter', you only have to look at the family photographs and home movies from my childhood to see that only white lives mattered. This worldwide reality was caused by centuries of slavery and colonialism – and exacerbated, in my own lifetime, in my own country, by decades of apartheid. To claim that all the wrongs of the past are history, now, and that white and black lives are thus equally important, is just as untrue in South Africa as it is in America.

Or even in France, as you know.

I feel about the Black Lives Matter movement the way I do about Women's Day. I wish with all my heart that I lived in a world where it wasn't necessary to draw people's attention to any one group of historically disadvantaged people. But if any of my male friends were so bold as to ask why we celebrate a Women's Day and not a Men's Day as well, the answer would be that there are already more than 360 men's days in every year. That is why it remains essential to have at least one Women's Day – or two, if we celebrate both the international Women's Day on 8 March and the South African Women's Day on 9 August.

Women may have far more rights than before, but the historical disadvantage is a long way from being erased. The same argument applies to the BLM movement. It is going to be necessary for a long time to come, to make white people aware of the problem – without their reacting with outrage or excuses.

My only consolation in the meantime is that things have changed in my own little world. Your eldest brother's life partner is black; no one in our family doubts that Black Lives Matter. I accepted long ago that I cannot change the whole wide world, but I can raise my children differently from the way I was raised.

Which doesn't mean I spurn everything my parents taught me.

On the contrary.

Pa taught me to work hard (and play hard) and always to get back up again, no matter how many times fate pulled the rug out from under your feet. He had a deep admiration for Norman Vincent Peale's self-help guide, *The Power of Positive Thinking*, which was a worldwide bestseller in the fifties. Even as a child I would roll my eyes whenever Pa started lecturing from this capitalist bible written by a Protestant pastor, and these days I am no less sceptical about Peale than about Billy Graham and other evangelist preachers who hawk religion to get rich. Yet I do know that Pa's belief in positive thinking spurred him on to a lifetime of endeavour, to work harder and study further.

Working by day and studying by night, he ultimately obtained a master's degree in industrial psychology, long after I had left school and when I was already working on my own master's degree. Ma had also studied further in the meantime – if you can't beat them, she must've thought – and obtained a degree in nursing.

In the end, then, we became quite an educated family. But Pa's parents' intractable condition for further study – either you became a church minister, or you were on your own – roused my suspicions early on about what grown-ups wanted you to become and not become.

I was about ten years old when I confessed to one of my teachers that I was thinking of becoming a doctor. Really only because my mother was a nurse and I cherished an impossibly romantic vision of doctors and hospitals. The teacher did not think that this was a good plan for the future.

Oh no, she said, to become a doctor you have to study for a terribly long time and then it will be difficult to find a husband. You would be old already, remember, and men simply don't like women who are better educated than they are.

Oh, I said, deflated. Because I did want a husband too, one day.

Today, I'd probably have to admit that this teacher did me a favour. Her sophistry may still stick in my throat, but I probably wouldn't have been a good doctor. I never liked science or maths, physics or biology. I liked blood even less. I am glad, now, that I didn't study medicine, just as I am glad that my father didn't study theology.

Just imagine, my dear girl, if your grandfather had been a clergyman and your mother a doctor. You wouldn't have been you, right?

What you are, what you have become, with a mother who writes for a living in Europe in a language that in Africa appears to be regarded as dying out, and with a grandfather who became a businessman and married a nurse because he didn't want to become a clergyman, is a fascinating new kind of global citizen. Your life is entirely different from mine at the same age, and yet I constantly recognise myself in what you do and the way you think and the things you dream about.

When I was twenty, as old as you are now, I knew no country besides South Africa. Except for the countries in the books I'd been reading since I was a child. And, of course, the ones in the dreams I dreamt.

The first time I ever flew in a plane was at the age of eighteen, on a flight between Cape Town and Johannesburg, to go home for a university holiday. How Pa was able to afford that flight, I will never know. It was after he was declared bankrupt and the furniture was carried out of the house and he and Ma had to get divorced to keep from losing everything. Because they'd been married in community of property, all their assets belonged to both of them. After the divorce, which their children only heard about much later and which few people ever knew about 'because it was just an emergency measure', they lived together 'in sin' for several years. Until Ma insisted on getting married again, because this sinful cohabitation, emergency measure or not, wasn't a good example for the children.

Or perhaps she just wanted to ensure that Pa didn't run off with another woman when she couldn't even drag him to court.

I can therefore boast that I was at my mother and father's wedding, something not many people of my generation and with my cultural baggage can say – not in the country of my birth.

And that is something else my daughter and I share, for all the differences in our early years – the fact that we were both at our parents' weddings.

You don't remember it because you were just nine months old, but there are a few photographs of you in a white dress smiling like a little blonde angel in the arms of the bride and groom. Our own little Cupid, you might say. Of course, photographs like these are nothing special in the country of *your* birth. Many of your friends' parents also got married only after they'd had children. Some never considered it necessary to get married at all. When you were at school, the country's president and his partner raised their four children together without ever putting a ring on each other's fingers.

Since the sixties, the whole concept of 'living in sin' has disappeared from France. While my mother still fretted about this in the eighties, and young Afrikaans people were still being shunted down the aisle in their droves before the bride 'started to show', the notion of a shotgun marriage had long ceased to exist in my future adopted country.

But at the age of twenty, all that lay very far in the future.

The only time I had ever been to another country was for a couple of weekends in Mozambique during my last two years at school in Nelspruit. Lourenço Marques, as the capital was known back then, was the closest I would come to a 'European atmosphere' in my youth. Hillbrow in the seventies was supposedly also cosmopolitan enough to feel like Europe, but I don't recall ever being in Hillbrow while I was at school.

Lourenço Marques was exotically foreign and decadently colonial. Everyone spoke Portuguese and ate Portuguese food. It was where I tasted prawns for the first time – the famously large and delicious LM prawns – and I was instantly besotted. It was where I saw posters for bullfights on lampposts for the first time. I didn't necessarily want to attend a bullfight – I knew I would feel too sorry for the bulls, given my tendency to always side with the loser – but I posed in front of such a poster, smiling and eager, for a Kodak moment that would look as if it had been captured in Portugal or

Spain. That was what I hoped, at least, given that I'd never been to Portugal or Spain.

There I am, leaning against the pole (at least not up the pole, as one of my mischievous hostel mates quipped) in a short, red halter-neck dress and these platform clogs that looked a bit like the ugly Crocs of a few years ago, but which felt much heavier on your feet. An Afrikaans teenager in a wild global city. Shame.

LM was a wild global city, of course, because there you could watch movies and listen to music that was banned across the border. It was where LM Radio broadcast from – and LM Radio was as indispensable to countless South African teenagers in the seventies as radio reports from England were to the French resistance movement during the Second World War. A lifeline to hope, proof that there were people elsewhere who felt the way you did, proof that you were not alone.

In another scene from *Childish Things*, two teenage girls are listening to the very last broadcast of LM Radio's weekly hit parade – at the end of 1975, on a farm in the Lowveld near the Mozambican border, as the Portuguese colonial dream in Africa became a nightmare.

'Just imagine, one day we'll be able to tell our grandchildren that we listened to the last broadcast from LM Radio!'

'They won't know what LM Radio was,' said my practical roommate. 'They won't even know what LM was. It's getting a new name.'

Just as I was about to start feeling blue, number fifteen on the Hit Parade was announced: 'Love Will Keep Us Together' by Captain and Tenille. Dalena cheered me up with a broad smile as she hummed along with the radio.

Love will keep us together. That was what I believed in 1975, when

I was seventeen: that love would be enough to tie everyone in the country and in the world together.

And yet the country was falling apart before our very eyes. Soon many of the boys in my matric class would also be in another country for the first time, but for them there would be no cheerful posing in front of bullfighting posters. They had to cross the border between the old South West Africa and Angola as conscripts, as forced recruits rather than as voluntary tourists, to do things that they would never be able to talk about to their loved ones.

That was my youth, cut off from the rest of humanity, like living inside a bubble of blissful ignorance. There wasn't even television when I grew up, something I still struggle to explain to you and your brothers every time you father refers to a TV programme from his French childhood and I can only give a blank shake of my head. We are contemporaries, your father and I, we were born in the same year. But we were raised in different worlds.

You were barely two months old the first time you flew between Europe and Africa – and you haven't stopped travelling since. You have been to Florida and New York in the USA, Tokyo and Kyoto, Amsterdam and Brussels and London and Venice, and several other European cities. Paris too, of course, but Paris – which had been an almost impossible dream for me in my youth – is just another French city to you, like Lille or Lyon, Marseille or Montpellier. A place where everyone speaks your language and where the food tastes familiar and the shops look familiar. Not nearly as exciting as foreign cities in faraway countries. You've dreamt of Cape Town since you were young the way I once dreamt of Paris – oh, the irony of fate – with the very important difference that you know what you are dreaming of because you have been to Cape Town several times. While I had to dream blindly, trapped inside my bubble.

Besides physical journeys, there were also the mental journeys you could venture upon from childhood, thanks to the internet and social media and the availability of culture all around you. You had barely started school when you watched Robert Aldrich's *What Ever Happened to Baby Jane?* with two of your brothers, all three of you complaining because your father and I were 'forcing' you to listen to the original American soundtrack rather than the dubbed French version. The old black-and-white movie with Bette Davis and Joan Crawford nonetheless left a lasting impression on all three of you.

And these days I hear you explain to your French friends how important it is to watch any movie with its original soundtrack, 'whether it is English or Arabic or Japanese'. Just what your father and I always told you.

Forgive me if it sounds as if I'm gloating about this small victory. A triumph of any kind is rare when you are raising children.

I almost said 'as you too will discover one day'. But I stop myself from entertaining such expectations of you. Who is to say that you will want to raise children one day?

I want my daughter to have choices, and having children should also be a choice. My great-grandmothers, whom I will tell you about in this letter, did not have that choice. They produced offspring year after year the way animals do, and like good Christian women prayed that at least some of the litter would survive into adulthood.

And they existed in a cultural wilderness, without the solace of great art or music or literature. Nothing but the Bible to comfort them.

Whereas you grew up in a forest of books. You were surrounded from birth with far more books than there ever were in my childhood home. Not that mine was entirely devoid of books, there's no need to feel sorry for me, but it definitely wasn't a book forest. The bookshelf in my parental home was more like a neat suburban garden. You'd come across nothing wild or unexpected there.

There were several encyclopaedias, and the Reader's Digest condensed versions of popular novels, and the comic-book versions of classics such as *Robinson Crusoe* or *Robin Hood* that Ma would buy us three children ahead of every long car journey. They were the only comics she condoned. All the rest – about American superheroes who could fly, or the even more alluring local photo stories such as *Mark Condor* and *Ruiter in Swart* – we were forced to read surreptitiously at the café or in the domestic helper's room. Pa's little paperbacks about the Wild West, written by Louis L'Amour, were allowed inside the house even though Ma probably turned her nose up at cowboy stories. Yet this American author, whose French surname was far better suited to soppy love stories, taught Pa the kind of life lessons that he would sorely need a good few times in his life.

There will come a time when you believe everything is finished. Yet that will be the beginning.

That selfsame cowboy-writer's wise words.

Ma was a passionate reader and her favourite genre was historical fiction, preferably British historical novels by popular writers such as Georgette Heyer, which she borrowed in vast numbers from the library. And she took us children along to the library from the start. I have an idea that the most passionate readers are born rather than made, and I was a born reader like my mother. My brother and sister also became enthusiastic readers in their adulthood, though, thanks to a reading mother who frequently took us to the library to choose our own books.

You were still a baby when you started coming to the library with us. And because you are the *laatlam* in the family, our bookshelves were already filled with enticing children's books. Your tastes, then, developed much faster than mine. You were barely seven when you confidently declared that *Alice in Wonderland* was the best book in the world. I had also read it as a child, but only realised years later what a miracle of a book Lewis Carroll had really created.

At the age of sixteen, rummaging through a pile of secondhand books at our neighbouring village's annual flea market, you picked up a weathered paperback copy of Camus's *L'Étranger* (*The Outsider*) and asked me what it was about.

'Well, it's quite difficult to describe,' I hedged. 'Camus was a philosopher, you know.'

'I know,' you said. 'And you know I like philosophy. Do you think I'll enjoy it?'

I recalled that as a thirteen-year-old you had devoured Jostein Gaarder's *Sophie's World*. And that your eldest brother was writing his doctoral thesis in philosophy. Philosophy didn't scare you – it fascinated you. I did think, though, that Camus's existentialism of the absurd might be a little advanced for a sixteen-year-old who had, until then, read mostly *Harry Potter* and John Green's modern young-adult novels.

But I didn't want to tell you that you were too young. It's a phrase I'd had to hear too often when as a curious child I'd wanted to read more widely than children's books.

'Why don't you try reading it, and decide for yourself?' I suggested.

You dived into that book the way one might dive into a cool mountain pool on a hot summer's day. Started reading in the car on the way home already, as if it were a gripping detective story, and didn't stop until you got to the last page. You read it a few more times after that.

'I don't understand all of it,' you said, 'but I love it.'

To me it seemed like a perfect example of the kind of enchantment you can expect when the right reader and the right book find each other at the right moment. It isn't rational, it cannot be predicted or explained, it's just, well, a kind of magic.

Your enthusiasm inspired me to read *L'Étranger* again too. I had forgotten – how could I have? – about those two opening sentences, still among the most striking first lines of any book. You read them in French, the way Camus originally wrote them. I translated them into Afrikaans for you, so you could hear what they sounded like in your mother's tongue. But in my student years I read them in English:

Mother died today. Or yesterday, perhaps, I don't know.

I still can't tell you 'what it is about', because like any good story it is about many things, but it starts with a son's relationship with his mother – and it ends with the death penalty. Camus himself said, 'In our society, any man who doesn't cry at his mother's funeral is liable to be condemned to death.' He later added, 'I only meant that the hero of my book is condemned because he does not play the game.'

Cordelia, the youngest daughter in Shakespeare's *King Lear*, also refuses to play the game – with tragic consequences for everyone. And as I type these words, it dawns on me how many books have been written through the centuries about the relationships between parents and children. It is probably the oldest and most universal story in the world, because we are all somebody's child. Even if we grow up without parents, even if we don't have children of our own, we all arrived on this earth as somebody's child.

The Bible is full of stories about what parents and children do to each other. In Genesis already we encounter Abraham, who is prepared to slaughter his only son like an animal, and Jacob, who deceives his father by pretending to be his own brother, and from there on it only gets worse. You don't know the Bible nearly as well as your mother does, because you grew up in a far more secular society. I regret that – not the secular society, but all the wonderful stories you will probably never read.

Fortunately, to compensate for your deficient Bible knowledge, you know a lot more about Greek mythology than I did when I was your age. You know the story of Oedipus, who unknowingly kills his father and marries his mother, and probably also that of Orestes, who deliberately kills his mother in revenge because she conspired with her lover to murder his father.

But I wonder if you know that clever Shakespeare borrowed this ancient story about Orestes to create *Hamlet*. Or that Orestes's father wasn't quite the innocent victim of female guile that Orestes wanted to believe him to be. Orestes's mother took her own revenge because his father had sacrificed their daughter Iphigenia to the gods – to turn the winds in his favour so his sailing vessels would reach Troy faster, where he wanted to wage war.

Which brings us back to the Bible, with a father who is prepared to kill his own child to pander to a heavenly power. And because I am a mother, who would not be able to bear it if my husband murdered my child, my sympathy has always leaned towards Orestes's mother. But ultimately all these ancient stories only serve to confirm Philip Larkin's poetic words: *They fuck you up, your mum and dad. / They may not mean to, but they do.*

That is another reason why I want to write you this letter. To apologise for all the unintentional and unconscious ways in which I may have, well, hopefully not fucked you up completely – let's just say for all the times I've disappointed you.

Disappointment is part of even the most beautiful love affair, part of life itself, but thank goodness forgiveness is also part of love. And thank goodness not all stories about parents and children are about twisted relationships. It may be the oldest story on earth, but it remains a story with endless possibilities.

And on the subject of disappointment, I may as well confess that I am disappointed that, in the past year or two, since leaving school, you are reading less than you used to. But not too disappointed, let me immediately add, because I recall how you rapped me over the knuckles just recently. 'Ma, just because you read *thousands* of books, it doesn't mean that I also have to!'

With typical teenaged hyperbole, I thought.

It is true that you still read more than most of your friends. But it is also true that you inhabit a world where images have become so much more powerful than words – and now you are studying in a visual field as well. You are learning to design video games, you create the characters, the background, the storyline.

At first I struggled to understand why you had chosen video games. Growing up, you never spent hours playing video games the way your brothers did. Like most girls, you preferred to spend your free time on social media, or you watched YouTube videos or made your own. Sometimes you even read old-fashioned books.

Until the day you explained to me that you wanted to create stories.

'Like you, Ma. I want to create stories but I want to do it with images rather than words. Video games are stories for the twenty-first century.'

Now I understand.

My own story I am nevertheless going to tell you in old-fashioned words – and hopefully I will create enough images with my words to hold your attention – so that you will know where your mother and your mother's mother's mother come from. And your mother's father too, of course, and that father's father's father. When you know where you come from, you don't lose your way so easily.

That is my hope for you, my dearest girl. That you won't get lost too far away, and for too long. Getting a little lost is indispensable. They say you do not really know a city until you have lost your way in it. I think that also applies to life. You haven't truly lived if you haven't strayed from the straight and narrow. Sometimes, like

Little Red Riding Hood, you have to wander off onto all sorts of footpaths to pick flowers and face wolves. Just ask your mother.

As long as you don't wander so far off that you cannot find your way back home.

And your home – just ask your mother – isn't Paris or London or Cape Town. Your home is anywhere on earth where your heart is. My heart is rooted in my language, and my language, as Fernando Pessoa said, is my only home. That is why I initially told this story in Afrikaans, knowing you were more likely to read this translated version.

Believe me, I am glad that I can talk to you in Afrikaans, particularly as several of my Afrikaans friends' children around the world no longer understand Afrikaans, but I realise that the language in which you read and write is the language in which you learnt to read and write at school. French, first, and then English. That is why I am especially grateful for translations.

Without translations I could never have read Pessoa's Portuguese words, would probably not even have known that he also grew up in South Africa. Without translation his magisterial *The Book of Disquiet* would simply have sailed past me, like those ships he writes about so movingly:

There are ships sailing to many ports, but not a single one goes to where life is not painful.

My own ship and those of my ancestors also carried us to places where life was painful. I want to tell you about these places, but also about the joy and wonder and beauty we discovered in every harbour.

Here begins my story.

2

ONCE UPON A TIME

I was born into words. Not book words – those only came later, when I began to read and write. (And after that, nothing would ever be the same again.) But in the beginning were spoken words and listening words. Rhyming words and magic words. Songs Pa sang to us and fairy tales Ma told us.

Daar's 'n apie op 'n stokkie voor my ma se agterdeur. According to Pa, this fun little rhyme about a monkey on a stick was my earliest performance of spoken-word poetry, long before I was old enough to remember such things myself. Like any young father, mine also believed that his first-born was the cleverest child on earth, and all visitors to our house were therefore compelled to listen to the baby rapping: *Daar's 'n gaatjie in sy broekie en sy stertjie loer daardeur.*

Words were all around me while I was growing up. Stories and anecdotes, lyrics and legends, sacred words and swearwords. Sacred words that could become swearwords and swearwords that at times sounded almost sacred. The never-ending miracle of words.

When as a young adult I was finally brave enough to embark on Nabokov's notorious novel *Lolita*, the opening paragraph knocked me off my feet.

Lo-lee-ta: the tip of the tongue taking a trip of three steps down the palate to tap, at three, on the teeth. Lo. Lee. Ta.

I am still struggling to get back up, in fact, even now, because how does a lover of words ever recover from such a sentence? The full glory of words – not just the way they look on paper, but also how they are shaped in the mouth to enchant the ear – that was what Nabokov revealed for me here.

Marguerite Yourcenar writes that the written word taught her to listen to the human voice, in almost the same way that the great classical statues taught her to appreciate physical movement. Life leads us to art, in my experience, then art leads us back to life.

And the art of writing begins with the sound of words. Everyone's first words, except for those of deaf babies, are heard, rather than seen, after all.

Unlike you, my girl, I didn't grow up with the ancient myths. In my early years I knew nothing of Greek or Roman or any other gods, except for the Big Guy in the Bible. *In the beginning was the Word*, I heard in church as a toddler. I didn't realise that it was a capital-letter word with a mystical meaning. It simply sounded right that everything should begin with words.

A word often seemed lovelier to me than the thing it referred to.

The word 'Vredelust', for example – the desire for peace – was far lovelier than the modern facebrick building, with its high-pitched roof and a steeple as sharp as the wrath of God, where the Dutch Reformed congregation of Vredelust gathered on Sundays.

It was the first in a long line of ugly Dutch Reformed church buildings in my life. Of course, not all Afrikaans churches are unsightly. In some of the older towns in the Western Cape there are stately snow-white buildings with elegant steeples, and the Free State is famous for its beautiful sandstone churches. But I grew up in the country's new suburbs, during the sixties and seventies, when new buildings were needed to accommodate growing congregations. And in the land of my birth, this was not exactly the golden age of religious architecture.

To this day, I suspect that church services on Sundays would have felt less like punishment if they'd been held in a more aesthetic environment. From childhood I yearned for an Anglican stone chapel surrounded by centuries-old gravestones, a Catholic cathedral with candles and paintings, a blue-domed snow-white chapel on a Greek island. That I had only ever seen such buildings in pictures did not make the yearning any less.

On the contrary.

And to this day I don't like organ music. Sorry, I know Bach's organ compositions are supposed to be heavenly, but they just bring up too many earthly memories. Of sitting quiet as a mouse, sucking on a peppermint, surrounded by women sprayed with too much cheap perfume and men who smelled of tobacco, to the sober drone of the shiny organ pipes.

Fortunately there were words in all the ugly churches too. I adored the lyrics of the old hymns, the psalms, the hallelujah songs. 'The Lord is my shepherd', 'Jesus loves me, this I know', 'O come all ye faithful'. I didn't know what 'ye faithful' meant, but I sang along with gusto because it sounded so beautiful. 'You in your small corner, and I in mine'. I heard 'a mine' and wondered what kind of mine I was singing about – was it a gold mine or a coal mine? And what was I doing in the mine? And why couldn't I come and sit in your small corner too?

The singing and the fascinating lyrics were really the only enjoyable parts of the church service – until they went and changed the words.

Then, all that was left were the Bible words, sometimes equally incomprehensible and yet also irresistible. *Let there be light. The valley of the shadow of death. I lift up my eyes to the mountains.*

But more enchanting than any Bible words – far, far lovelier, the way Snow White was far, far lovelier than her cruel stepmother – were the words of fairy tales. That I knew from the start.

Once upon a time.
This is how all stories begin.

It is how my own story must begin as well, because when I was born in the late fifties, the eldest child of Yvonne Swart and Danie van der Vyver, my parents, my grandmothers and grandfathers, my uncles and aunts, had long been characters in their own stories. I grew up with the stories they told, the funny family anecdotes and the heartrending legends that, constantly repeated, turned into the most delightful yarns. Not that all my ancestors were liars, but any story handed down from generation to generation inevitably gets distorted.

Like *telefoontjie* – the 'telephone' game my English friends called Chinese whispers – where everyone sits in a row and the first person whispers a phrase in the second one's ear and the second one whispers whatever they heard in the ear of the next person in line, and so on until the last one says the phrase out loud. And then everyone falls about laughing because the phrase that finally emerges is usually altered beyond recognition. 'Monstrosity' becoming 'warm sausage tea'.

And if by some chance a rude phrase could be conjured up from the original words, we laughed even harder. Because 'dirty words' and scatalogical innuendos were always hilarious. Some words, which usually had to do with certain body parts, were so forbidden that we couldn't say them at all. When we absolutely had to refer to our genitalia, we used pet names like *tottermannetjie* or *snoefie*.

Always diminutives, of course, a linguistic quirk of Afrikaans speakers and just another one of our many weird habits that I battle to explain to you, like why we kiss each other on the mouth.

In France, of course, the mouth is reserved for romantic and erotic kisses. But that was how I was raised, my child, weaned on words, my little boat bobbing on a sea of stories. Everything was true, the lies sometimes even more so than the so-called truth I would later be taught at school, and that was how I understood instinctively from childhood that more truth may hide in fiction than in boring factual books.

My father's mother, an Afrikaans Johanna Maria Saayman who, somewhere along the way, became an anglicised Hannah, was raised in a family of sixteen children in the vicinity of Riversdale. To me – with just one brother and one sister – growing up with fifteen brothers and sisters seemed inconceivable. Something that belonged in a storybook. No wonder I reached back to this romanesque family when I started to write *Entertaining Angels*. Like many fiction writers I packed bits of my own history into my first adult novel, like the raisins or nuts you add to a pudding to make it taste better. The raisins aren't the most important ingredient – you're writing fiction, after all, mixing the batter in your imagination, but the raisins make it personal. *Your* pudding, and no one else's.

'My prettiest sister died of wet hair,' Grandma Hannie always told her. 'One evening she got caught in the rain and she went to bed with damp hair. The next morning she was lying in bed with her hair wound round her body like a golden cloak. Stone dead.'

Grandma Hannie was the youngest of sixteen children who had all come to bizarre ends.

One brother broke his neck when his horse shied at a ghost one night . . .

It was the ghost of the sister with the wet hair, the family whispered. She was taking revenge because he'd snipped off a tress of her hair after her death. He'd apparently wanted to give his daughter a doll with real hair.

The real Ouma Hannah did indeed have an exaggerated fear of wet hair, and from childhood I was warned of dire consequences if

I didn't dry my hair properly before going to bed. And there really was a story about a sister who got very ill. I can't remember whether she survived, but I later realised that Ouma Hannah had been a child when the so-called Spanish Flu hit in 1918. If her big sister got the flu that year, she would more than likely have died, even if her hair had been bone dry.

This is perhaps a good example of how a sterile fact can be fertilised by a rich imagination to give birth to fiction.

But it is important to bear in mind that raisins are a manufactured product. They are grapes that have been dried. I suppose you could say that the true events of my life are the grapes. Whenever I want to use 'the truth' in a story, I first need to turn the grapes into raisins. Every time.

Ouma Hannah's large family spent the Christmas holidays in Stilbaai, back in the days before it became Noisy Bay. That was how she came to refer to this bustling coastal town where she and my Oupa Willie van der Vyver retired, and where I also spent many holidays as a child. Back then, Stilbaai was still a village without stop signs or shopping centres, although a bridge did connect the caravan park in the East with the harbour in the West on either side of the river. In Ouma Hannah's day, they went on holiday in ox wagons and horse-drawn carts and were ferried across the river in a pontoon – and that pontoon would be overloaded almost to the point of sinking with everything needed to sustain such an enormous family throughout the festive season, from live chickens for slaughter to canisters filled with rusks and biscuits to jugs of ginger beer. And clothes, of course, dresses and hats and bonnets, because in those days girls wore a great deal of clothing, even in summer, even on the beach. And they always had to have a hat or bonnet on their head.

Until the day she died at about ninety, Ouma Hannah could pride herself on the loveliest peaches-and-cream complexion, the result surely of protecting her face against the sun from childhood. As an adult she never used expensive skincare products. Her policeman husband controlled the purse strings too tightly for any such vanity. But she was of a generation that believed a pretty girl didn't have to look like a thin slice of bread that had been toasted too long. A white *mosbolletjie*, soft as a pillow, that was more my ouma's style.

I was unfortunately born two generations later, a pale blonde who longed to be browner and, as a teenager, also thinner and harder, more English toast than Afrikaans *mosbolletjie*. So I spent hours frying my skin in the sun on that same Stilbaai beach, often with a rumbling tummy, not because there wasn't food in the house, but simply because I believed that the thinner I was, the more desirable I would be. With neither hat nor sunscreen, take note. Without anyone ever warning me against premature wrinkles or skin cancer.

Or perhaps Ouma did warn me that a girl should keep her face out of the sun. Just like she warned me that whistling girls and crowing hens always come to some bad end, and against doing needlework on Sundays (not something I ever felt like doing on any day of the week) because 'you'd be sticking the needle in the Lord's eye'. She also tried to convince me that my frayed jeans made me look poor, fashionable or not, and on one occasion she turned up the hems on my new jeans with meticulous and loving care – after I had spent an entire afternoon unpicking the hems because I was aiming for a scruffy look.

But of course no one listens to their grandmother.

Nor did I listen closely when she talked about those long-gone family holidays in Stilbaai. Or about how the Saaymans had to leave the farm and move to the city during the gruelling years of the Great Depression. They ended up in a working-class Cape Town neighbourhood like Epping or Maitland, where her mother had to turn their home into a boarding house to keep the vast family alive.

These reduced circumstances were a heavy blow to the young Hannah Saayman, who had dreamed of becoming a music teacher but in the end couldn't even finish school.

Of course, now that there is hardly anyone left whom I can ask about my grandmothers' and grandfathers' histories, I regret not listening more carefully when they talked about their younger days.

Especially this Ouma Hannah, who really, really loved to talk.

When she and Oupa Willie had retired to Stilbaai, they would still sometimes visit us in the suburbs of Cape Town, to see doctors or to shop, and often use the opportunity to see a movie as well. And if Ouma enjoyed a movie, she liked to retell it to whoever was prepared to listen, from the opening scene to the final scene, in the finest detail. Pa and Ma were seldom all that keen to listen, but they'd be trapped inside their bedroom in the evenings when Ouma and Oupa would come home from the bioscope, and then Ouma would simply plonk herself down on the bed and start talking . . .

The concept of the spoiler meant nothing to her. She might even have thought she was doing Pa and Ma a favour by giving them a blow-by-blow account, so they wouldn't have to spend the money on seeing the movie themselves.

She was a proud woman, proud of her Van der Vyver husband and her four Van der Vyver children, but nothing made her prouder than her Saayman background. If her children or grandchildren displayed a talent of any sort, for anything from playing the piano to counting their toes, she put it down to their Saayman blood. Or it was the Kasselmans' good genes – her mother had been a Miss Kasselman. Between the gifted Saaymans and the virtuous Kasselmans the table was set where talent was concerned, with precious little room for any other guests.

I believed until just the other day that the Kasselmans had injected a bit of German blood into my gene pool. The same way I believed that the 'saay' in Saayman meant 'sow' and that the surname referred to a man who planted seeds.

Imagine my surprise, darling Mia, when I heard that while the Kasselmans may in fact have hailed from the German university town of Kassel, they could equally have originated in Cassel in the Flemish-speaking north of France. And of course I don't know which Kasselmans I come from, because I didn't listen when my grandmother talked about her family.

It amuses me nonetheless to think that it could have been the French Cassel – because that is a stone's throw from Lille, where you father grew up and where all my French in-laws still live. It is almost too good to be true, for a storyteller who is always looking for storylines, that I may unknowingly have completed a circle when I married a man from the north of France. And I know that Ouma Hannah would have loved this story, whether or not it was true.

I also discovered only recently that Saayman is most likely a distortion of Seeman, which means that this grandmother's ancestors weren't seed-sowers or farmers as I had always believed. Not people from the soil, but people from the sea. Like the Van der Vyvers, who once upon a time lived beside fish ponds – *visvywers* – near the sea. Which means that sailor blood runs even more thickly in my veins and in the veins of my loved ones than I had realised. Not only was Ma's Scottish ancestor a sailor on a ship that ran aground off the Cape coast, but it turns out there were seafaring Dutchmen on Pa's side too.

The part of my ancestry that I am most proud of these days is also thanks to the Saaymans. The legendary Khoi woman Krotoa, who is the subject of several books and movies, had a daughter called Pieternella (the eponymous protagonist, along with her mother, in Dalene Matthee's novel, *Pieternella, Daughter of Eva*). This daughter got married in Mauritius to one Daniël Zaaijman, a cooper originally from Vlissingen in Zeeland. Pieternella and Daniël returned to the Cape and became the founders of the South African Zaaijmans, Zaaymans, Zaaimans, Saaymans and other versions of the same surname – even a few anglicised Simons.

This I only heard about after my grandmother had died, and that may have been just as well, because I don't think she would've been particularly proud of being a descendant of Krotoa. She was a product of her age, and in her day Afrikaners certainly didn't boast about their 'non-white blood'. Today we have scientific proof that all old Afrikaans families had non-European ancestors as well. Of the mishmash of mainly Dutch, French, German, English and Scottish genes, more than three per cent can be traced back to the slaves who were brought to the Cape Colony from other countries. And around one percent of the genetic cocktail comes from the Khoisan, who truly were the 'first people' at the southernmost tip of Africa.

It is without question something to be proud of, in these times of racial friction where white South Africans are frequently told to 'go home' by black South Africans, back to Europe where their ancestors came from. Like the writer Thomas Wolfe, I believe that you can never go home again – especially not when your 'home' is on another continent. But if anyone in my native country ever dared tell me that I didn't belong there, I would at least be able to produce my foremother Krotoa from the !Urill'aelona tribe as my trump card.

And yet the most important reason for my pride is more personal. Krotoa was apparently a clever child with a gift for languages, a girl who even as a teenager had already mastered Dutch and Portuguese and became an interpreter between the European colonists and her own people. From an early age, then, she earned her living from words. It is only natural that, more than three centuries later, I still feel an affinity with her and her work.

Because I have also had to act as interpreter, between my own background in Africa and the French environment where my children live, every day for the past twenty years, I know how terribly difficult it can be, sometimes, to reconcile different worlds.

Pa's father, Willem Johannes van der Vyver, was a fairly rare phenomenon in the Afrikaans rural community of the early twentieth century. He was the only child of Danie and Nelie van der Vyver, also from the Riversdale region. As far as I know, there was no brother or sister lost in infancy. It was always just him and his parents.

I can scarcely imagine what a shock it must have been for a shy only child – he was not a talkative, gregarious man – to find himself amid Hannah Saayman's enormous family, with such a multitude of brothers and sisters and cousins. I assume that some of Hannah's siblings died before they reached adulthood, but there was still an awful lot of them left. Perhaps, like so many only children, Willie had dreamed of a bigger family. But to acquire more than a dozen brothers- and sisters-in-law so suddenly must have been terrifying all the same.

Of my eight great-grandparents, only Oupa Willie's parents were still alive when I was born. Of my great-grandfather Daniel Cornelius van der Vyver I remember nothing, aside from a few blurry images of his funeral in Riversdale. I was so young when he died that I am almost convinced these images were constructed from what grown-ups would later tell me rather than from my own experience.

And yet.

I have a faint memory, like fragments of a dream that you struggle to piece together, of a large farmhouse in the Riversdale district where our family stayed over either before or after the funeral. It wasn't the departed oupa's farm – he had died in a modest little house in the town – but perhaps a house belonging to a brother or a nephew. And I remember it as a haunted house, with unearthly sounds in the night, like chains being dragged across wooden floors. I even remember one of the grown-ups saying something about the house being haunted by a slave, and my being afraid of the slave ghost for years afterwards. But I couldn't mention it to Pa, because he would just have laughed and said that ghosts don't exist. And Ma would have comforted me and started talking about something else to distract me.

I still wonder about the slave's chains clattering across the wooden floors. Had it all just been my overeager imagination? Not only the sound of the chains, but the memory of the sound of the chains too?

How will I ever know?

My great-grandmother I remember well, because I was already at school when she died. And Pa filmed her for one of the first home movies he made with his 8 mm camera. Nelie van der Vyver, born Cornelia van Zyl, was a tall thin woman in black with snow-white hair scraped back into a tiny knot behind her head. Of course she hadn't worn black clothes or had white hair all her life, but after her husband died she only wore black. In those days the period of mourning for widows was seven years of black dresses, apparently followed by seven more years of purple and sombre colours, and given that Ouma Nelie died when she was still in her black period, I never saw her in any slightly more cheerful colours again.

Sometimes I try to picture her in purple attire, like in Jenny Joseph's beloved poem, 'Warning'. (*When I am an old woman I shall wear purple / With a red hat which doesn't go, and doesn't suit me.*) But my great-grandmother just wasn't the sort of woman who would do silly things in old age to make up for the sobriety of her youth. She would be sober and clad in black until the day she died.

Oupa Willie wasn't a very tall man, but he was as thin and sinewy as his mother, and as sober too, until he also died when he was already in his nineties. What I remember about him in particular is that he was unusually dark-skinned – browner, in fact, than many people who were classified as 'coloured' during the apartheid years. And that this dark skin may have been a source of embarrassment to Ouma Hannah.

I heard her say any number of times that Willie had jaundice as a baby – a severe case, it seemed, that had caused his skin to go dark. I swallowed the story hook, line and sinker, of course. Years later I learnt that untreated jaundice in babies could indeed have serious consequences, such as hearing loss and even brain damage. But I have never heard of another baby who sustained a lifelong change in skin colour.

Willie was a hard man – you had to become hard as nails if you wanted to be a policeman in the Old South Africa – who beat his eldest child and only son with a police sjambok until blood ran. It was not viewed as abuse – it was simply corporal punishment in those days, recommended by the Bible. *Do not withhold discipline from a child; if you punish him with a rod, he will not die. You shall beat him with the rod, and shall deliver his soul from hell.* That is what it says in Proverbs 23. And Oupa Willie took every bit of advice in the Bible very seriously.

His eldest son, Danie, later became my father, and although he was never as devoutly religious as my grandfather, he nevertheless continued the family tradition of corporal punishment for his only son. My father beat my brother with the belt of an old Voortrekker uniform – a choice of rod that strikes me as no less telling in its irony than my grandfather's police sjambok – but at least not until blood ran. And my brother never had any children, as you know. The tradition of Van der Vyver fathers who beat their sons hopefully ended with my father.

In fact, the entire Van der Vyver line, with or without heavy-handed fathers, would have ended anyway had I not been so bold as to become an 'unwed mother' and pass on my maiden name to my son. My grandfather had been an only son, my father an only son, my brother an only son, and my Daniel is once again the only Van der Vyver son.

I didn't realise how important the tradition of family names was to Oupa Willie when I was young. In old Afrikaans families the first-born son was named for his paternal grandfather and the first-born daughter was named for her maternal grandmother. Then the second son was named for his maternal grandfather and the second daughter for her paternal grandmother, and the third son got the father's name and the third daughter her mother's name, and if there were still more children (and in old Afrikaans families there were frequently more, as evidenced by Ouma Hannah's multitude of brothers and sisters), they would be named after other relatives. But most important of all was the eldest son's name, because he was responsible for continuing The Line. The daughters would lose their surnames anyway when they got married, and if they didn't marry, well, it was unthinkable for any decent Afrikaans woman to have a child outside of holy matrimony.

I know, my girl, you were born outside of holy matrimony, just like your brother Daniel, and in France no one bats an eye about it. In France I am generally considered a decent woman. But had I lived in South Africa during the first half of the past century, I might have been as scandalous as Nathaniel Hawthorne's Hester Prynne, with a big red letter A for Adulteress pinned to my chest. A scarlet woman, long before Margaret Atwood's fictitious handmaids with their red cloaks became a new kind of scarlet woman.

(Two books, by the way, that you really should read when you get the chance, *The Scarlet Letter* and *The Handmaid's Tale*; there are all sorts of dots that can be joined to form a clearer picture of unwed motherhood through the ages.)

There were 'indecent' girls in the old Afrikaans families too, of course, ironically enough often the victims of their own innocence and ignorance, but a pregnancy out of wedlock was such a blot on the family name that the girl was usually rejected, banished to the most distant darkness of a wicked city life, as far away as possible from her rural family. Or the 'bastard child' would be hidden or given away, or raised as a *laatlam* by its grandmother, without knowing that his sister was in fact his mother.

It was a different era. A different world. That is the only way I can explain this sort of cruelty to my children.

In my Van der Vyver family, where for several generations there had been just one son, an unusually heavy burden of responsibility rested on these only sons to carry on the family name. My father got his oupa Daniel Cornelius's name, and my father's son was supposed to be named after his oupa Willem Johannes – but then my mother went and put a spanner in the works. She was probably ahead of her time, but she couldn't see why children had to be burdened with a string of old-fashioned family names if they ended up being called something else throughout their lives. No one ever addressed my father as Daniel Cornelius. He was Danie, Daantjie, Daan, DC, but never Daniel. My mother wanted her children's Christian names to be the names by which they were known.

Such a simple idea – and yet also radical enough to cause a revolution, like so many simple ideas in history.

My mother came from a family where the men on her father's side didn't set such store by the continuation of The Line. Just as well, since she had no brothers and The Line came to an end with her and her only sister in any event. Her mother named her Yvonne, a nod to the French Huguenots from which that mother was descended, and that was all. No second name. My Huguenot grandmother had good reason to be suspicious of family names, and especially of second names, but that is a story for another day. For now, suffice to say that a single Christian name that would also serve as your given

43

name throughout your life was extremely rare among Afrikaans girls who were born in the early thirties. My mother was Yvonne, and nothing but Yvonne, until the day she died.

(She did relinquish her surname when she married, though. Her rebelliousness did have its limits.)

Ma was pragmatic enough to realise that she couldn't break away from family names altogether. She chose evolution over revolution. I was the eldest daughter, therefore I was (kind of, in a way) named after my mother's mother, the very same Huguenot grandmother with the unmentionable second name that I will tell you about shortly. Ouma Tina's first name, Martina, became Marita. Just that, no second name, a Christian name that would also become my given name for the rest of my life. Ma also chose the easiest spelling possible, not Marieta with an e or Maritha with an h or Marietha with both an e and an h, because she hoped that it would make my life easier.

That hope was dashed, Ma had to admit later on. Most people still want to write it with either an e or an h. Some even with both an e and an h.

And my French in-laws cannot pronounce it at all. I became 'Megite' to all your father's brothers and sisters and to all my French friends.

But that is not my mother's fault. How was she to know that I would one day live in another country? Besides, I am grateful every day that I have only one name for the French to mangle. Imagine having to haul a long trail of Afrikaans family names through my French life.

My sister was christened Hanli, because she was (kind of, in a way) named after my father's mother, the Johanna who became Hannah.

The grandmothers accepted it, even felt flattered that they'd ended up with namesakes one way or another. It was when my brother had to be christened that the story turned into a drama. My mother wanted to call him Wiaan, kind of named after his paternal grandfather, Willem Johannes, but she surmised that this grandfather wouldn't be satisfied with 'kind of'. That was why she made an exception and gave him a second name. He was christened Wiaan Johan – not the full family names, to be sure, but at least with the same initials as his grandfather, so that there would be another WJ van der Vyver in The Line.

Oupa Willie was still not satisfied. Ma and Pa hoped he would accept it, in time, but it never happened. To him, a grandson with the same initials was like a bouquet of artificial roses. They might look like real roses, but they had no scent. And he knew his roses, this green-fingered grandfather. My brother was already heading into adolescence when Oupa begged Ma and Pa one more time to change the child's name to Willem Johannes. He even offered to pay for an official name change.

That was when Ma realised how strongly he felt about the matter, because Oupa Willie didn't like to pay for anything.

'If I had known it was that important to him,' Ma said, 'I suppose we could have christened the child Willem Johannes.'

But by then it was too late. You don't tinker with the name of a child who is already almost a teenager. Besides, by this time my brother himself had a say in the matter, and he wanted to stay Wiaan rather than turn into Willem.

Like my mother, I couldn't understand the Van der Vyver men's obsession with family names. And yet I named my son after my father, because I realised how happy it would make my dad. Perhaps I had learned from my mother's experience with the Willem Johannes saga.

What I most certainly did learn from my mother was to insist on my child's Christian name also being his given name.

I have always thought Daniel a desirable name, more desirable than Daantjie or Danie or Daan, so it wasn't difficult to name my son Daniel. And although I didn't know when he was born that he would one day grow up in France, it is fortunately also a name the French are familiar with and can write and pronounce. Unlike mine.

In France, where corporal punishment has long been prohibited in schools, no teacher ever hit Daniel. And given that there has never been any violence in his home environment, it is almost unthinkable that this youngest Daniel van der Vyver in The Line might one day become a father who hits his son.

Your French grandfather never raised his hand against your father – or against any of his eight children. And they did not become criminals or devil worshippers, as my Afrikaans ancestors feared would be the fate of children who did not know corporal punishment. They became responsible adults who do not hit their children.

When I mention almost in passing that even I as a girl received corporal punishment from teachers at school – on my hands and not on my backside, which I suppose is something to be grateful for – I can see the shock in your and your brothers' eyes.

I know I grew up in a cruel, religious society, I know that the country of my birth has become a place of terrifying violence where fear reigns supreme, I know the government has been reproached for years because 'nothing is being done' to reduce violent crime. And yet, when the Constitutional Court recently decided that it was against the law for parents to beat their children, the announcement was met with furious indignation. 'Why don't they stop the farm murders and the gang violence instead? Or all the men who murder their wives? Why come and interfere with our right to beat our own children?'

I observed this indignation from a distance, with a growing sense of despair.

46

Nearly all violent criminals were once children who were raised violently. Some are still only children when they become criminals. How do you ever break this chain of violence if you don't start with the way children are raised?

'My love she speaks like silence,' Bob Dylan sang when I was a teenager. I was crazy about the song, mostly because I misunderstood the second line, much like I had misunderstood that hymn about sitting in some kind of mine. Instead of 'without ideals or violence', I heard 'with no idea of violence'. Now there was something to strive for, I thought. Being someone with no idea of violence. When I finally realised that it was 'without ideals', I was quite disillusioned. Who wants to live without ideals?

But more than four decades on, I still think it would be wonderful to be someone with no idea of violence.

Wonderful – and impossible, if you were born where I was born.

Fortunately I never got to know Oupa Willie's cruel side. I remember him as a prim and quiet man – not a sports enthusiast or a passionate rugby supporter like my father and so many other Afrikaans men; gardening was his only pastime and his greatest passion. His flower garden in the Cape Town suburb of Thornton was a feast for the eye, with roses and dahlias spilling onto the sidewalk and a small pond with goldfish in the centre of a modest little suburban lawn. During his retirement years in Stilbaai, he got an impressive vegetable garden going behind the house and spent most of his time there.

The only earthly possession that he was really attached to was his car. Not an expensive or flashy car, just a little jalopy, really, but always buffed to a shine on the outside and pristine on the inside. His car offered a degree of independence, even after he and Ouma Hannah became too frail to live on their own and moved into Stilbaai's old-age home. By his late eighties his hearing was very poor and his eyes not much better, which made him a menace behind the wheel, but he stubbornly kept on driving. At least no longer on the open road, definitely not to the city, just trundling around Stilbaai, mostly. Especially during the off season, in the quieter parts of the town where many residents knew his car and probably rushed to get out of the way when they heard him approaching in the wrong gear.

On one occasion Pa drove with him to Riversdale and spotted a couple of geese crossing the road, from a distance. 'Deddy,' cautions Pa well ahead of time, 'there are geese in the road.'

But Deddy doesn't hear him, because he's deaf, and it doesn't look like he sees the geese either, because he's not slowing down.

'Deddy!' Pa says again, louder and with urgency, as the geese are a lot closer now. 'There are geese in the road!'

Deddy doesn't even brake.

'Deddy!' Pa shouts when they hit a goose and feathers fly everywhere. 'Now there's a dead goose in the road!'

'Never mind, they're Gert's geese, he has plenty,' says Deddy as he drives on, unperturbed.

That was the last time Pa got into the car when Oupa was driving.

Imagine if those geese had been children, Pa kept muttering.

Not long after that the family convinced Oupa to sell his car.

It was a heavy blow for Oupa.

But even worse was when the management of the old-age home decided to turn a patch of ground in front of the building, where Oupa had planted a small garden to keep himself busy, into a tarred parking lot for visitors.

After this, Oupa Willie sat at a window and waited to die. What else could he do, if he could no longer drive or garden? He had never been a reader or a talker, he wasn't really interested in sport, he never really listened to music or watched TV.

My final conversation with him, there at the window in the old-age home, was about the white Volkswagen Polo I had just bought. I had never been interested in cars. I bought this one simply because it was a 'demo model' that the salesman offered to me at a special price, and after the trip from Stellenbosch to Stilbaai it was dirtier on both the inside and the outside than Oupa's car had ever been. But he questioned me about my new car with intense interest. It may have been the longest conversation my grandfather and I ever had.

Soon afterwards, he died. Not of any particular illness as far as I could tell. Old age, the family said.

But I always suspected that he died from longing for his garden and his car.

In reality we had started saying goodbye to Oupa Willie a very long time before he died. Every Christmas holiday for at least twenty years, from when Oupa was seventy, Pa would warn us three adult children that we had to get ourselves to Stilbaai 'because Oupa isn't well'. This could be his last Christmas.

Year after year, we'd go to spend the 'last' Christmas with our grandfather.

For about two decades.

In time it became a family joke, our grandfather becoming thinner and paler, short of breath and sickly towards the end of every year, but during the Christmas holiday recovering literally before our eyes. By the end of the holiday he'd be in such fine fettle you'd swear he would live to a hundred. But then he would gradually start to decline again, until by the end of the year Pa would once again rally the children to go visit Oupa because this could be his last Christmas.

No, I don't believe it was affectation or attention-seeking. Oupa Willie had never been an affected, attention-seeking kind of man. I do believe that longing can affect your health. My grandfather's body was deteriorating because his heart was sore, that was how I explained it to Daniel when he was a toddler and we were headed for Stilbaai to visit my grandfather and his great-grandfather for the 'last' time, one more time.

And when my grandfather was surrounded by his offspring, his sore heart was mended, and therefore also the rest of his body.

Now that my own father is well into his eighties, I notice the same phenomenon in him, this unaccountable cycle of decline and revival that coincides with the absence or presence of his offspring.

Maybe as we grow older we all become sick with longing, for people who are far, for things that are past. The older I get myself, the better I understand the word 'homesick'. That you can literally become sick because you are missing home – or whatever 'home' may mean to you.

When Oupa Willie finally died, after twenty years of saying good-bye, I really did want to say goodbye one last time. I sent word to my aunt that I would come with her to the funeral home early on the morning of the funeral, to view my late grandfather in his coffin. I was already past thirty by this time, had already given birth to two children and lost one, and I thought that the time had come for me to look death in the face.

Perhaps it was just another case of Mister Thought not knowing a thing. Or of the body not heeding the mind. Because on the night before the funeral my body betrayed me, turned against me like never before. Out of the blue I caught a sky-high fever and spent the whole night either sweating, tossing and turning, or shivering from cold. At one point I even became delirious.

Or that was what my family told me afterwards.

Thankfully we had all gathered in the same holiday house for Oupa's funeral – Ma and Pa in the main bedroom with little Daniel, my sister and I in the other bedroom, our brother on the couch in the sitting room – so I didn't have to brave this unexpected illness on my own. My loved ones could fetch pills and damp cloths to help bring my fever down. And they could look after my child, who was quite frightened by the sight of his strong and healthy mother lying shivering and pale in a bed.

I was especially grateful that my mother was a nurse. I convinced myself that she would not allow my fever to get so high that I died. Because somewhere in the course of that long night I wondered whether I had tempted fate when I decided I was old enough to look death in the eye. Perhaps it wouldn't be necessary to go look at my dead grandfather. Perhaps I would simply die right here myself.

You cannot control your thoughts, of course, when you are feverish.

To this day I don't know what happened to me that night.

At daybreak the fever 'broke', as the old people used to say, and I fell into a deep sleep, like falling into a black well. When I came to my senses, I was well enough to attend the funeral. I had however missed the chance to go to the funeral home with my aunt in the early morning to look at my grandfather one last time.

I had to wait until I got to France soon afterwards, before I could look at a dead person for the first time.

In this Catholic country there is a centuries-old tradition of viewing the body. Whether the departed is in your immediate family or the neighbour across the street, you say your farewells face to face.

It's just another thing that you, my French daughter, learnt to do at a much earlier age than I did.

You were still in high school when your French grandfather Victor died, just like me when I lost my first grandfather. Unlike me, who was never even asked whether I wanted to say goodbye to my Oupa Corrie after his death, you went with your father as a matter of course to view your departed grandfather.

The Calvinists among whom I was raised didn't care much for hanging around with their dead. The body was nailed shut inside a coffin as soon as possible, nothing to see here, keep moving, the spirit that is destined for heaven is the only thing that matters anyway. Someone once told me it was because of our heat that the old people had to seal off the body so quickly (before you could smell it), in the days when farms were still a very long way from undertakers and most people's coffins lay waiting for them in the attic. But surely there are warm countries in South America and elsewhere that do take leave of their dead in the Catholic way before the coffins are sealed?

I have now lived in France for long enough to believe that this kind of final goodbye is a better way to find closure when a loved one dies. It is indeed what it means to face death. Not only the death of your loved one, but also your own inevitable demise.

During Oupa Willie's funeral service, Pa made a speech in the church and was so overcome that he couldn't carry on talking. It made a deep impression on me, because I can count the times I have seen my father cry on the fingers of one hand. What had made Pa cry, he admitted to all of us in that Stilbaai church, was the thought that now there was no one left who would pray for him every day.

Oupa Willie had without a doubt been the best sayer of prayers in our family. Although I didn't really turn out religious, I would still like to remember my Afrikaans policeman ancestor as someone who prayed passionately. Like in the poem 'Die eerste steen' (The first stone) that Pieter Odendaal dedicated to Adam Small, I would like to convince my descendants that my grandfather was a good man.

My father is a good man, mister small

. . .

even though he sometimes shouts at taxis

and even though he and his god
were kind of okay with everything

I hope you will believe me when I tell you that your great-grandfather was a good man?

3

THE OTHER SIDE OF THE STORY

And then there is Ma's family, where most of the people die sooner than on Pa's side, with the result I know even less about them than the scraps of information I was able to gather about Pa's ancestors. The Scottish Patersons and the blue-eyed Swarts, the Du Plessis with the flared French nostrils, and the Standers I only discovered when I started writing this letter to you, my darling girl. All these ancestors died either long before I was born or during my childhood.

When you write about characters from the past, whether they are great historical figures or your own insignificant relatives, you find yourself in a dark forest trying to follow the faintest of paths. Like Gretel in the Brothers Grimm fairy tale, you are sometimes lucky enough that someone has left you a trail of pebbles. (Yes, I will always return to fairy tales, in my life and in my writing, like a carrier pigeon flying in wide circles just to get back home. If my language is my one true homeland, as Pessoa put it, then fairy tales have become my one true home in that homeland.) Often these pebbles are strewn by older relatives who tell you stories when you are small – although these stories can also lead you astray. But soon you find yourself in a place where the path is completely overgrown. Then you have to use your imagination to cut down trees and pull up shrubs until you can find your way again.

I recently read the great French author Marguerite Yourcenar's *Mémoires d'Hadrien* (*The Memoirs of Hadrian*), partly because I hope that the best real or fictional memoirs will help me find my way back to my own past, and this novel about the ancient Roman emperor Hadrian is widely regarded as among the very best. There is also the fact that Hadrian records his memories in the form of a letter to a loved one, his adopted grandson and successor, Marcus Aurelius. But the real reason, I may as well confess, is that Yourcenar is apparently a distant relative by marriage. At least according to one of your French aunts who has started researching the family on the internet. (Until I heard that, I had no interest in Yourcenar at all.) Now I regard this news as almost as gratifying, for the cultural fertilisation of my daughter's family tree, as my own distant connection with Krotoa.

Because Yourcenar, who was born in 1903 as Marguerite Antoinette Jeanne Marie Ghislaine Cleenewerck de Crayencour (and here I was, thinking that my Afrikaans forebears had too many Christian names), was a truly formidable trailblazer of a woman. Her father was French, her mother Belgian, and when she gained American citizenship in 1947 she had her writer's surname registered as her official surname. (Yourcenar is an anagram of Crayencourt, minus one c.) She translated Virginia Woolf's *The Waves* into French, which strikes me as a surprising association between two women authors I admire, one of whom now turns out to be a relative by marriage on top of it all. But in France she is remembered above all as the first woman elected to become a member of the prestigious Académie Française, in 1980.

The signs on the bathroom doors of this chauvinist institution were apparently changed to *Messieurs/Marguerite Yourcenar* – as if the eminent gentlemen found it unthinkable that more women would follow in her footsteps.

You know by now that your mother admires women who open doors for other women – and Yourcenar opened far more than just the bathroom doors in the French Academy.

She wrote something about her research for Hadrian's biography that I would like my daughter's heart to know:

The facts of my father's life are less known to me than those of the life of Hadrian. My own existence, if I had to write of it, would be reconstructed by me from externals, laboriously, as if it were the life of someone else.

That is what I am doing here, reconstructing my existence from externals.

But it is also what has occupied me for the past forty years, in all the fiction that I have written.

My mother's mother, whom I knew as Ouma Tina, got a fictitious doppelgänger named Ouma Lina in my first adult novel, for example. She was 'The Grandmother Who Was Afraid of Everything' (a chapter title in *Entertaining Angels*), or at least of everything except climbing trees. Right into old age she remained a secret tree climber.

Ouma Tina had indeed been a fearful, nervous type of person, just like the fictional Ouma Lina, but Ouma Tina never, as far as I know, climbed the fig tree in her suburban backyard. As far as I know. Because a year or three ago I overheard a younger relative regaling some friends with the story of our tree-climbing grandma. My impulse was to say, whoa, that isn't true, I made it up in a book! But then I thought, what if it were true? What if Ouma Tina had in fact been a secret tree climber, and even though I never caught her in a tree (remember, it was a hidden vice, like my mother who smoked in secret for years), I had somehow guessed it?

I suspect that fiction writers sometimes capture 'the truth' quite unintentionally, like a child who lowers a fishing line with a hook into a pool of water with no hope of catching anything bigger than a *klipvissie*, and unexpectedly – oh, the joy! – finds a proper edible fish wriggling on the hook.

Grandma Lina wasn't only afraid of water, but also of lightning and germs and illness, and the dark and death, in roughly inverse order of importance. If she heard the rumble of thunder – fortunately a rare occurrence, as she spent her entire life in the Cape Colony – she covered all the shiny things in her house. It was a formidable task because everything in her house shone . . .

She drew the curtains and threw sheets over the mirrors and even hid the bathroom taps under facecloths. And while the lightning played eerily round the house, she inspected the kitchen like a drill sergeant to make sure that no spoon or fork ventured forth from a drawer to attract the destructive impulses of a bolt of lightning.

The real Ouma Tina really was afraid of water and never learnt to swim. Which makes it rather ironic that she married into Oupa Corrie Swart's family of fishermen. (The Swarts and the Patersons of Hermanus were said to have more seawater than blood in their veins.) And because she had such a high-strung temperament, always waiting for the next disaster to fall upon her or her loved ones, she couldn't relax for a moment when the family went to the seaside. While her daughters cavorted in the waves, she watched them from the beach like a zealous life guard.

Because she couldn't swim, she wasn't a reliable lifeguard, of course. Nor did she wear a bathing suit, possibly didn't even own one. Like my other grandmother, she didn't favour a suntanned appearance. She remained fully clothed while she kept vigil on the beach – dress, petticoat, perhaps even shoes and stockings.

One day my mother's sister Suzette was playing with a beach ball in the sea at Gordon's Bay when the tide suddenly came in and she found herself in deep water. She clung anxiously to the ball until a man, spotting her from the rocks at one end of the little beach, jumped in and brought her back to the shallow water. Meanwhile, Ouma Tina had charged into the sea fully clothed to save her child.

Heaven knows exactly how my grandmother thought she was going to save her daughter while she herself was drowning. Most likely she just started powering through the waves blindly, because if her child had to die, she wanted to die with her.

The real Ouma Tina was also really afraid of lightning (and of many other things) and waged a lifelong, obsessive kind of war against germs and dirt. Especially in her own home. She sometimes got up in the middle of the night to scrub the kitchen clean one more time. Literally everything I ever heard about this grandmother led me to believe that she had an obsessive-compulsive personality, but in her day no one had ever heard of OCD.

During my childhood, when I displayed signs of obsessive-compulsive behaviour myself, OCD was still not a well-known phenomenon. But that's another story. For now, let me just say that I marvel at the way people almost boast about this syndrome on social media these days. A while back I posted a picture on Facebook of a tart that had been cut in a very irregular way (it wasn't me who had cut it, I should probably add), which made several virtual friends openly declare that this manner of tart-cutting could make their suppressed obsessive-compulsive tendencies run amok. There was a good deal of self-deprecating humour in the comments, which made me realise anew that social media, for all its attendant evils, can in fact help many of us acknowledge our own weirdness.

I thought that I was the only person in the twenty-first century who literally detested talking on the phone, for example. Thanks to Facebook I recently discovered that hundreds of people I know – people whom I have always considered well-adjusted and emotionally well-balanced individuals – shared this phobia. Which instantly made me feel less weird.

I know, my dear girl, that I have always encouraged you to embrace your otherness – and you began to accomplish this at a much younger age than I did. Pride of place on our fridge has for years belonged to a photograph of one of your father's great musical heroes, Frank Zappa, with his curly hair tied in ponytails on either side of his long moustached face, which make him look like a strange spaniel. Printed above his face is one of his famous sayings: *Without deviation from the norm, progress is not possible.*

And as a young teenager you painted a great *cri de coeur* on your bedroom door: *Normal people scare me.*

Which made me feel quite proud.

But even in our otherness we seek out other people who are different in more or less the same way as us. We remain herd animals no matter what. Those of us with OCD tendencies look for others with similar disorders. Whether it is ubuntu or merely a case of misery loving company, we are all looking for our tribe.

My strange Ouma Tina, I now know, was part of my own tribe.

She was born on a farm in the De Rust district, the umpteenth daughter of a tenant farmer who was desperate for the family names to survive. By the time she was born all the girls' names in the family must have been accounted for, and Petrus du Plessis got the hideous notion to christen this baby girl Marthinus Petrus. In those days a man's word was the law, especially in his own house, and women, like children, were to be seen rather than heard, but the baby's mother, Susanna Stander, actually put her foot down. How she managed it no one knows, but Petrus partly gave in. Fine, the first name could be changed to a girl's name, Marthinus could become Martina, but Petrus stayed Petrus.

That was how my ouma Tina was burdened with the names Martina Petrus, which caused her to be mercilessly mocked throughout her school days, and ultimately led to her revolutionary refusal to give her own daughter a family name.

Of my great-grandmother Susanna Stander I know absolutely nothing – I don't believe I ever saw a single photograph of her –

except that she made a stand against her husband at least once in her life. And that seems to me an important thing to know, important enough to relay to my daughter.

Your mother's mother's mother's mother, your grandmother's grandmother, put her foot down when it came to the male tradition of family names. And your mother's grandmother did it again when she christened her daughter Yvonne. And your mother's mother did it again when she christened me just Marita, instead of Martina Petrus.

That is your tribe, my child, women who can put their foot down.

For Tina du Plessis school mostly felt like punishment, and not only because her second name was Petrus. Exams and tests roused all her fears and phobias, and oral exams were a dreadful torture for such a shy introvert. About the fictional Ouma Lina I wrote:

If a teacher asked her a question, she stuttered and stammered and sometimes even dissolved in tears. When an inspector visited the class, she began to tremble so badly that two children had to hold her desk steady.

It probably sounds like exaggeration, but these were the kinds of stories my mother told me about my grandmother. I cannot recall Ouma Tina herself ever sharing anecdotes from her childhood with me. (She certainly wasn't what you would call a chatterbox.) But there was one story in particular, probably also relayed by my mother, that left an indelible impression on my young mind.

Tina du Plessis was an Afrikaans schoolgirl in the days before Afrikaans was officially recognised as a language, and speaking the 'kitchen language' was discouraged in cruel ways in classrooms throughout the Cape Province. At times Tina du Plessis was forced to stand in a corner for hours wearing a cone-shaped hat, probably made from cardboard, with the word DUNCE written on it – as punishment for letting a few Afrikaans words slip out.

It was the first time I'd heard the word 'dunce'. It means stupid person, Ma explained. Poor, poor Ouma Tina, I thought, and burst into tears. Evidently more of an empath than was good for me then already, an emo before that word existed.

I only learnt years later that the dunce cap – which was widely used in schools during the Victorian era in particular and even gets a mention in Dickens's novel, *The Old Curiosity Shop* – was derived from a very clever man's name. John Duns Scotus was born in the thirteenth century in the village of Duns in Scotland, and as a Franciscan monk he frequently asked his pupils to wear a kind of 'wizard's hat' to help them concentrate better. He held an obscure theory about wisdom rising like warm air to the sharp end of the hat from where it would descend to the brain. As might be expected, with time Duns's hat became an object of ridicule – until in the end 'Duns's hat', corrupted to 'Dunce hat', was employed as a visible humiliation for 'stupid' pupils.

Tina du Plessis didn't finish school, but this was the consequence of material poverty rather than poverty of the spirit. Before she even started school, her family were forced to leave the farm and move to town – the result of the disastrous collapse of the ostrich feather market in 1914 – and soon after Standard 7 she went to work for a shopkeeper in Oudtshoorn to help keep the large family alive. A few of her siblings died young, but at least seven made it into adulthood. Unfortunately for her father, nearly all of them were girls.

Working in the shop (I seem to remember it was a pharmacy) brought her into contact with Oudtshoorn's most famous resident, the Afrikaans author, language activist and politician CJ Langenhoven. The young Tina sometimes had to deliver parcels at Arbeidsgenot, the house where Langenhoven lived from 1901 until his death in 1932. Sagmoedige Neelsie, as he was popularly known in reference to his gentle nature, was probably the first ever Afrikaans literary celebrity and made a lifelong impression on my unliterary Ouma Tina.

She didn't become a language activist, though. Despite the detested dunce cap of her school years, despite Langenhoven's impassioned parliamentary addresses that contributed to Afrikaans finally being recognised as an official language in 1927, Ouma Tina's everyday spoken language was always peppered with a few English words. If you were cold, you put on a jersey, not a *trui*. Her youngest daughter's beautiful paper dolls from the fifties, that I was allowed to play with every time we went to visit Ouma, she called 'ka-touts'. Or that was what I heard for many years, until one day I suddenly realised that she meant cut-outs.

In *Forget-me-not Blues* there is this flat cardboard box with old paper dolls, played with literally to shreds, which in the story is handed down from the grandmother to the mother and from the mother to the daughter. I used it as a kind of symbol of all the secrets, all the hidden knowledge and wisdom, that women pass on to one another from generation to generation.

Ouma Tina did indeed leave those old-fashioned paper dolls to me, and I did in turn give them to my daughter.

When you were small, most of your friends had never even seen a paper doll – let alone played with one – but you spent hours playing with those fragile little dolls from the fifties. Drew them outfits, which you cut out and tried on them, just like I did once upon a time, and thought up new names to write on their cardboard backs. When you left home to become a student, you stowed them in a small blue toy suitcase in your bedroom.

I came across this little suitcase recently when I was cleaning your room for guests. Shame, the three remaining dolls are looking decidedly tattered by now, more like landmine victims with missing feet or hands than the glamorous Hollywood stars they depicted in the fifties. But their outfits have remained magnificent, the glittering evening gowns and smart coats and elegant casualwear of those bygone days.

The only one that still has all her limbs is a sexy brunette (although she lost her head somewhere along the way because her neck is attached to her body with yellowed Sellotape) and on her back are various names (written by at least three different hands) that were given to her by the girls in my family over the past half century. Hilde, Annemarie, Neli, Franci, Gina and Noeline.

I lifted her out of the little suitcase and held a few of the breathtaking evening gowns in front of her bent cardboard body, and at that moment I understood exactly how Marcel Proust's narrator felt when he dipped the famous madeleine biscuit in his tea. For some people, their childhood can be summoned by a particular taste or smell or sound. All I have to do if, like Lewis Carroll's Alice I want to return to the Wonderland of my childhood, is hold Hilde-Annemarie-Neli-Franci-Gina-Noeline for a little while.

Langenhoven died long before I was born, and I never could quite understand the Sagmoedige Neelsie hero-worship. But the way my grandmother spoke about him made me realise for the first time that writers can command respect, even among people who don't really read.

I don't know if this has anything to do with the desire I'd had for as long as I can remember to become a writer. I do, however, know that Ouma Tina was the only one of my relatives who ever met a famous author face to face. On more than one occasion. In his own home.

She was without a doubt a member of my tribe.

In Ouma Tina's wedding picture, which has been hanging in my bedroom for years, she is a lovely blushing young bride with a veil of fine lace attached to a coronet of flowers on her head. (The photograph is one of those old-fashioned, yellowed black-and-white portraits, so of course I cannot actually see the pink flush on her cheeks, but it is nevertheless clear that her cheeks are a shade darker than the rest of her face.) The toes of a pair of satin shoes peep out from under a flowing white dress, and in her arms she holds an enormous bouquet of roses like a baby across her chest.

Unfortunately this is not how I remember her in the flesh. She died 'young', before her sixtieth birthday, of a stroke that came out of the blue. But in those days women in their fifties were already much older than they are today, and she wasn't a woman who paid much attention to her appearance, so I remember her as an ancient grandmother who wore ugly loose-fitting dresses and flat shoes. I never saw her in a pair of trousers or in any kind of 'casualwear'. And although her hair stayed jet-black until the day she died, it didn't exactly help to make her look younger.

To top it all, in the last decade of her life she grew a beard. Not like the Bearded Lady in a circus freak show of old, of course, but there was an unmistakeable thin moustache between her French nostrils and her upper lip. My sister flatly refused to kiss Ouma, because her moustache was prickly. I was the dutiful big sister who dutifully kept kissing Ouma, even though the moustache pricked me too. What I found far creepier than Ouma's facial hair were the bulging varicose veins that curled around her legs like blue snakes. I couldn't stand to look at them; I would far rather keep my eyes on her face and brave the moustache.

Now that my sister and I have both been through menopause, on some mornings we also spot a prickly chin hair that's shot up overnight when we look in the mirror, and we think of our grandmother with affection. Before we reach for the tweezers and pluck the hair out. Because no matter how much we loved our grandmother, for the chocolate cake she baked for us and the coin she hid in the

Christmas pudding and the paper dolls she allowed us to play with, we do not want her moustache.

Ouma Tina was the first person whose death really made me cry. The news hit me like a thunderbolt when I was about twelve. There had been no warning, she hadn't been sick, she was suddenly just *gone*.

It was an ordinary weekday afternoon after school in our house in Pretoria. I was in the bathroom drying my hands when I heard Pa's footsteps in the passage – which immediately made me sense trouble, because he was supposed to be at work. In their bedroom he started talking to Ma, his voice ominously soft. 'I have bad news . . .'

When I heard him say that Ouma had suffered a fatal stroke, I sank onto my haunches as if I'd been punched in the stomach, and literally roared with pain. Then ran sobbing to my sister's bedroom and shouted: 'Ouma is dead! Ouma is dead!'

This melodramatic reaction continued to embarrass me for years afterwards. My mother's reaction was much more subdued than mine, even though it was her mother who had died. I wondered whether it meant that for the rest of my life I would become hope-lessly hysterical every time a loved one died.

A half-century later I have lost several loved ones – family, best friends, former lovers, my former husband, even my oldest child – but I have never again reacted with such absolute lack of restraint. I have learnt that you can get used to anything as you grow older, even to losing people you love.

Ma reacted to Ouma Tina's death 'better' than I did because she was older than me and had more experience of death.

Possibly also because she didn't want to upset her children unnec-essarily. That is what you do when you have children, I have also since learnt. You pretend to be stronger than you are because you want to protect them.

But the first time hurts.

I have learnt that a song by Cat Stevens that I often listened to as a teenager, 'The First Cut is the Deepest', doesn't only apply to the first time we are wounded by love. It is also true of our first intense acquaintance with death.

In the previous century's early thirties, the young Tina du Plessis married Corrie Swart, a postman from a family of fishermen from Hermanus and Gordon's Bay, a gifted raconteur, singer and angler. He was rakishly attractive too, with sea-blue eyes and blond hair and a finely chiselled nose, something between Brad Pitt and Robert Redford in their younger days. His Christian names were Cornelius Jacob, son of Lukas Swart and Maud Isabelle Paterson.

Or perhaps it was Isabelle Maud Paterson.

I have to guess, because my knowledge of the Patersons is wreathed in a fog of myths and legends and plain old-fashioned lies, with the odd fact rising above the fog here and there like a mountain peak. One such mountain peak is that the family's progenitor had been a sailor from Inverness in the north of Scotland, and that the Patersons belonged to Clan MacLaren, along with names such as Law, Lowe, Lawson, Lowrie, Laurie and others that sound nothing like MacLaren.

Another mountain peak of a fact is that this Paterson found himself on the British troopship *Birkenhead* on 26 February 1852, when it sank at Danger Point near Gansbaai. There weren't enough serviceable lifeboats on the ship – the same disaster that would befall the 'unsinkable' *Titanic* a few decades later – and hundreds of soldiers who were on their way to Algoa Bay to fight in the umpteenth Xhosa War were ordered to stand to attention on the deck and go down with the ship.

Grandfather Paterson, however, was a wild sailor, not a disciplined soldier, so he leapt into the stormy sea and started swimming for land. On washing ashore somewhere between Gansbaai and Hermanus, he went AWOL – his surviving commanders would assume he had been among the casualties – and married a local woman. According to scandalmongers in the family she wasn't white, but how would we know?

They had children, I have no idea how many, but enough to carry on the Paterson line all the way to my Oupa Corrie's mother – and the heroic tale of the Scottish sailor who refused to be sucked into the depths of the ocean with his ship was handed down from generation to generation. Take note that no one in our family ever questioned his bravery. That he swam for land rather than waiting to die didn't make him a coward. On the contrary. He was likely smarter than the soldiers who blindly obeyed orders, is how we see it – or just more inclined, perhaps, to think for himself. And it must have taken courage to brave the enormous waves, let alone the sharks that circled the sinking ship for hours, feeding on survivors and the dead. Gansbaai is known to this day as the best place in South Africa for tourists to view dangerous sharks up close, after all.

Anyone who has read *Entertaining Angels* will recognise the story of the sailor on the sinking ship. When little Grietjie first heard about this ancestor she admired him instantly, just like I did when I was told about my Scottish forebear. Why would anyone (except the captain) *not* jump from a sinking ship and try to save his own life?

I knew from childhood that my ancestor's ship sank 'somewhere near Hermanus', but I only established fairly recently that it was at Danger Point. It immediately shed new light on my youthful memories – and here I am literally referring to the very bright light of a lighthouse that was erected at Danger Point at the end of the nineteenth century to prevent another ship from running aground there. I never visited the lighthouse as a child – I would have known about the memorial plaque for the victims of the *Birkenhead* if I had –

but I do remember the lighthouse's sweeping beam of light well.

When I was in primary school our family spent virtually every weekend in a timber cottage in Franskraal. When I lay in my bed at night waiting to be lulled to sleep by the sound of the sea, the beam would light up my bedroom wall, then disappear, then light it up again, regular as the ticking of a clock. Some people count sheep to fall asleep. In my primary school years I counted the rotations of the lighthouse at Danger Point. Blissfully unaware that it was beamed from exactly the place where my Scottish ancestor's South African story began.

Danger Point. What a marvellous place for a family legend to come into existence.

Danger Point was coincidentally also where I came very close to my own death for the first time. Or maybe nothing is coincidence.

When I was eleven, I begged Pa and Ma to buy me a snorkel and goggles for Christmas, as I wanted to go diving for perlemoen with the uncles and male cousins in the family. We were celebrating Christmas at Franskraal and Danger Point was, of course, the best diving spot. It didn't occur to anyone that it might not be the safest place for an eleven-year-old girl to go diving for the first time in her life.

And I was seemingly fearless – when I think of all the fears and phobias I battle with these days, I seem to be talking about a different person – or perhaps just so brainwashed by all the heroic tales of sailors and fishermen on Ma's side of the family that I imagined I was part mermaid.

On a sunny summer's day when the waves didn't seem all that high, my cousin Leon and I charged into the ocean at Danger Point. Ma and Pa and a few other grown-ups were sitting on the rocks drinking wine, mouths watering in anticipation of the haul of perlemoen Leon and I were going to bring back in the bag that once had oranges in it and that now hung from our inflated inner tube, because that would be our dinner. Tenderised and cooked in butter with flavourful rice . . .

I had barely hit the water when an enormous freak wave struck me from behind and sent me spinning around like laundry in a washing machine. The saltwater poured into my snorkel and down into my lungs, and I ripped the tube out of my mouth and struggled for all I was worth to just get my head above water. The moment I burst through the surface gasping for air the next wave hit me and dragged me below again – this time with considerably less breath or fight left in my body. When at last I stuck my head out above the water again and saw that another wave was about to crash over me, I knew that this was where I would drown at the age of eleven. I saw Ma on the rocks, far away in the distance, watching me over the rim of her wineglass, but I had too little breath left to shout. I could only wave my arms desperately for help.

And I saw Ma waving cheerfully back.

When later on as a student I came across Stevie Smith's best-known poem 'Not Waving but Drowning', I immediately understood, deep down into my lungs, what it meant.

I was much too far out all my life
And not waving but drowning.

These are lines that still punch me in the stomach every time. Fortunately a stranger, who was also in the water at Danger Point looking for perlemoen that day, saw that the child was in trouble and saved me from drowning.

I didn't go diving again that day – and I never again walked into the sea without fear. I remain scared of waves to this day. That child's fear of drowning is something your body never forgets, no matter what your mind is trying to tell you.

69

Oupa Corrie wasn't there the day I almost drowned, but he often came to Franskaal with us. He wasn't a diver; he had a great respect for the ocean and preferred to fish from the rocks, a safe distance away from freak waves and other perils. And when he went fishing in Franskraal, my sister and my brother and I were sometimes invited along. During these fishing expeditions he sang for us, like Mario Lanza in *The Student Prince*, in a clear tenor voice that travelled far across the water. In my unstoppable imagination even the fish couldn't resist Oupa's singing voice, because we seldom returned home without a substantial catch.

But what impressed me even more than his singing were the stories he told his grandchildren next to those waters. Especially the ghost stories. Like his fishermen ancestors, he believed in ghosts and premonitions and all kinds of supernatural phenomena.

The story I remember best was about a small group of fishermen who had to spend the night in a cave on the False Bay coast after they were trapped there by the tide. I like to imagine that it was the cave on the little beach at Kogel Bay where, in my student years, I whiled away many pleasant hours among unsober friends – although I wasn't yet familiar with Kogel Bay's cave the first time I heard the story.

According to Oupa's tale the fishermen got a small fire going to keep them warm, but every time the coals started dying down they would hear someone approach from the sea. They couldn't see him properly in the dark, but they soon realised that it had to be the ghost of a dead fisherman; when they stoked the fire, he disappeared, but just as they fell asleep and the embers started to cool, they'd hear him steal closer again. Shlupp, shlupp, shlupp, through the shallow water. After a while one of the fishermen was so desperate for a bit of shuteye that he grabbed a burning log out of the fire and threw it at the skulking ghost. The log flew straight through the apparition and landed in the water with a hiss. The ghost was evidently the hell in, as you can understand, and for the rest of the night the fishermen didn't sleep a wink. Even with the fire burning, they could hear him constantly. Shlupp, shlupp, shlupp . . .

I remember the terrifying sound effects Oupa made while he was telling the story. I wanted to cover my ears so I wouldn't hear the awful 'shlupp, shlupp, shlupp', but I didn't dare miss the rest of the story, so I just squeezed my eyes shut to concentrate harder on Oupa's voice. And that 'shlupp, shlupp, shlupp' kept me awake at night for weeks.

Today I suspect that everything I learnt as a writer about the art of storytelling began with Oupa Corrie's ghost stories.

Like any good storyteller, he never allowed the facts to interfere with the flow of his narrative.

But these weren't 'lies' – they were just a different kind of truth. A truer truth, I think these days, the kind you only find in fiction. Whenever Oupa lied on purpose, it was for the sake of the story. Like the time he and my eight-year-old brother returned from a fishing expedition beaming with pride and with a big fish that Wiaan had supposedly pulled out of the water. We all took photographs of Kleinboet's first fish, the small boy with the skinny legs and the enormous fish in one hand and the fishing rod in the other, the sea of Franskraal bluish-grey in the background. While Oupa described down to the finest detail how Wiaan fought the fish until he could lift it out of the water in triumph. And Wiaan's smile kept growing wider as his bare boy chest grew broader.

Years later, after Oupa Corrie had died, my brother confessed that, while his hands had indeed been on the fishing rod, Oupa's hands had rested on top of his and done all the right things to get the fish out of the water. Oupa Corrie took so much pleasure in telling the story of his grandson's first catch that the grandson didn't have the heart to contradict him.

Corrie Swart was one of a horde of siblings, several of whom had apparently been 'blue babies', children who were stillborn, while others also didn't survive into adulthood. As far as I can tell, his Paterson mother gave birth to about sixteen babies, just like Ouma Hanna's Kasselman mother. And Ouma Tina's Susanna Stander-who-put-her-foot-down was also the mother of a multitude who failed to make it into adulthood.

Of my four great-grandmothers, only Nelie van der Vyver was spared the trauma of multiple births and frequent infant deaths.

Every time I think of these women who lost so many children at such a young age, I can only shake my head in astonishment. I watched just one child die in infancy, and to me it was so terrible that I didn't know how to carry on living. How on earth did my great-grandmothers do it? It is too easy to say that it was a different era, that infant deaths were part of a mother's life. How does any mother face life after the death of a child?

As far as I am concerned, all these mothers were unsung heroines, women who had to bear the unbearable because they had no choice.

I want you to know about them, my French daughter, about your brave female ancestors in Africa, because their sacrifices made my life, and your life, possible.

Oupa Corrie died of cancer when I was seventeen. He had been sick for a few months and spent the final weeks of his life in a Cape Town hospital waiting to see his Transvaal grandchildren one last time. At the start of the summer holiday, when the school year ended, we drove straight to Cape Town to 'say goodbye to Oupa'.

'He's ready to go,' Ma told us three children. 'He's just waiting for you.'

As a nurse Ma probably knew better than most people when someone was ready to die, but I was puzzled nonetheless. If you were as sick as Oupa was, surely you couldn't decide when you wanted to die? You just got sicker and sicker and then you died, was what I thought.

But Ma was right.

Oupa was emaciated almost beyond recognition when we went to say goodbye, a bag of bones in a bed in Conradie Hospital, but I didn't want to believe that it would be the last time. With typical adolescent selfishness I was looking forward to my summer holiday in Stilbaai, not inclined to hang around in the hospital while Oupa died. I convinced myself that I would see him again, once we'd had a bit of a holiday.

We had barely reached Stilbaai when the news came that he had died. He had waited for us, indeed, before he'd drawn his last breath.

Many years later, when you were born, Mia, the granddaughter my mother desired with all her heart, she was dying of cancer herself. She would have come to France for your birth, her plane ticket had been bought and everything had been arranged, but barely a month before your birth she became too sick to travel. From the moment you were born, I tried to get a photograph of you to your grandmother, to reassure her, to introduce her to you, to allow her to greet you before she died. But twenty years ago there were no smartphones or Skype or social media yet, photographs couldn't be sent from one continent to another in a flash, and I couldn't dial an overseas number from the hospital.

I had to wait until the hospital allowed me to go home before I could phone my mother – and because my baby was born by Caesarean, the hospital refused to discharge me within a day or two. French hospitals can be inhumanly strict about rules like these and they wanted to keep me in bed for at least a week. In the end I managed, through a combination of pleading and threatening (and desperate plans to escape from the hospital in the night if all else failed), to get home after a week.

I called Ma right away. It was early evening, the time of day when she was usually so drugged from pain killers that it had become difficult to have a meaningful conversation, but that evening was an incredible exception. Her mind was as clear as her voice. She asked eagerly about her granddaughter. How tall was she? What did she weigh? Did she have hair or was she bald? Was she sleeping well? Was she drinking enough milk?

'She sleeps like a dream, Mamma,' I said.

'She takes after her grandma,' Ma said with a weak little laugh. 'I am also going to sleep well tonight.'

The phone woke us before daybreak the next morning. I knew immediately what it meant, even before we picked up. My mother would never wake up again.

She had waited to greet her granddaughter before dozing off one last time.

Oupa Corrie's funeral, a few days before Christmas, meant another trip from Stilbaai to town. His final resting place is beside Ouma Tina in the Stikland cemetery, a depressing necropolis in the northern suburbs, on the fringe of a busy main road that becomes Voortrekker Road a little further on. Even back then I thought it the ugliest street in the world (despite not knowing many other streets in the world in my teenage years), a mecca of car dealerships with Sanlam's charmless headquarters towering above everything like a capitalist cathedral.

This is why I have never taken you to see your great-grandparents' graves, my love. It is something entirely different from the centuries-old churchyards and peaceful graveyards in the French countryside where I sometimes take a stroll to meditate on mortality. There is no peace to be found where those great-grandparents of yours lie.

All I remember about the funeral is that I rode in my uncle's car in the funeral procession. With my sister and brother too, surely, because Ma and her sister were in the car at the front, behind the hearse. As we drove, my uncle played a Neil Diamond tape – and just then 'Morningside' started to play, a song I didn't know because Neil Diamond wasn't cool enough for my seventeen-year-old musical tastes.

The old man died, is how it starts, *and no one cried . . .*

It tells the story of an old man who made a table with his own hands and carved the words 'For my children' into it, but when he dies, no one wants the table.

If it were a movie, this would have been the perfect soundtrack. This I realised even at that tender age, as I rode in my dead grandfather's funeral procession, looking at the ugliest street in the world through a fog of tears. Sometimes life truly is more improbable than fiction or film or anything else we can invent.

And to this day, I find 'Morningside' one of the saddest songs on earth.

4

HERE BEGINS MY STORY

Reality is a crutch for people who can't handle science fiction. Apparently this clever saying originated with the American science-fiction writer Gene Wolfe, but for many of us story people it applies, really, to all fiction.

I am not saying that I would ever want to trade my real life for a fictitious one. (Well, maybe sometimes, when things are going particularly badly, for a day or two.) But I wish almost every day that I could live longer so that I could read more fiction.

At the same time, I don't want to miss out on the heartbeat of life while I spend months giving mouth-to-mouth to a story I am creating. Most fiction writers spend their lives gingerly walking the thin line between reality and imagination. Fall off one side, and you could easily drown in your own sea of stories. Tumble down the other, and you could crash-land in reality, left so bruised and maimed that you are no longer capable of creating stories.

That is why I like to read writers' memoirs, in the hope of discovering how they manage the balancing act on that thin line. It's the only non-fiction that excites me, in fact – although some claim that writers' memoirs are sometimes more fictional than their fiction.

It's not deliberate deceit, as I wrote in the preface to one of my own non-fiction books – it is merely the constraint of an occupational hazard.

If you have to use your imagination day in and day out to keep the home fires burning, it can be difficult to abstain from that and confine yourself to the boring truth.

I know, my darling child, it does seem as though with this quote from *Retoer: Pretoria Provence* I am apologising in advance for all the lies I am about to tell here. But I promise you that I will do my best to write as honestly as possible. Just as long as you remember that honesty and truth aren't necessarily one and the same.

Every time my siblings and I talk about specific incidents from our childhood, I am struck by the fact that we each remember our own unique version. One of us might, for example, be able to describe the decor in the finest detail, but can only vaguely recall the action or the dialogue. Another might be able to recall the dialogue word for word, but remember nothing about the surroundings. Ultimately, we end up with three different stories, all three of them equally 'true' (or not), because each story is its narrator's own version of the truth.

Memories sometimes lie in relation to facts, but facts also lie in respect of memory. That is how Anthony Burgess puts it in the preface of his exceptionally entertaining memoir, *Little Wilson and Big God*, which I devoured like a thriller about three decades ago. Burgess uses his preface to apologise for everything that 'the daughters of memory' have turned into fables and, while he's about it, for everything else that might possibly require a pardon, from crudeness to self-indulgence:

I have spent much of my life apologising, asking for pardon first and then deciding what I should be pardoned for afterwards.

It sounds so damn familiar, I thought when I read these words, as if Burgess had also been an Afrikaans girl in the latter half of the last century, doomed by a Calvinist upbringing to mumble please, thank you and – especially – sorry her whole life.

I didn't realise how often I apologised until I met your father. 'Why are you Afrikaans girls always saying sorry?' he wanted to know after he had met a few of my women friends as well. I couldn't even begin to explain – how could he ever understand the environment in which my friends and I grew up? – but I made up my mind that my French-Afrikaans daughter would not be as sorry a sorry-sayer as her mother.

And to accomplish that, I had to set an example and become less apologetic myself, of course. Easier said than done. After a twenty-year battle, a sorry or a 'scuse me still slips out now and then, like someone with Tourette's syndrome who keeps being tripped up by swearwords. But I stay in the fight, because I want my daughter to assume her rightful place – to 'take up space', as the South African Miss Universe Zozibini Tunzi put it recently – without apologising to anyone for doing it.

There's another first, isn't it, your mother sharing a beauty queen's advice with you. But I take good advice wherever I find it.

Aside from writers' *Confessions*, as Anthony Burgess called his autobiography – in tongue-in-cheek emulation of St Augustine – I have always found writers' journals and letters a source of reading pleasure and wise counsel. It is true that journals have become an endangered species, just like old-fashioned, handwritten letters on paper. Present-day writers prefer to capture their daily thoughts in blogs on the internet, and most writers have long succumbed to the speed and convenience of email.

It's maybe only teenage girls who still pour their hearts out in their journals – and then only a particular kind of introverted and word-hungry teenager, the kind that I used to be and the kind you were until just the other day, my dear girl.

Because as a teenager I would have hated it if anyone else had read my journal, I was never even tempted to read yours when I came across it by chance while looking for something in your room. Until one day I realised that you sometimes left your journal out on purpose, on the kitchen counter or on the coffee table in the sitting room, open at a specific page, like an invitation: *Read me, Ma, here is something I am struggling to say to you, something I am trying to write because I cannot say it.*

And every time I read such an entry, which probably only happened three or four times, I left you a sign that I had been there. Slipped a feather or a postcard or a snapshot between the pages before I closed it again. But we never talked about it, because it dawned on me that there are things that a daughter struggles to say to her mother while they are looking each other in the eye. Details that might upset a mother, especially about the intense mood swings of the teenage years. But if a mother is very lucky, a daughter will find other ways to communicate with her.

Music was always your and your father's mode of communication when everyday conversations became too difficult. You both make music, you with you light-blue ukulele, he with his harmonica or his electronic synthesiser, you sing and he writes lyrics, and one of his loveliest songs he wrote for you when you turned thirteen. 'Ma fille' is about a father who is looking at his sleeping daughter, with her hair fanned out on her pillow like a star (*Comme une étoile sur l'oreiller / Ses cheveux se sont étalés*), and imagining her getting older every year.

In two days she'll be sixteen / She is neither woman nor child . . .
Tomorrow she'll be seventeen / She is part woman, part child . . .

And then she turns twenty, *no longer a child*, but still and forever *ma fille, ma fille*. My daughter, my daughter.

I am so grateful, my girl, that writing has always been an alternative form of communication for you and me. The postcards I sent you from when you were a baby, the passages in your journal that you permitted me to see, the very long letter I am writing to you now . . .

In the past nearly all writers kept journals, and wrote an astonishing number of letters, and I still find I have much to learn from the personal documents of famous authors.

At university I couldn't really relate to Virginia Woolf's novels – they were beyond my modest comprehension, I decided – but then I discovered her journals in the library. *The Diary of Virginia Woolf*, which was edited by her husband, Leonard Woolf, covers the two decades from 1918, when she was in her thirties and really starting to develop her own voice as a writer, until four days before her suicide in 1941. All her famous novels were published during this period – from *Mrs Dalloway* and *Orlando* to *To the Lighthouse* and *The Waves* – and her journal entries shed fascinating light on the everyday life of someone who is in the process of becoming a truly great writer. Despite her demurral that, as she writes in 1933:

I will not be 'famous', 'great'. I will go on adventuring, changing, opening my mind and my eyes, refusing to be stamped and stereotyped.

The woman I got to know in these journals was so far removed from the cold, intellectual writer I had pictured when I took on the first of her novels as a young girl that it gave me the courage to try to read a few of her novels again. I still didn't 'understand' everything when I reached for *The Waves* once again, but I was beginning to understand that the literary arts can move you profoundly, that they can reach into your heart, even if you don't necessarily 'understand' each word.

And I will remember for the rest of my life that Woolf's final journal entry wasn't about her depression or about the horror of England being caught up in another world war, but about the evening meal she had to cook.

And now with some pleasure I find that it's seven; and must cook dinner. Haddock and sausage meat. I think it is true that one gains a certain hold on sausage and haddock by writing them down.

Other writers' work I already knew fairly well by the time I read their letters, like the two Russians who stand back to back on my bookshelf to this day, Vladimir Nabokov and Anton Chekhov. In both cases the letters showed me a side of their characters that made me newly curious about their fiction. Art leading to life, and life leading back to art, over and over again.

Nabokov is famous for his razor-sharp intellectual aloofness, but his *Selected Letters* turned him into an ordinary person for me. Or no, perhaps not an 'ordinary person' – his life story was too extraordinary for that. But his writer's voice suddenly sounded less coldly elevated than in his novels. And Chekhov's *A Life in Letters* allowed this doctor-playwright-short-story-writer to emerge from the pages as a warm, generous, humorous man that I would have liked to have known as a friend.

I know all too well that a nice personality is no prerequisite for literary talent, but if you discover that one of your favourite writers was also a nice person, you'll only be more eager to read their work again.

I should probably add that I have a thing about letters – as anyone who knows my books can infer. One of my collections of columns and essays is even called *Franse briewe*; it doesn't really consist of letters, it's the double entendre of 'French letters' in English that was irresistible when we were looking for a title. French letters are what in my youth were known as FLs or 'effies' – or rather *not* known, because the mere words were enough to make us giggle and blush.

Condoms, my child, which you have known about since childhood, and which would never make you giggle, unless your mother used the French word in the wrong context. The problem is that *préservatifs* is a false friend of the English word 'preservatives', so I have on more than one occasion assured French guests at our table that there were no condoms in our food.

In most of my novels readers will also find a letter or two, and one of them is even written in the form of a letter from start to finish. *Just Dessert, Dear* was my light-hearted attempt to put a modern spin on the most famous epistolic revenge novel in literature, Choderlos de Laclos's unsurpassed *Les liaisons dangereuses*. It's the kind of challenge that a writer with a letter mania has to tackle sooner or later, even if only to get it over and done with and carry on writing.

For me letters are a way of hearing the natural voice of my fictional characters, that inner voice that is close to a speaking voice but still remains a written voice. Not quite as raw or as crude as a journal voice, because a letter is always intended for at least one other reader besides the writer; but also not as sanitised and sterilised as a book voice that has to satisfy thousands upon thousands of readers.

This may also be the most important reason why I decided to pour this story into the mould of a letter to a loved one. I believe that it will help keep me honest if I stay as close as possible to my inner voice. While I constantly remember what Christy Lefteri, the young British author of *The Beekeeper of Aleppo*, wrote in her debut novel a decade ago:

Only a story never told is true in entirety.

I also frequently think of the journalist Léon Daudet's audacious answer when a reader complained that his memoirs, *Fantômes et vivants* ('Ghosts and the Living'), contained rather a lot of lies. Of course, he conceded, otherwise he'd be nothing but a train timetable. In mitigation I should add that he was the novelist Alphonse Daudet's son, and married to Victor Hugo's granddaughter, so it is probably understandable that he found fiction more alluring than journalistic facts.

I don't want to sound like a train timetable, my dear girl, but it's high time I got to the main character in the story, or I could start sounding like Tristram Shandy. If I were ever forced with a gun to my head to choose only ten novels that have had a lifelong effect on me, *The Life and Opinions of Tristram Shandy, Gentleman* by Laurence Sterne would be quite high up on the list. I read it in my twenties, when my taste in books was still largely unformed. (Like my taste in food and art and music and male companions and quite a lot of other things at that stage.) I only discovered much later that Susan Sontag viewed Sterne as the English-language writer who may have had the greatest influence on world literature after Shakespeare and Dickens. And that the philosopher Nietzsche claimed that *Tristram Shandy* was his favourite novel, which made me decide that I was in good company.

Assuming, of course, that you consider Nietzsche good company. *Tristram Shandy* is a bonfire of a book that was published in nine volumes between 1759 and 1766, in which an eponymous narrator carries literary digression to such entertaining lengths that he doesn't get to his own birth until the third volume.

Believe me, I don't want to break Laurence Sterne's record, but I must make just one more detour to tell you how my mother and father got together. After all, if that hadn't occurred, I would not be here to write this letter. Or you here to read it.

But by the end of this chapter I'll have been born. Promise.

Yvonne Swart was born in December 1934 in Cape Town, not really an only child, but because her sister only arrived thirteen years later she spent her childhood on her own. I sometimes wonder whether this solitude was the reason for her lifelong love of reading.

I believe that some people are born readers – and that others, in the right circumstances, with the right sort of encouragement, can also become readers. The difference is that made readers will never be quite as hungry for books as born readers. For a born reader, reading is an urgent need rather than a vague desire, an indispensable necessity like eating or sleeping.

Had I grown up in a rural backwater early in the previous century as one of sixteen children, like some of my ancestors, without anyone to set the example of reading or any books in the house except for the Bible, I would only have been able to satisfy my hunger for reading much later. Had my mother not been a solitary child in a Cape Town suburb, with enough time to read and access to libraries, she may also not have been able to enjoy the luxury of a lifelong love of reading.

But I suspect nonetheless that, like me, my mother was a born reader.

She was a clever child who skipped a grade in primary school, as children could do more easily then than now, because she was being terrorised by an unfair teacher. Because her mother, my Ouma Tina, had herself run the gauntlet of taunting classmates and harsh teachers at school, she didn't hesitate to have little Yvonne moved to the older class.

Yvonne was nearly five when the Second World War broke out – and almost eleven when it finally ended in 1945. Her earliest and most vivid memories were of Cape Town in the war years. The blackout curtains that covered windows at night, the darkness of the city streets, the fear that the enemy might bomb Cape Town. It is possible that her ever-fearful mother honed her anxiety, because my father (who was also born in Cape Town, in the same year as she was) has no such clear memories of wartime fears.

Neither of my grandfathers went to fight in the war. They were working-class Afrikaners, not exactly admirers of the British Empire, but nor did they hate Great Britain as a result of the Anglo-Boer War. None of my ancestors took part in the Boer War – they were all from the Colony, as they referred to the Cape Province. And the reason for that is that none of my ancestors had been part of the Great Trek from the Colony into the uncharted north.

Neither of my grandfathers, then, bore a grudge because the Tommies had burnt down their farms or let their families die in concentration camps. They were never tempted to side with the Germans against the English, as some well-known Afrikaners did indeed do. No, my grandfathers lived meekly under the colonial yoke and spoke English when they had to. In fact, my mother's father spoke excellent English and ensured that his two daughters could also speak the conqueror's language better than the conqueror himself – a tactic that some Afrikaners apparently considered a kind of soft vengeance.

And yet my grandfathers didn't volunteer to fight on the side of the colonial ruler either. Perhaps they were peace-loving, perhaps they were just fence-sitters. They weren't political animals, that much was certain.

At least one of Oupa Corrie's brothers did go to war on the side of the British and was taken captive in North Africa. Like most men who return from war, he never shared the horror of his experiences with his family. All my mother ever heard was that this uncle suffered from a phobia about flies for the rest of his life. 'Because there were so many flies in North Africa.'

But not all Yvonne's wartime memories were unpleasant. In *Forget-me-not Blues* I devoted a whole chapter to the war years in Cape Town, and my mother's reminiscences were the foundation on which I built it. For a scene in which a child and her mother travel from the suburbs to the city centre by train to shop and go to the bioscope, I obviously needed to research the scenery. Old photographs and newsreels on the internet helped me describe Adderley Street in the forties, the names of the buildings and the shops, Fletcher & Cartwrights for Fashion and Foods, the trams and the soldiers in uniform on all the streets, but my mother's memories brought the scene to life. Like grand old Stuttafords where an elderly gentleman in uniform with a cap on his head pushed the buttons of the elevator for the customers and announced each floor *as if it is some place he has always wanted to go, a white beach with palm trees or another planet, and then all the shoppers squeeze out through the doors a little more eagerly.*

Ma didn't really describe any such gentleman, I had to use my imagination to see and hear him. But Ma did at some point mention something about a 'lift attendant' in a grand department store, and that was enough to form the outlines of a picture I could colour in myself. Ma also helped me understand that war could sometimes be almost exciting for a child, as it was for little Colette in the book, as long as it was happening in some distant land.

Colette wouldn't tell her mother, of course, but there are times when she rather enjoys the war. At school there are drills in case of a bomb attack, then they must dive under their wooden desks with their arms held above their heads, which usually ends in giggling and joking. Much more fun than arithmetic or Bible study.

And then there was the music of the war, Vera Lynn's sentimental songs that my grandfather could sing so beautifully – 'When the Lights Go On Again', 'The White Cliffs of Dover', 'We'll Meet Again' – and which brought tears to Ma's eyes until the day she died because it reminded her of the deprivations of the war. The strangest thing is that these days I am also moved to tears when I hear Vera Lynn sing, even though I don't share any of my mother's wartime memories.

As if sadness is inherited.

I can't help wondering if you will also get weepy one day when you listen to the songs of your own mother's war. Probably just as well that Rodriguez's 'Sugar Man' or Bernoldus Niemand's 'Hou my vas, korporaal' aren't tearjerkers like the music from the Second World War.

For my generation of South Africans, the war was much closer than for my mother. It was waged in our backyard, on the borders of our country and inside our neighbouring countries. It was part of the Cold War between the USA and the Soviet Union, and there was a Communist or a terrorist hiding behind every bush. At least according to the scary stories we were told. There wasn't much public sentiment about our Border War, aside from the messages from pining family members that Esmé Euvrard would read out on her radio show, *Forces' Favourites*, on Sundays.

And unlike my mother, even as 'my war' was raging throughout the eighties, I had stopped regarding it as a just war.

My mother's mother was the kind of old-fashioned mother who couldn't talk to her daughters (or to anyone else) about matters of the flesh. When at about eleven or twelve Yvonne's breasts started to develop, her mother sent her to the school nurse to be informed about menstruation and the sins of Eve. About sex and reproduction no details were forthcoming.

And yet deciding to ask the school nurse for advice was more than many other mothers did back then. For many girls of my mother's generation, their first period was a traumatic experience for which they were in no way prepared. Imagine, you suddenly start to bleed and the blood is coming from a part of your body that you are never allowed to touch, that you have never been able to examine up close, and that you cannot question anyone about.

No, my child, I am glad that you cannot imagine it.

Another unusual decision Yvonne's parents took was to send her not to whichever high school was nearest, but instead to what they considered to be the best Afrikaans school on the Peninsula. Although it meant having to commute to the city centre by train and by bus every weekday for five years, at Hoërskool Jan Van Riebeeck she encountered a wider variety of classmates than would have been possible in the modest neighbourhoods of Thornton or Goodwood. Children from rural towns and farms who lived in the school hostel, rich men's children from the finest houses in Oranjezicht and Tamboerskloof, the clever and privileged children of Afrikaner intellectuals and artists, but also children who came from small flats and 'broken homes' in the city's poorer neighbourhoods.

And yet, as in Henry Ford's famous comment about which colours Ford cars could be painted – 'any colour as long as it's black' – this wider variety only meant different shades of white. My mother was thirteen when the National Party came to power with its policy of separate development. After that, everything around her just kept getting whiter and whiter, like a washing-powder advert.

By the time she went to high school she already knew what she wanted to do when she'd finished her schooling. Florence Nightingale was her role model, but even before she read about the Lady with the Lamp's trailblazing work during the Crimean War, she was dreaming of hospitals and a white uniform. According to Ma she had 'always' wanted to be a nurse.

Just like I have always wanted to write.

Because my mother had been so certain about her calling since her childhood, because she practised it with such passion throughout her life, I thought that everyone just knew from childhood what they wanted to become. Granted, I was too shy to tell anyone what

I wanted to do because it sounded so far-fetched, and I assumed I would have to find a day job to keep myself alive – in case I couldn't find a rich man to do it – but writing was what I wanted to do.

For my mother, as for me, it wasn't even a question of what you wanted to do one day. It was simply what you had to do, or your life wouldn't be worth living.

I only realised after becoming a mother myself that most children have no idea what they want to do when they finish school. Only then did I begin to understand how rare it was 'always' to have known your calling. And how lucky my mother and I had been to share this experience.

The choice of 'respectable' careers for young women was, of course, far smaller in my mother's time – more or less limited to becoming a teacher or a nurse – and even in my own time it wasn't nearly as bewildering as it was for you.

Just imagine, Mia – you are training for a career that didn't even exist when I was your age. The first full-length animation film, Walt Disney's *Snow White*, was made when your grandmother was a child. (And she adored it.) When I was a child there were already a good many animated films, but animated games were something I couldn't even imagine. The closest I came to any sort of electronic game as a teenager in the seventies was a pinball machine. And even that was something I knew from a song by The Who rather than from personal experience. Respectable girls like me, shame, weren't supposed to hang around pinball machines and Pinball Wizards.

In the early fifties a bright-eyed Yvonne Swart enrolled at the nursing college at Groote Schuur Hospital. She traded her parental home in Thornton for the nurses' hostel near the hospital and embarked on an independent adult life in the city. Those five years of studying and working between school and marriage were probably the happiest years of her life – even though she never said so herself, because her husband and children would have felt slighted. But whenever she talked about her Groote Schuur years, she sounded happier than usual.

Among dozens of pictures on a pinboard above my desk is a tiny, black-and-white snapshot of my smiling future mother and three nursing friends posing with a skeleton. They are wearing dark capes with straps across the bodices of their white uniforms and white caps on their heads, and they are holding the skeleton up between them as you'd hold a drunk man to keep him upright. One bony arm is slung around my mother's shoulders on the right of the picture, the other around the shoulders of the nurse on the left, with the third nurse down on her haunches in front of them and the skeleton's legs hanging down on either side of her neck, as if she's about to carry him on her shoulders.

This was the skeleton they used in class to study every bone in the human body, Ma told me later. I seem to remember that he even had a name, Bob or something, and I assumed that he had previously been a living person. It never even occurred to me to ask Ma whether it might have been a synthetic skeleton.

As if it were the most natural thing in the world for my mother to stand smiling with her arms around death itself.

It is true that her work at Groote Schuur brought regular contact with death when she was still young. She loved to entertain us kids with stories about the hospital ghosts, whom the nurses on the night shift, in particular, became better acquainted with than they might have wished. And when at the age of 54 she was diagnosed with terminal cancer, she returned to Groote Schuur, this time as a patient in the oncology department where she frequently had chemotherapy.

It wasn't what she would have wanted, of that I am certain.

No one wants to get cancer at 54 and realise that they will be dead in a few years.

But if she absolutely had to get cancer and absolutely had to be treated in a hospital, there was some consolation in it being her beloved Groote Schuur. Almost a kind of homecoming.

While Yvonne Swart was nursing at Groote Schuur she met Danie van der Vyver, and in June 1957 they were married. She was a beautiful bride – and I'm not just saying this because she was my mother and your grandmother – in a breathtaking dress, with a tiny waist and a wide skirt and a long veil with which her future children would play wedding for years to come. And the children came quickly, because eleven months after the wedding the first one had already arrived. That would be me, and when I was nine months old, she was pregnant again with the next one.

Wait, hang on, we're at my birth at last – but we still need one final flashback for you to understand how Danie van der Vyver fits into the picture.

My father was born in the same year as my mother, in the same city, and like her he was the eldest child in a working-class family. And yet his childhood memories sound completely different from hers. Which just goes to show that we all make up our own stories, from when we're young.

Pa cannot remember his life as an only child, because before his second birthday a little sister had arrived and, by the time he was seven, two twin sisters. All three of his sisters were christened Maria. They got one other name each, at least – the eldest was Maria Johanna Catherina, and the twins were Cornelia Maria and Johanna Maria – but the tradition of family names required them to be named after specific female ancestors, and there was evidently a surfeit of Marias in this family. Fortunately they weren't called Maria 1, Maria 2 and Maria 3. As was the custom they each received a given name that was derived from their first Christian name, and

I got to know them as Tannie Marie, Tannie Cora and Tannie Joan.

Pa's primary school was in Maitland, and his high school between Goodwood and Epping. Working-class Cape Town neighbourhoods, like those where Jeanne Goosen's characters in *We're Not All Like That* would have lived in the fifties. When Pa was a child in the thirties and forties, these neighbourhoods were not yet exclusively white, because the National Party was not yet in power and separate development was not yet the official policy.

But even then, people were separate. Although Pa never talked about this when he talked about his childhood.

What he did talk about was the mischief and the *kwajongstreke* he got up to. *Kwajongstreke* is an archaic Afrikaans word that I haven't used in years and the sound of it will probably make you laugh, the way you burst out laughing every time I say, '*Goeie genugtig*, Mia!' when I'm upset. (These days I sometimes abuse old-fashioned phrases like these to defuse possible conflict, because I know you won't be able to keep a straight face.) *Kwajongstreke* were pranks of the sort that naughty boys kept themselves busy with in Pa's schooldays – and Pa was bloody naughty. It was as if he drew on his innate competitive spirit – which made him an excellent athlete – to ensure that he would always be the naughtiest child in the class, the school, the neighbourhood.

This competitive streak did not extend to schoolwork. Being the naughtiest child in the class was more important than being the cleverest child. Naughty, sporty boys are nearly always more popular among their classmates than well-behaved, clever boys. So it was in Pa's day, long ago in South Africa, and alas, so it still is in France, where until just the other day his grandson and namesake also aspired to being the naughtiest rather than the cleverest boy in the class. *Plus ça change*, as you French like to say.

One of the young Danie's antics that plays out like a movie scene in my head was the time he and a friend hid between the ceiling and the roof of the school hall because they wanted to drip water from a bucket onto the school principal's head while he was delivering his homily during assembly. When they crawled along the ceiling to reach a point exactly above the principal's head, a rotten plank gave way and Danie dropped from the ceiling with bucket and all to land at the feet of the astonished school principal, soaking wet. To the great delight of the hall full of children, of course.

If I remember correctly, he broke a bone somewhere, although that didn't prevent the school principal from giving him a hiding. And when he got home, his sister told his parents about this latest *kwajongstreek* – and then his father gave him another hiding.

This did not deter him from further *kwajongstreke*.

He was accustomed to hidings; he had been taught that boys didn't cry, and this was probably only the first of many broken bones. Ma always claimed that over the years Pa broke every single bone in his body on the rugby field – except for his neck, she always added gratefully – and that all these broken bones would one day take a toll in his old age.

Ma didn't live long enough to witness Pa's old age, but her words came true. Pa's joints have stiffened and his knees have given out, his wrists ache and his vertebrae are crumbling. Not all of it because of rugby, to be sure, but the way he punished his body on the rugby field certainly didn't help.

Pa carried on playing club rugby long after school, and when the injuries became too much for his ageing body he became a referee. And when he was too old to run around after the players with a whistle, he became a coach and kept serving in the management of his club. The clubs changed over the years as my eternally restless father moved his family across the country, but I remember the Goodwood clubhouse when I was very small, Harlequins in Pretoria, Gardens in Cape Town later on. These days he watches the most important matches from the couch, and pretends that his beloved game no longer gets him quite so excited or upset, but you only have to look at him while he's watching rugby to know that it isn't true.

There is no getting away from it: most Afrikaans men have rugby in their blood. Something else my French husband and children struggle to understand. There are passionate rugby supporters even among my gay Afrikaans friends. In my father's case it isn't just in his blood, it is in his bones. Yes, all those broken bones of yore, all freely sacrificed to a sport that has become a kind of religion.

And from which I felt excluded when I was small.

Why, I don't know, perhaps only because words were always more important to me than balls. Or because I wished the literary arts could make people celebrate and cheer the way sport did?

But I didn't have a choice, I literally grew up next to the rugby field, wherever Pa was playing or blowing the whistle on Saturday afternoons. I even have a flash of memory about a joyful boat ride to a game on Robben Island. Pa's club went to play there – against the prison warders, of course, not against the political prisoners.

I was blissfully ignorant about the island's most famous prisoner, who would one day become president of the country.

But surely Pa and Ma must have known about Nelson Mandela?

If they did, they didn't allow a rugby match to be spoilt by a guilty conscience or moral discomfort. It was just another game. The only difference was that the players and their families were conveyed to the field by boat, and that a few of the guys got a bit seasick.

Decades later, when I went with you and your father and hundreds of other tourists to look at Nelson Mandela's former prison cell, I winched up this memory from the darkness of my subconscious.

'So you were actually there while Madiba was in prison, Mamma?' you asked, your eyes wide with admiration as if I had gone to visit Madiba carrying a bunch of flowers.

'Yes, I was there,' I answered.

I was there, in that beloved country, during the darkest days of apartheid. I watched my father's team play rugby on a field near Nelson Mandela's prison cell.

And sometimes, my dear girl, it's no use saying that I didn't know. It doesn't make me feel any better to claim that I was too young. Because the adults around me must have known – and I loved many of the adults who knew.

And here I go pushing my writer's finger into an open wound that so many white South Africans who were born right up until the eighties still carry around with them. Most of the time we don't really talk to each other about it, because it hurts too much to remove the bandages and display the gaping wound to others. Most of the time we prefer to stay silent, as though the wound might heal by itself if we just keep ignoring it.

Our wound is the complicity question. Even if we are lucky enough to be able to say that we were not complicit in the sins of apartheid ourselves, either because we were too young or because we did in fact rise up against it after we became aware of it, we are still burdened with the complicity of our parents and grandparents. Our earlier ancestors, the ones we did not know personally, we can perhaps still consider objectively, but what about our beloved fathers and mothers, our grandmothers and grandfathers, our uncles and aunts, all those good, kind, religious people (even though they and their god had been 'kind of okay with everything'), whom we could never consider objectively?

If we are lucky enough (pure chance, once again) that our closest relatives weren't political leaders, or members of the security police who had to do the dirty work, we can perhaps still convince ourselves that they had no choice. They were products of the time and the place in which they were raised, they did what 'everyone' around them did, they simply listened to figures of authority and obeyed orders. And yet they inadvertently became part of what the American-German philosopher Hannah Arendt described as 'the banality of evil'. The kind faces of perfectly ordinary people who act immorally because 'everyone' around them is doing it.

But we continue to love these people, because they are our family, because their blood flows in our veins, because we have to judge their lives against the backdrop of their era.

After all, most of the great historical figures who are still admired today would come off badly if measured exclusively against present-day moral standards. Most of them were slave-owners, or racist, or homophobic, or religiously intolerant, oppressors of women, beaters of children, guilty of innumerable sins that may not have been considered sins in their time.

And yet.

Some people, and some nations, are guiltier than others. The Germans, who are still weighed down by the burden of their Nazi past, even have a word for this 'battle to overcome a negative past'. It is a very long word, as German (and Afrikaans) words tend to be: *Vergangenheitsbewältigung*. It is a concept found in political, philosophical and literary studies. A way to help the next generation – Bertolt Brecht's *Nachgeborenen* – process the horrors of the Holocaust.

We white South Africans do not have a word to help us deal with the recent past. Archbishop Desmond Tutu's Truth and Reconciliation Commission was a one-off event. Granted, it did go on for a long time – with weekly televised summaries from 1996 to 1998 – but when it was over, it was over. Most white people heaved a sigh of relief and put the bandage back on the wound and carried on living.

But it is not a self-healing wound. It has now started to fester and stink underneath those bandages. We will simply have to find a way to talk to one another about our own complicity and that of our loved ones – without accusations or intolerance. With empathetic understanding for historical circumstances. But above all, also without indignant excuses or cries of, 'Look what's happening now! In the New South Africa!'

Apartheid can no longer be blamed for everything that goes wrong in present-day South Africa. But nothing that happens in the country today can ever exonerate the sins of apartheid.

My father had another overriding passion that also influenced my childhood. He loved cowboy movies almost as much as rugby. (And several of his beloved Westerns, in which the 'Indians' almost always came off second best, would also not pass a contemporary test for political correctness.) Because of Pa's two great passions, my siblings and I slept in a car nearly every Saturday night.

Often, there'd be a party in the clubhouse after the afternoon's rugby game, a lively affair where Pa played the guitar and sang naughty songs and the grown-ups twisted to the music of the sixties till late at night, while the children all lay asleep in cars in the parking lot. And when there were no rugby parties, I still spent most Saturday evenings in a car, because then Pa would load his family into the brown Opel or the black Valiant to watch a Western at the nearest drive-in bioscope.

In the first decade of my life I swear I saw every cowboy movie ever made in Hollywood. The start, at least, never the end, because we children would go to the drive-in in our pyjamas, and while the trailers and adverts were showing we would run around outside with the other children, in their pyjamas, below the gigantic movie screen. As soon as the main feature started, we would all run back to our respective cars – and within ten minutes we would usually be fast asleep in the back seat, dead tired and oblivious to the movie.

Back home Pa would carry our sleeping bodies to our bedroom, and the next morning we would wake up in our beds with only vague recollections of tumbleweeds rolling in the wind and shots being fired and horses galloping. Almost as if we'd dreamt it.

Pa himself would never fall asleep while watching a Western, no matter how tired he was from working at the bank all week and attending classes in the evenings and studying at night. Some cowboy flicks he even watched more than once, from start to finish, without being bored for a second. His enduring favourite was *Shane*, with blond Alan Ladd as the lonesome cowboy, which he and his friend Bertie watched over and over in the fifties. Bertie eventually named his son Shane, and I sometimes wonder whether my brother might not also have been Shane if my grandfather hadn't been so adamant about family names.

It was thanks to Bertie that Pa met Ma, apparently on a kind of double date, Bertie and Danie together with Yvonne and a friend. Yvonne already knew about Danie, actually, because their parents lived just a few streets apart in Thornton. And Danie regularly cruised past Yvonne's house on the corner of Kafferboom Road. (The street is now called Coral Tree Road, my child, I checked recently on Google Earth just to be sure.) She thought he looked like a blowhard, this guy with the Brylcreem in his dark hair, always driving with one hand on the wheel and the other hanging out the window or holding on to the roof of the car. That, at any rate, was what she told her friend Verity, when they'd sit on the stoep and watch the guys drive by.

But when she ended up on this date with the blowhard, and could see and hear him up close, she apparently liked what she saw and heard. I don't know whether they would have touched each other on the first date, but if they had, they surely liked that too. Soon they were sweethearts, although neither of them had any experience of sex.

Thanks to her nursing training, Yvonne did at least have the necessary theoretical knowledge, and when they got engaged she drew pictures for her future bridegroom to explain the female and male body. What went where, and what could be expected if this or that was done, and so on.

The unbelievable innocence of Danie van der Vyver. It sounds like the title of a book. But both, indeed, were afflicted by the kind of innocence that is inconceivable to young people today. Morally and politically my parents and their contemporaries may not have been innocent, but when it came to sex, they truly were babes in the wood.

He'd just turned twenty-three when they were married, she was a scant twenty-two, but they learnt quickly. Barely eleven months after the wedding, on 6 May 1958, their first child was born.

I believed until just the other day that I was born on a Wednesday, because Ma always quoted a line from an old English rhyme to me: *Wednesday's child is full of woe*. Imagine my surprise when a month or so ago I looked at the 1958 calendar on the internet and realised that 6 May had been a Tuesday.

Had I known, I could have avoided a lifetime of woe. I may instead have tried to be more graceful, because *Tuesday's child is full of grace*, according to that rhyme of Ma's.

But it's too late now. Sadness, melancholy, woe have become part of my nature. It is like discovering only in adulthood that your beloved parents are not your biological parents. I will always feel like Wednesday's child, even though I am really Tuesday's child.

5

LET'S BEGIN AT THE BEGINNING

Some blessed beings can apparently trace their earliest memories back to infancy. They will tell you that they remember a white curtain stirring in the breeze while they lay in a cradle. Or a streak of bright sunlight on a wooden floor where they crawled before they could walk. Or a ginger cat that belonged to the family when they were three years old.

Not to be needlessly sceptical, but I believe that such images are often inserted into our memories by photographs, or the stories older people tell us, or just an unusually fertile imagination.

Maybe I am just jealous; despite my own fertile imagination, I cannot clearly recall a single image from before my fifth birthday. Sounds, yes, smells too, I believe – our sense of smell is after all our most primitive sense, the one that connects us to our animal nature more than the others – but every time I 'see' an image from my earliest years I realise that I am really thinking of a photograph or an anecdote. Like the picture of me as a dark-haired baby rocking in a swing made from half a tyre, somewhere under a tree in someone's yard. Or another one where, as a toddler – when my dark hair had grown out white blonde – I'm standing in a bucket, waist-deep in water, laughing. In some other backyard that I cannot recall at all.

I looked for these two black-and-white snapshots the other day and added them to the pinboard above my desk. To remind me of all my memories that don't really belong to me.

Writing about your own past is like diving into a deep ocean. The further down you swim, the darker everything becomes, the harder it is to hold your breath. And when at last you push upwards, to burst through the surface gasping for air, holding a shell you found at the bottom, that shell is always less impressive outside the water. Smaller, less shiny, more ordinary.

That is what I'm doing now, looking for shells in pitch-dark water, feeling my way around.

In his novel *Light Years*, American author James Salter writes about a character who looks back at her life, an older woman who has completed the required pilgrimage through vanity and envy to reach a wider and calmer world. I read his words with an involuntary nod of recognition, especially the final sentence:

Like a traveler, there was much she could tell, there was much that could never be told.

That *much that could never be told* remains any writer's greatest challenge – an even greater one in memoir than in fiction. Perhaps that's another reason why I'm casting this memoir in the form of a letter to my daughter, so that I always keep in mind that someone very close to me will read my words.

And behind you, my dear girl, are all the other people I write about here.

In a novel I can harness my imagination to disguise reality, but in a memoir I have to write about things that really happened and people who really lived. Or who are still living, which only makes everything more complicated.

That is why I have always insisted, with only half my tongue in my cheek, that I was too young to write an autobiography. Too many people still have to die before I can write about them honestly. But sitting and waiting for people to die around you is a rather macabre way to pass the time. Especially if your own way of living and lifestyle choices can't guarantee that you will outlive everyone around you.

Life is short, writes Maggie Smith (the American poet, not the British actress), *and I've shortened mine / in a thousand delicious, ill-advised ways /. . . I'll keep from my children.* Exactly, I thought the first time I read the poem 'Good Bones'. Me too.

I turn 62 this year, and at least two Afrikaans author friends of roughly the same age have died in the past three years. Ryk Hattingh unexpectedly, of a heart attack, one week after we had enjoyed a joyous reunion at a literary awards do in Cape Town. Although he too had undoubtedly shortened his life in various *delicious, ill-advised* ways. And Harry Kalmer more slowly, of cancer, but still far too quickly, too soon. Untimely.

I wanted so badly to read more of Ryk and Harry's words.

And if I were to die tomorrow? That was the question I had to ask myself. What is the one book I would still have wanted to write? The answer came to me instantly, as if a light had gone on in the back room where I'd always packed the thought of a memoir away. I wanted to tell my own story, in my own words, to my daughter.

You are old enough now, and our relationship has always been sufficiently forthright that I don't have to shy away from any of the traditionally 'awkward' topics between mothers and daughters. Unlike my poor Ouma Tina, who couldn't talk to my mother about her body or menstruation or sexuality, these days most modern mothers and daughters can hopefully talk about these things.

Even though it often remains an impersonal kind of conversation. Mothers still struggle to share their personal experience of sexuality with their daughters, and precious few teenage daughters have the confidence to share their own sexual experiences with their mothers. This I realised with shock a few years ago, when I accompanied you to the local sexual health clinic and the doctor on duty congratulated us on our good relationship. High school girls almost never brought their mothers along to the clinic, she explained. Because teenage girls in France don't need their parents' permission to obtain contraceptives from a state clinic, by far the majority of them prefer to keep their parents in the dark.

I looked at you, astonished, mindful of all your friends with their pretty, modern and youthful mothers – all much younger than me, at any rate – and asked if it was true that they didn't bring their mothers along to the clinic. You shook your head and said they couldn't talk to their mothers about that sort of thing.

Sexual candour has nothing to do with age, I realised that day. It is a process that starts the day your daughter is born, it is shaped by everything you do and everything you say, as well as by the way you react to everything she says to you or shows you from childhood.

I may have had an unfair advantage over other mothers because by the time my daughter was born, I was already well-known – or notorious, rather – as a writer who wasn't afraid to write about sex. Perhaps it was simply a matter of practising what you preach. I would've felt like a fraud if I had tried to write as honestly as possible about sex in my fiction but couldn't talk about it to my only daughter.

If you, my only daughter, had not felt free to discuss your emerging sexuality with me, I would have failed somewhere along the way. If I am brave enough to write honestly, I should be brave enough to live honestly, because living well is still more important than writing well.

When I write about the first years of my life, the *much that could never be told* is more than just a moral issue. I am constrained by more than the fear of injuring loved ones, or the discomfort my attempts at honesty could cause in my own small circle. I am above all restricted by the physical impossibility of remembering far back enough.

One writer's beginning. This could also have been the title of my story, mindful of Eudora Welty's *One Writer's Beginnings*, a slim little book full of wisdom that meant a great deal to me when I was unsure of myself as a beginner writer.

Now I am unsure of myself as an experienced writer, as you know, my girl. The uncertainty doesn't disappear with age. On the contrary. The older you are, the more other people expect from you, the higher the demands you make of yourself, the greater the uncertainty. It's just one of many things I didn't know when I started writing.

And the reason I am telling you this is because I suspect that it applies to all creative professions.

It does strike me that Welty's title refers to 'beginnings', in the plural, while Afrikaans doesn't really have a suitable plural form for the noun *begin* – and yet I know that my story had many beginnings.

For me, as for Welty, who divides the memories of her youth into three sections ('Listening', 'Learning to See', 'Finding a Voice'), listening was also a beginning. One beginning among several possible ones. I've told you how enchanted I was by the sound of words when I was small, haven't I?

The repetitive sounds of songs and fairy tales and games are what I especially remember from my toddler years, rather than any images.

Some bedtime stories Ma had to tell again and again, like 'Little Red Riding Hood', with its rhythmic, question-and-answer ritual that me and my siblings could never get enough of. *But Grandma, what big eyes you have. All the better to see you with, my dear. But Grandma, what big ears you have. All the better to hear you with, my dear.*

We drew out the pleasure of the questions for as long as we

could. Grandma's nose, hands, feet, everything we could think of, was questioned, and if Ma hadn't stopped us, we would probably have strayed underneath grandma's nightgown as well. (*But Grandma, what big boobies you have. But Grandma, what a big bottom you have.*) Until at last, giddy with joy and quivering with fear, we got to Grandma's mouth.

All the better to eat you with, my dear!

And the next night we would want to hear it all again.

Pa wasn't a big storyteller, but he sang us bedtime songs. 'My hartjie, my liefie' (My little heart, my little love) was my eternal favourite. Probably no coincidence that it was the first song my French daughter learnt to sing in her mother's language.

Well, you were too young to keep a tune, and you weren't really talking yet – in any language – so it was actually just a babbling re-frain. What on earth was the meaning of *soh-sah-weh*, one of your French aunts wanted to know after you had been in her car for half an hour, during which you'd 'sung' non-stop.

I had no idea – until the next time you started 'singing' in my car and the penny dropped that *soh-sah-weh* was your version of '*son sak weg*', the sun setting far beyond the blue mountains in this beloved little song.

And then there are all the soothing, rhyming, repetitive incan-tations of children's games. In Afrikaans we didn't play catch or house, we played catch-catch or house-house, as if repeating the word would double the pleasure. *Aan-aan. Huisie-huisie. Bok, bok. Wolf, wolf. Aljander, aljander.*

Whenever I am tempted to regret all the games my French chil-dren will never know, I am reminded that many Afrikaans children don't play *Aljander, aljander* either any more. It is cold comfort – how can the loss of words ever console one who loves them? – but it makes me feel less guilty, at least.

Had you grown up in South Africa, my darling girl, it is equally unlikely that you would have played *Wolf, wolf, what is the time?* with your friends.

Different times, different games.

Had you grown up in the country of my birth, you would also not necessarily have known all the old-fashioned sayings and idioms I sometimes have to dive for in the depths of my deepest memories. Now at least I can make you laugh when I try to translate some of the untranslatable phrases into French, like the one about Mister Thought who planted a feather.

Poor old Can't died from pushing a wheelbarrow.

Nephews and nieces produce little pieces.

After fun, tears will run.

Cover your mouth with your hand, says the hen to the hound, says the hound to the bees, if you cough, yawn or sneeze.

This last one you actually knew as a toddler and can still rattle off in Afrikaans ('*Sit jou hand voor jou mond, sê die hoender vir die hond*'), because it was the most fun way for you to learn 'manners'.

But then the damn COVID-19 virus hit, while I was writing this long letter to you, and suddenly the silly rhyme became worthless. Now you have to learn *not* to touch your mouth with your hand. 'Cover your mouth with your elbow, says the hen to the crow'?

Many of these sayings were already past their sell-by date when I raised you. 'Curiosity fills prisons and empties churches.' 'Children should be seen and not heard.' Such warnings you would never hear in our house – not in any language.

Others were so entertaining that I used to share them with you just for fun. 'If you eat lying down, you'll grow horns.' 'Hiccups mean you've stolen sugar.' But if you want to stop hiccupping, you have to try to remember the last time you saw a white horse. This was one of my mother's tried and tested remedies, which also worked for my French children.

And then there were sayings or customs that I would never have been able to explain to you, phrases buried so deep in my memory that they had ceased to exist – until I started digging down to my subconscious.

Like Ma shouting '*Koes!*' whenever we drove under a bridge. At this call to duck, everyone in the car would cover their heads with their hands as if the bridge might collapse on top of us. Everyone except the driver, usually Pa, who had to keep his hands on the wheel. Where on earth did that game come from? Maybe it originated with Ma's mother, back when there were still very few bridges; maybe a family member was afraid of being crushed by a bridge. But in our car it was a funny little ritual that made us laugh, nothing to be taken seriously.

I grew up in the suburbs, after all, and we regularly travelled on highways with bridges.

At some point the ducking game stopped, probably even before I went to school, and I forgot about it. Never asked Ma about it. Never established whether any other families played it as well. And now Ma has been dead a long time and I will never know the origin of that '*Koes!*'

Now it is merely a sound – a single syllable – that encapsulates all the secrets, all the silences, all the unanswered questions of my earliest years. But also all the exuberant joy that words can bring.

My first visual memory is of a journey, an endless train ride with my grandmother across the Russian Steppe, my doll and I clad in identical little coats with fake fur collars. Of course I wasn't really in Russia, but years later, when I read about the Trans-Siberian railway, I was reminded of my winter journey with my ouma Hannah. Eventually movies like *Dr Zhivago* and *Reds* blurred my memories even more, and to this day this journey soon after my fifth birthday seems vaguely Russian to me.

It is probably fitting that the first images I remember were un-locked by a journey. I would become a lifelong traveller, both figu-ratively and physically, never home in the same place for too long, always planning my next escape. And to this day things become untethered when I travel – fears and joys, questions and biases, but above all my imagination.

Before I tell you about that first journey, I should at least sum-marise the preceding five years, that part of my existence of which I have only secondhand knowledge. I was there, but I wasn't there. I was a character in a story that my mother and father told me.

Born on the rainy back of Table Mountain, in the Mowbray ma-ternity home, where the Rosenkowitz sextuplets would make world headlines sixteen years later, the first surviving sextuplets in history. As a young adult this was often my answer when someone asked me where I was born: 'In the same hospital as the Rosenkowitzes.' When I changed gynaecologists in my thirties, after the traumatic ex-perience of my first child's birth, I gave my new doctor the custom-ary answer about the Rosenkowitzes' hospital – and then he nodded modestly and said yes, he had been the obstetrician at that birth.

I knew, then, that I would be in safe hands for the birth of my next child.

It was as if I had completed a circle. Many more circles waited in my personal life and in my career, and some would always remain incomplete, but the storyteller inside me always wants to connect the dots and come full circle. I look for endings to chapters in order to start new chapters.

My siblings arrived in quick succession. This was before wom-en gained access to reliable contraception, and I was barely nine months old when Ma became pregnant with my sister. And when Hanli was barely a year old, our brother was on his way.

One of the many unanswered questions in my life is how on earth my mother kept her head above water. She had three children under the age of four before her twenty-seventh birthday. In a cramped little house in Thornton, with no domestic helper or washing machine, let alone a tumble dryer, and disposable nappies didn't exist. In the wet Cape winters, nappies and baby clothes that wouldn't dry were strung up all over the house.

I know, things were even tougher for my great-grandmothers with their dozens of children, and in the early sixties millions of my mother's fellow citizens were raising their children in shacks and tin shanties, without electricity or running water or sanitary facilities. Compared to them, of course, Ma was privileged.

But the misery of women I didn't know, I can only imagine. My mother's frustration I can feel inside my own skin. I know she was a clever woman who couldn't wait to go back to work.

Or just to read a book for a change.

Whenever she spoke about those difficult early years of motherhood, the longing for books shone through, almost more than the frustration about all the wet bloody washing. There was no time for novels; she started reading magazine stories to fill the void, short stories she could get through between feeds and nappy changes and other tasks. But read she would.

After the birth of her third child the contraceptive pill was starting to liberate women around the world from continuous pregnancies, but her husband badly wanted another son. Or even a daughter, if it really couldn't be helped.

It's not that Pa was ungrateful for his two daughters. It's just that he wasn't quite as grateful as when Ma gave him a son.

He wasn't at the hospital with Ma when his children were born. In those days fathers were excluded from the labour ward, doomed to pace up and down in waiting rooms while chain-smoking, like cartoon characters. Or if the labour lasted throughout the night and into the next day, they had to go to work. Paternity leave was a ridiculous notion, almost as ridiculous as a woman wanting to be a rugby referee. In those days the respective territories of men and women were demarcated with painful precision, with boundaries as impenetrable as the Berlin Wall.

This is 1961 we're talking about now, when my brother was born and the Berlin Wall was built.

Pa never smoked, neither in a waiting room nor anywhere else, and he dutifully went to work in his office at the bank while Ma was in labour. Each time he hoped that all this pain and suffering would produce a son, but he was glad in any event when the call came with the news that his wife had given birth to a healthy, normal little girl. Both the first time and the second time.

By the third birth he had perhaps stopped hoping, because when the call came and he heard that he finally had a son, the astonishment and joy made him sit back down on the chair in his office so heavily that the legs broke. He landed flat on his backside on the floor, but immediately jumped up and borrowed a colleague's scooter and raced to the Karl Bremer Hospital in Bellville to admire his son.

For years my sister and I had to listen to the story of how Pa broke the chair in his excitement. We never asked why no chairs had been broken when we were born, we simply accepted that was how it worked. Every father wanted a son.

But Pa's second son never arrived. Ma was pregnant three times after Wiaan's birth, and each time she lost the baby very late in the pregnancy. Each time it was a little boy.

After the third failed attempt the doctors warned that it would be dangerous to fall pregnant again, and she had a hysterectomy when she was still in her early thirties. I didn't know what a hysterectomy meant. I had hardly been aware of Ma's last three pregnancies. I vaguely remember that she went to hospital and had to stay in bed when she came back home and announced to us children that there wasn't going to be another little brother.

The news didn't exactly break my heart. It was difficult enough to be a responsible big sister to one wicked little brother. I wasn't really keen on more.

I only realised years later that a hysterectomy was a serious operation, that my mother's uterus had been removed when she was so young, and that she had handled the awful experience with so little drama or self-pity that we children can scarcely remember it. It was the way she approached all illnesses and accidents and operations, strong and unselfish, right up to her final illness.

There were other journeys, too, before the train journey with my grandmother. The one that Ma and Pa talked about often was an adventurous road trip to Natal where we camped in a small tent under subtropical trees. There were monkeys in the trees and my brother was still a baby who slept in a suitcase. I don't know why, there probably hadn't been money for a carrycot, but I like to imagine that I can see the baby lying among the clothes in the suitcase, with monkeys peering at him from the trees. And yet I know that this is another secondhand picture. I remember nothing about that trip.

But the journey on the night train with Ouma Hannah, from Cape Town station through the Swartland and Namaqualand to Keimoes near the Orange River (the final stretch in my pharmacist uncle's Mercedes), where we went to visit Tannie Marie and my cousin Riana, is a beacon in my life. As if I had been blind before, and was afterwards miraculously able to see. During that endless train journey (which in reality probably only lasted a night and a day), I started to observe my surroundings and store my observations in my memory, and during the lifetime Ouma and I spent in Keimoes (perhaps a week or so), things happened every day that I would remember for the rest of my life.

As far as I'm concerned that was where my life really began, in a train on the way to Keimoes.

Not quite as mournful as the Briel family's song about the train to Pretoria that your father plays so often for our French guests to tease me. They don't understand a word but the Hawaiian guitars and quivering voices make them roar with laughter.

In Keimoes my cousin and I baked mudpies for the fairies and one night we left our baking outside. The next morning we found only a few dry crumbs on the table in the backyard. Now convinced that the fairies adored our mudpies, the next night, of course, we wanted to do it again. I will always be grateful that Tannie Marie played along night after night to reinforce our belief in fairies. I was a naive child, with no older cousins to rub my nose in 'the truth' before I was ready to hear it, and I managed to keep believing in fairies and Father Christmas and other imaginary beings for an unusually long time.

Or maybe it was just self-deception – a defence against the harshness of reality? – as Griet confesses at one point in *Entertaining Angels*:

'It was one of the biggest disappointments in my life when I heard that Father Christmas was my own father in my mother's dressing gown.'

'You always believed in that kind of thing more easily than the other children,' Hannes said thoughtfully. 'Father Christmas and the Easter Bunny and the Tooth Mouse.'

'I still have an extraordinary capacity for self-deception . . . But when I first started doubting Father Christmas . . . It was like pulling a cornerstone out of a wall. The whole wall collapsed.'

At the end of the visit to Keimoes, Ma and Pa came to fetch me by car. When I suddenly saw my whole family in front of me, Ma and Pa and little sister and brother, after the longest separation of my short life, I burst into tears. It was the first time I realised that it was possible to cry from happiness, not only from hurt or frustration or fear, and it was a revelation that left me bewildered.

It was likely the beginning of an emotional life I could recall, because most of the other memories from that year also involved violent emotions. The incredible disappointment when, one night shortly before Christmas, we were looking at the stars and I asked Ma and Pa where the star of Bethlehem was that we sang about in church, and Ma said no, we couldn't see it, it had only appeared that one time in the Bible. So I would never see that star with my own eyes, I realised, which made me wonder how many other things in the Bible I had also misunderstood.

The start of my disillusionment with Bible stories, perhaps, or at any rate the beginning of the end of a blind faith in everything written in the Bible.

Because once you start asking questions, you can't just stop. Especially not if the grown-ups around you don't seem to know the answers either.

That was also the year I became aware of a fear of death, because an elderly neighbour died and her domestic helper came to tell Ma that she knew the woman was dying when she noticed how cold her feet were that morning.

'Death starts at the feet, you know,' she said.

This gave me such a fright that every night for months afterwards I would feel my feet in bed to check that they were warm enough, that death wouldn't sneak up on me in my sleep.

Still, it remained only a vague fear – I couldn't honestly believe that a child like me would die just like that – until one day in my Ouma Tina's house it dawned on me that anyone could die at any age. Including me, this Marita with the pet name Hatta – which I got because my younger brother and sister couldn't pronounce my name correctly – this little girl, with blond hair and blue eyes and far too many freckles, could cease to exist tomorrow.

This intense realisation of my own mortality hit me in the toilet in my grandmother's house. I wish it had been somewhere more aesthetic, more suited to philosophical speculation, beside the sea or under a tree, even beside the cannas in my grandmother's front garden or in her sitting room with the piano and the Tretchikoff on the wall, but it was in the 'lavatory', as Ouma called it. 'Levetrie', as it sounded to me. The only wall ornament was an old-fashioned cistern with a long chain you had to pull to flush the toilet.

We cannot, unfortunately, choose the origins of our great metaphysical questions.

I sat in the toilet for a long time, completely paralysed with fear, until I had the bright idea to start praying. If I could reach some sort of agreement with the Lord Jesus, I figured, I might be spared, at least until I was an adult. I decided forthwith that I would become a missionary one day, and save hundreds of little heathen children in Africa, if only I could stay alive until I was old enough to set off on my mission.

As you know, I never did go and save little heathen children.

I was spared in spite of this. To my astonishment I became an adult and started writing books. Sometimes I think the main reason why I started publishing so early was because I remained convinced that I could keel over at any moment. That would have served me right for not keeping my promise to become a missionary.

After that day in my grandmother's toilet, I could never again live without the knowledge of my own mortality, as an animal or a very young child lives. It was a shadow that always walked beside me, sometimes a very long shadow, sometimes barely visible, but always there. It impelled me to get a foot in the door of the publishing world as soon as possible. Before I keeled over.

Some of my friends in journalism also dreamed of writing fiction one day, but they were prepared to wait patiently for that 'one day' to arrive. I couldn't afford to wait. I went looking for my 'one day', grabbed hold of it and pulled it closer, did everything in my power to turn 'one day' into right now.

But for the past few years I have often visited schools in South Africa, to encourage children to read Afrikaans books and write Afrikaans words, and sometimes I feel as if I did indeed become a kind of missionary after all. We may no longer talk about little heathen children, but I do believe that here and there I have converted a child to appreciate the wonder of the word (with a lowercase 'w'). And that makes me happier than any other kind of missionary work ever could have.

I find it strange that I remember Ouma Tina's house in Thornton better than the house where my family lived at the time. Even though I always thought the Tretchikoff print above the couch in Ouma's house was the one of the famous orchid wilting on the stairs, presumably because I was subconsciously drawn to the decadence and sexual suggestiveness in that painting. The flower with its blushing reddish interior, the open safety pin with which the corsage had been pinned to someone's shoulder, the cigarette end and the streamers higher up on the stairs, mementoes of a wild party.

It was only when my mother's sister recently assured me that it had been one of Tretchikoff's more innocent paintings of poinsettias that I searched for it on Google, and instantly recognised the real painting of windblown red-brown flowers. Of course, my grandparents would have preferred the less decadent picture. It was wishful thinking that had made me remember the voluptuous orchid in their prim sitting room.

It was a reality check, reminding me once again that I cannot always trust my own memories.

Of my first home in Thornton, near Ouma's house in Kafferboom Road that has now become Coral Tree Road, I have no visual recollection. All I know is that there must have been a small garden. Throughout my childhood the family teased me because as a baby

I was often discovered outside in the garden, eating snails until the slime streaked down my chin.

Look, I know babies eat the strangest things. You, my girl, chewed right through the sponge rim of your playpen in my writing room – even after we had sprinkled pepper on it and covered it in mustard – as if you were trying to eat your way to freedom. In the end I had to get rid of the playpen and pay someone to watch you two days a week while I tried to write. But I have never heard of another baby snacking on raw snails.

When in my teenage years I started displaying an inclination towards Francophilia, my mother claimed that those garden snails in Thornton had been the first sign.

The first exotic dish I braved during my first visit to Paris, then, was a bowl of snails with garlic butter. It was in one of those cheap tourist traps in the so-called Latin Quarter where the food is almost inevitably disappointing. But I convinced myself that any kind of cooked snail had to taste better than the slimy junk food I had swallowed as a child.

By my fifth birthday we were living in Boston, in a house whose outlines alone I remember, like a picture in an old colouring book that was never coloured in. It was in one of the avenues that run parallel to Voortrekker Road, possibly Third Avenue, close enough to the busy main road that you could sometimes hear the drone of the traffic. Long before that sad ride in my grandfather's funeral procession I found Voortrekker Road devoid of any appeal, but my brother was a born wanderer, an adventurous runaway, a miniature version of Tom Sawyer for whom Voortrekker Road was as alluring as the mighty Mississippi River.

There was a wire fence around the house, overgrown with a green creeper, but that never prevented his escaping. He was barely two years old the first time he sailed through a hole in the fence and disappeared without a trace. He was eventually found in the main road, a small figure fearlessly toddling around, mesmerised by the traffic and the bustle. They patched the hole in the fence, but it was like trying to stop water from flowing through your fingers. The mini Houdini of Boston always found an escape route.

I was far more timid than my brother. The wide world on the other side of the fence looked much too dangerous for me to brave on my own. Besides, Pa and Ma said I wasn't allowed to leave the yard, and I tried really hard to be obedient.

I was a painful goody two-shoes in my earliest years, really, the apparent fate of many oldest children who are constantly being told to set a good example for the younger ones. Your French father was an exception. He managed from an early age to serve as a warning rather than an example to his seven younger brothers and sisters, with all his wild adventures they wouldn't want to emulate.

Our home was an ordinary little suburban house with two bedrooms and a stoep in front, and a backyard with an inflatable pool and a tricycle which we children used as a diving board. We would stand on the seat of the tricycle and jump into the water amid much shrieking and laughing and a great deal of splashing. Given that the inflatable pool was barely deep enough for the water to reach our calves, the hosepipe was usually left in the pool to ensure that just as much water flowed in as was splashed out.

In my teenage years we would have proper swimming pools at two other houses, with deep water and a Kreepy Krauly, but no swimming pool ever gave me the same exuberant joy as that little inflatable pool in the backyard.

I remember none of the furniture or decor in our Boston house. The house wasn't empty, naturally, it's just that everything in the house was already there when I started consciously observing my surroundings, so it made no impression on me. Except for the pictures of dogs on the wall above my bed – and that I only really remember because one day the pictures were suddenly no longer there.

At least one of these pictures, probably cut out of magazines, was of a German shepherd dog. An inexplicable choice, because I was afraid of 'wolf dogs', as we called them, after a supposedly friendly German shepherd belonging to friends had tried to bite my sister. I supressed the fear, the way children do when they cannot articulate their emotions, but I was plagued by the most awful nightmares night after night. I would wake up sobbing and call to my mother. She sometimes had to sit beside my bed for hours while I stared fixedly at the ceiling, too scared to fall asleep again and have another nightmare.

All I was ever able to tell Ma was that I had dreamt about snakes.

Ma enquired everywhere about what we could do to prevent these recurring nightmares, but found no solution. She even started reading psychology books to discover the origin of the snake dreams, and probably began to suspect that it stemmed from sexual fears. The symbolism of snakes and Eve in the Garden of Eden is notorious, after all. But of course she couldn't share this suspicion with her five-year-old daughter.

Eventually, at her wits' end, she removed the pictures of the dogs from the wall, apparently intending to replace them with more sentimental pictures for me to look at before I dozed off at night. Pretty flowers or little lambs or something. But it never became necessary to put up anything else on the wall. Within hours of the picture of the 'wolf dog' being removed, the nightmares vanished. And I never had bad dreams about snakes again.

With hindsight, I can speculate that the wolf dog may indeed have triggered an unconscious sexual fear, given that I listened to Ma's telling of 'Little Red Riding Hood' so incessantly. This fairy tale has so often been scrutinised and analysed by psychologists and philosophers – the red of the little girl's riding hood symbolising menstrual blood, the wolf in the forest alluding to the dangers of a first sexual experience, the possibilities are truly endless – that it is difficult just to dismiss it as an innocent children's story. And perhaps in my sleep my fear of the wolf was transmuted into a fear of another animal with sinful and sexual connotations, and that was how the snake slithered into my dreams.

But it remains speculation. A young child's inner life remains a pitch-dark cellar.

Even when the former child returns as an adult to shine a dim torch of self-examination into the darkness, there will always be more darkness than light.

I remember an incident at a children's party over which I agonised for years, consumed by guilt, secretly convinced that it marked me as cruel beyond redemption. A seemingly nice Dr Jekyll that could at any moment turn into a hideous Mr Hyde.

The party was held at a house across the street, a dozen little girls in frilly dresses and patent-leather shoes and bobby socks who all stood in a circle belting out a shrill version of 'Happy Birthday'. I may have felt a little left out because I didn't really know the birthday girl; I was probably only invited because I lived in the same street or because the birthday girl's mom didn't know enough other children. I was terribly shy, remember, definitely not the sort of child who made friends easily and immediately became the centre of attention.

The only child who looked even more out of place than me was a considerably younger little girl, probably someone's little sister who'd been dragged along. Perhaps I was jealous because some of the older girls made a fuss about her. Or maybe she just had one of those faces that are asking to be punched.

Because that was what I did.

I punched her.

Or maybe I pinched her or pulled her hair – the gruesome details

I have mercifully wiped from my memory – which made her sob.

Of course, I wasn't so foolish as to launch my attack in front of the other children; I did it furtively when I came across her in the passage. Hopefully she was too young to tell anyone why she suddenly started crying so bitterly. Or maybe she did tell because I was never invited to play at that house again. Or maybe I stayed away of my own free will, like a criminal who feels too guilty to set foot at the scene of his crime again.

Because I felt terribly guilty. It was my first real experience of sin and guilt. Like in Dostoyevsky's *Crime and Punishment*, you might say, except that I succeeded in hiding my crime and was therefore never punished in any way. Which only made me feel more guilty.

At the end of that year we moved from our house in Boston to the brand-new suburb of Welgemoed, where I could begin a brand-new life as an innocent and harmless Dr Jekyll. I was given a second chance to become the good little girl I so badly wanted to be, despite the dark side of my kind temperament that I had discovered at that children's party.

Later on I learnt that many young children steal or lie shamelessly or hurt smaller children, apparently without ever feeling truly guilty about it, and that most of them do not become monstrous adults. I sometimes wished for a life that was equally carefree and guiltless, like children's author WO Kuhne's cheerful Huppelkind, who had replaced the disobedient Red Riding Hood as my role model. Huppelkind was an Afrikaans version of the sweet Christopher Robin in the Winnie-the-Pooh stories, always skipping and hopping along.

These days, I think that an early encounter with my dark side – the disturbing knowledge that I was capable of senseless cruelty, that I could hurt a defenceless smaller child for no apparent reason – wasn't a bad training ground for a future fiction writer. It made me understand instinctively that we can all be good or bad, that it is often only circumstance or chance that separates 'good people' from 'bad people'. I now know that my first sin wasn't all that despicable – I managed, somehow, not to become a violent sadist – but it did prepare me for the shadows that I would eventually find in myself and in the people around me.

But I still wish I could apologise to that crying little girl at the children's party. In imitation of St Augustine and the *Confessions* of Anthony Burgess, I am writing down these confessions of a distinctly unsaintly author, in the hope that someone may read them one day and recognise herself as the child who was bullied at a birthday party in Boston in the early sixties. And that she will forgive me.

6

MALINGERING

I wanted to call this story *Reisiger*. But Elsa Joubert has already chosen *Traveller* as the title for a memoir, and she belongs to the older generation of Afrikaans writers I admire too much to try to imitate.

And yet I have started noticing the phrase 'like a traveller' more frequently in other writers' work, like in this quote from James Salter's *Light Years*:

All the past, he told himself, all that had been so difficult, that he had struggled with like a traveler with too many bags – idealism, loyalty, all your virtues, your decency – they will be needed when you are old, they will preserve you, keep you alive.

It is an echo of an earlier quote from the same book (*Like a traveler, there was much she could tell, there was much that could never be told*), but this time it was the phrase 'with too many bags' that caught my attention.

We are all travellers with too many bags, too heavy for us to carry alone. Our roots are part of our baggage, of course. As Gertrude Stein rightly remarked: *But what good are roots if you can't take them with you?*

Sometimes it is complicated for me and my French-Afrikaans children to exist "between countries", like travellers trapped on a train that has come to a stop between stations. I use this image on purpose, my dear girl, because it is an experience with which you're familiar. The high-speed TGV trains in my adopted country have a way of sometimes stopping in the middle of nowhere, most often because someone has jumped in front of them. This is apparently a popular French form of suicide, a final desperate cry of *Je m'en fous!* (I don't give a damn!), to ensure that your death also disrupts the plans of a lot of travelling strangers.

When you are stopped between stations like this, you cannot get off the train. The automatic doors are locked, and even if you could smash an emergency window to escape you would already be too far from the station where your journey began to return to it. And possibly even further away from the station to which you were headed.

In my case, the original station is South Africa, and the destination France, but it is not the everyday France where I have now lived for more than two decades. (With one foot still in South Africa.) It is an idealised dream station that I will never reach. Because dream stations don't exist.

All that matters is the journey.

And that's okay, you know? It isn't 'easy', but we must be wary of getting too comfortable in our comfort zone.

Lauren Elkin issues a similar warning in her entertaining memoir of urban meanders with the title *Flâneuse: Women Walk the City in Paris, New York, Tokyo, Venice, and London*:

Beware roots. Beware purity. Beware fixity. Beware the creeping feeling that you belong. Embrace flow, impurity, fusion.

The difficulties of my school days are also part of my baggage, even though they barely tip the scale in the magnitude of human experience. I never knew desperate poverty or hunger, I did not lose my home or my family in a war or a natural disaster, I never had to flee empty-handed to a country that didn't want me.

I was a privileged white child in an era when anyone with a white skin in the country of my birth was privileged purely because of that. Even the poorest white children were so much more privileged than any black child. This is a simple fact that is still denied by many white South Africans, because 'white privilege' has become a rousing war cry among our black compatriots, but it remains a fact.

When we talk about privilege, Roxane Gay writes in *Bad Feminist*, people immediately start playing a meaningless and dangerous game she calls the Privilege Olympics. Is a wealthy black man more privileged than a poor white single mother? Is a disabled homosexual Asian man more privileged than an able-bodied heterosexual black man?

These are futile questions, says Gay, because privilege is always relative and contextual. Almost everyone on earth is more privileged than someone else somewhere on earth.

And yet no argument can change the fact that, in South Africa in the sixties, I was privileged in many more ways than most other people in the country. And it is important that you know this, dearest girl, because that is the lens through which you need to read everything I tell you about my school days.

My first school year in Totius Primary School, within walking distance of our house in Boston, did not start out well. Despite my excitement about learning to read and write, I found it hard to adjust to school life.

I was just five years old, probably not yet emotionally equipped to leave the shelter of my home and find my place among hundreds of older children at school. In the early sixties there weren't really psychological tests to determine whether children were school-ready. The rule was simply that you could start school at five provided you turned six before the end of June, otherwise you had to wait another year.

If you therefore turned six on 30 June, it was a done deal, but if your birthday was one day later, on 1 July, it was like playing al-jander, aljander, as we called our version of the game oranges and lemons. You lost your head because 'the last man's dead'. Nothing you could do about it; you were out of the game and could only watch as the other children carried on playing. Or as they went off to school while you waited until the next January.

Most children I knew didn't attend a crèche or kindergarten be-fore starting school either, because most mothers were housewives, or hired 'maids' to watch the children. If, in addition, you had no older brothers or sisters who would mentally prepare you for life at school, no one in the family who could be a reassuring presence somewhere in a terrifying school playground, the first weeks of Sub A could be fairly traumatic.

But I didn't sob in class on my first day or cling to my mother. I was too shy to cry in front of the other children, and I really wanted Mamma to be proud of me in my brand-new blue uniform, lace-up shoes polished to a shine, short white socks spotlessly clean, a boxy brown suitcase in my hand. My hair brushed back from my face and twisted into plaits so tight I could barely blink. Possibly another rea-son I didn't cry. To cry you need to be able to blink your eyes against the tears, at least.

But I was so terror-stricken that for several weeks I was doubled over with stomach pain in the mornings before school. My moth-er the nurse soon determined that I didn't have stomach cancer, or worse. The pain was certainly psychosomatic, but that didn't make it any less awful. It is impossible to say to a young child, 'You stomach isn't really sore, it's your head that is making your stomach sore.' It made no difference to me whether a malignant tumour or my head was causing the pain. All I knew was that my stomach really hurt.

Over the course of the year the inexplicable stomach ache gradually disappeared – but that was far from the end of my aches and pains. You and your brothers won't believe the physical and psychological health problems I had in my primary-school years, because I may well be the healthiest person you know. When everyone gets sick around me, I am invariably the last one standing, playing Florence Nightingale.

I suspect that my astonishingly good health as an adult has to do with the eight years during which I was a single parent to Daniel. You sometimes hear mothers say that they simply cannot afford to get sick, they simply have to stay on their feet to care for babies and toddlers. This is even more true of single mothers, who are solely responsible for a child's physical and material welfare.

Whatever the reason, I am genuinely grateful for my strong constitution, because as a child I was closer to being the proverbial ninety-pound weakling – although of course I didn't weigh anything close to ninety pounds. In my second year at school, I was so pale and thin that the teacher once kept me back in the classroom during break to feed me sandwiches, while she tried to winkle out as discreetly as possible if there was a money problem at home. Shame, she evidently thought, the child isn't getting enough to eat.

Ma was quite offended when she heard about this, because we most certainly weren't starving at home. I was just unbelievably 'picky' (as Ma used to sigh) – nothing orange like carrots or pumpkin would pass my lips, nothing green like lettuce or gem squash or just about half of all vegetables, nothing 'strange' that I hadn't tasted before, like tinned mushrooms or tinned asparagus. The list was endless, and doubtless very frustrating for Ma.

'What did Miss have on her sandwich?' Ma wanted to know.

'Cheese,' I replied. (Cheese was about the only food I always liked to eat.)

Ma sighed again and declared that a child could not live on cheese alone. It was her maternal duty to teach me to eat a proper balanced diet, and Miss should keep her nose (and her cheese sandwiches) out of our family's business.

Ma probably also sent a note to school, because Miss never offered me one of her delicious cheese sandwiches again.

Early in my primary school years I started getting terrible migraines as well. Same as you, my darling daughter. That pain was most certainly not psychosomatic, although of course it was literally 'in my head'. I remember the awful pressure on one side of my head, the blind spots and the nausea, the hours I spent lying in dark rooms groaning, and how nothing could ever bring any relief until I finally vomited. Then the worst was instantly over, as if a stone had been lifted from my head, and I could open my eyes again to face the daylight.

In primary school you were also felled regularly by migraines. I could think of no way to comfort you except to say that it would hopefully stop once you got to high school. Because that was what happened to me. Sometime during my early teens my migraines disappeared and never came back; apparently to do with hormonal changes.

I was endlessly relieved when yours also disappeared when you reached adolescence, because it doesn't always work that way. Some people's migraine attacks only start in adolescence; some women suffer for decades, until the migraines recede at last during their menopause, while for other people it remains a lifelong torture.

And if you *have* to experience regular pain (it's part of being human, they say), surely it is preferable to endure a few years of excruciating pain while your body is still young and your memory short, rather than to live with it for the rest of your life.

Besides, there is something to be said for intense pain at a young age. It helps you understand other people's pain and hopefully makes you more empathetic throughout your life.

My nurse mother always had empathy with pain and illness, but precisely because she was a nurse she had no patience for hypochondriacs and shamming.

After we moved to Welgemoed I was amazed to learn that nearly all my classmates could pull the wool over their mothers' eyes when they wanted to stay home from school. There were all sorts of ways to do it – besides putting on a performance of groaning and moaning – such as secretly plunging the thermometer in hot water just before your mother placed it in your mouth. There were tips and recipes for vomiting that children shared with each other in whispers. You mixed toothpaste and banana and I don't know what else and then you became so nauseous that you started throwing up on the spot.

But none of these tips helped me one bit. Ma would take one look at me and bundle me out of bed and off to school without mercy.

'Stop shamming,' she would say. 'There are lots of children in hospital who are really sick. Children who dream of going back to school again!'

All the sick children in the world couldn't make me want to go to school on days when I had to write a test for which I had not studied enough. Or when the test had anything to do with numbers or arithmetic. There was no point in even studying for those kinds of tests because all of it was incomprehensible and unlearnable.

Besides, Ma's sermonising about sick children in hospitals had as much impact as her warnings about hungry children in Africa when I was being 'picky' and didn't want to eat my food. What did that have to do with me, I wondered. It wasn't as if all the sick children would miraculously recover if I dutifully went to school every day. Just like the hungry children wouldn't suddenly be fed if I ate all the food on my plate.

But when my sister and brother and I were really sick, then Ma tended to us lovingly and even spoilt us a little. In those days children contracted all the contagious diseases that they're inoculated against these days – measles, mumps, German measles, chicken pox, the whole caboodle. The three of us infected one another as a matter of course, and time and again we all got sick at the same time. Then Ma would bring us toast with Marmite in bed, with sweet milky rooibos tea, and red or green jelly as a special concession.

When we were healthy, there was dessert just once a week, usually on a Sunday. And only if we had finished all our food.

When we were sick, Ma cut us a bit of slack. We could eat jelly and Marie biscuits as our main meal. Of course, not at every meal or even every day. 'Then you'll never get better,' Ma said, and she was probably right. I would stay in bed with no complaints for weeks on end if I could be rewarded with jelly and Marie biscuits.

Ma also fetched us books from the library, brought us paper and crayons and board games like Snakes and Ladders, and sometimes even bought us a few comic books. (Educational classics in comic form, of course, rather than the 'real comics' with American superheroes that we would have loved to read.) If we were being exceptionally good, not picking at our chicken-pox scabs or smacking one another around the head or complaining that we wanted to go play outside, we might even be rewarded with a coveted annual. One of those thick annuals, like *Boys' Own* or *Girls' Own*, packed with comics and stories, could keep us happily in bed for days.

But as soon as we were well, as soon as we could no longer infect other children, we were banished from this secret garden of earthly pleasures. Sent back into the cruel world of school and sums with no more sympathy. And heaven help you, as Ma liked to say, the next time you wanted to pretend something was wrong in order to skip school.

Of all the characteristics I inherited from my mother, this impatience with feigned illness was the one that surprised me the most when I became a mother myself. And to emphasise the eternal irony of fate, I had to raise my children in a country full of malingerers. The French have many admirable qualities – rationality, a passion for good food and personal freedom, respect for artists and intellectuals – but complaints, strikes and malingering just happen to be national pastimes.

It is sometimes very hard for me, the Calvinist daughter of a nurse mother, not to roll my eyes at all the shamming I see around me. By your mother you will be known, whether you like it or not.

I hope you will remember this, Mia, and forgive your mother in advance for all the hereditary sins with which she has burdened you.

Most of my early hereditary sins probably came from my neurotic Ouma Tina. By my seventh birthday I was increasingly displaying signs of obsessive-compulsive behaviour: a constant dry cough that made my family fear I had contracted a life-threatening lung disease, gasping for breath like someone who was suffering from severe asthma, continuous blinking as if I was short-sighted.

There were other aches and pains too, but of those I can remember nothing, either because I was too young or because they were so distressing that I have deliberately forgotten all about them. (I suspect it's the latter.)

As a last resort Ma and Pa took me to see a child psychologist – an unusually drastic decision in those days. I was the only child I knew who received 'psychological treatment'.

Even worse, I was, as far as I could tell, the only person – child or adult – in the northern suburbs of Cape Town in the mid-sixties who ever saw the inside of a psychologist's consulting room.

It wasn't something I wanted to boast about on the playground. I already felt 'different' from the children around me, shyer, less socially adept, more inclined to live in my own imaginary world, and my greatest desire was to be exactly like everyone around me. To be accepted as 'one of us'.

After a few sessions the psychologist suggested that I should spend more time with children my own age (my unvoiced heart's desire), that Ma and Pa should see to it that I was kept so busy that I would be too tired for anxiety attacks, and that I should 'play more and think less'. Perhaps not phrased in exactly that way, but that was how my parents understood it.

And that was how the Save Marita From Thinking Too Much campaign started in our house.

I was given a bicycle as a birthday present and quickly learnt to balance on two wheels, I started taking swimming lessons and ballet lessons and attended the Kinderkrans (a children's religious movement that provided a bit of biblical indoctrination amid all the playing), I joined the Voortrekkers and learnt to march and sometimes went camping in the mountains with my teammates. (No, it wasn't like the Hitler Youth, my child. Well, not really.)

The Kinderkrans and especially the Voortrekkers probably caused problems of their own later on in my life, giving rise to religious and political questions that no one wanted to answer, but at that stage it didn't matter. Ma and Pa were relieved, the campaign was apparently successful, my anxiety attacks and obsessive-compulsive tendencies were under control.

They succeeded – at least, for a few years – in getting me to play more and think less.

Of course, not all my memories of my first school years are unpleasant. I remember my first teacher better than most of the other teachers who would cross my path at five different schools over the next twelve years. Some of them I remember for all the wrong reasons, too. But my Sub A teacher was a radiant exception.

It is perhaps inevitable that the first woman who spends more time with you than your mother leaves a deep impression on your young mind. That was how it was in my day, and how it was for you too, although you were already at school by your third birthday, like nearly all French children whom the government tries to introduce into the education system as early as possible. All in aid of realising that sought-after equality in the French national motto, *Liberté, Egalité, Fraternité*, so that children from impoverished homes don't find themselves at too great a disadvantage by the time they start school. But it does mean that you, unlike me, were too young to remember your first teacher's name.

Some of my South African friends and contemporaries had a black childminder during their preschool years who seemed more like a mother to them than their own white mothers. For them, this 'nanny' was the first woman who could fill their mother's shoes. But for me it was Miss Hanekom at Totius Primary School.

Our family only got a house with a 'maid's room' in Welgemoed a year later, which made it possible to employ a full-time domestic helper. Ma went back to working a full day and Dolly Titus from Kenhardt became our second mother, taking care of us throughout my schooldays, even moving with us to Pretoria eventually, where she didn't know a soul but where she finally met her soulmate. When we moved to a farm in the Lowveld, she came along again. But towards the end of my schooldays she resigned to go marry her soulmate and live with him in Eersterust in Pretoria.

Then she disappeared from our lives without a trace.

I don't know what her husband's name was, I don't know if she had children, I don't know if she spent the rest of her life in Eersterust. I don't even know if she is still alive. I know absolutely nothing about the woman who had been 'like a mother' to me for a decade.

How do I explain that to you, my French daughter?

How do I explain the shameful prevalence of 'maids' rooms' in white suburbs throughout the country, of women who were 'like family', to borrow the title of Ena Jansen's book on the subject, but who never ate a meal at the table with the family or accompanied them to church or to the beach?

What kind of 'family' is treated like that?

In France, no one we know has a live-in childminder or domestic helper. Here, you have to be extravagantly wealthy to have domestic staff living on the premises. But in my childhood in South Africa, most white middle-class families could afford live-in help. There was no minimum wage. The fact that they were given a room and meals was often the excuse for paying them as little as possible.

Most of the good, kind, religious people I have already told you about didn't believe that they were treating their childminders badly. Like most slave owners in previous centuries, who felt no qualms about slavery. It was simply the way things were. If you were born into the right social class and with the right colour skin, you or your family owned slaves.

In South Africa skin colour was even more important than social class. Even working-class whites had black or coloured 'chars', women who came once or twice or more times a week to wash or iron or scrub floors, or 'nannies' to help watch the children. ('Char' comes from the British 'charlady'.) Many white children literally grew up on the back of a black nanny, bound tight against her body in a blanket all day long.

I was an adult before it became the fashion for white mothers and even for white fathers (completely unthinkable in my childhood) to keep their babies close to their bodies in wraps or slings. That was how your father and I carried you around in your first weeks and months – and it was soon clear that you were happiest when you could feel our body heat and hear our heartbeat. Something black women in my native country seemed to know instinctively, because that was how they had always kept their own children and their employers' children content.

I will come back to Dolly later – it is impossible to tell the story of my childhood without honouring her as one of the main characters – but first I must pay homage to Miss Hanekom. To me she seemed as beautiful as Snow White in Walt Disney's animation film, of delicate build, with porcelain skin and rosy cheeks and black hair, sweet-tempered with a gentle voice, the nearest thing to a fairy-tale princess I had ever seen in the flesh.

One day she asked whether anyone in the class had a little sister at home. A few children put up their hands and I conquered my shyness just long enough to also get one hand in the air at halfmast. Soon afterwards Miss Hanekom visited our home and asked my mother if my little sister could be the flower girl at her wedding later that year.

This request sent my emotions racing around like bumper cars at a showground and caused some quite violent collisions. I was overjoyed and proud that my little sister had been chosen, rather than anyone else's little sister, but also terribly disappointed about not being chosen as flower girl myself. And once I caught sight of the long pink princess dress that was made specially for the flower girl, and heard that her hair would be teased up into a high bun, I wanted to cry with envy.

Miss Hanekom was clever not to have chosen one of the girls in her class, as that could be considered unfair, and because a pre-schooler in her family had already been chosen to play page boy and carry the rings on a little satin pillow, she was simply looking for a flower girl the same age. That was how Mamma explained it to me when she saw how badly I wanted to wear that princess dress. But I was unconsoled. I felt that I had been weighed and found too light. Or too heavy, in this case, too old, too big for the little page boy. Spurned. Rejected.

Handling rejection is never easy, especially when you're barely six years old.

But I didn't hold it against Miss Hanekom. She remained my heroine right up to the end of the year and to this day I remember her as the fairy-tale princess who gave me the key to unlock a castle full of knowledge. The person who taught me to read and write. The greatest gift anyone could have given me.

It was only that little page boy I might have poisoned, given half a chance.

A year or two later, my father's twin sisters had a joint wedding, and again, to my deep disappointment, I was rejected as flower girl. This time it was my little cousin Sandra who got the chance to show off in a short pink ballet tutu with little ballet shoes and a tight bun. As a consolation prize my sister and I were named the official confetti girls. We stood at the entrance to the church with baskets full of confetti, wearing identical party dresses with bell sleeves and billowing skirts – hers yellow and mine light-blue. But we weren't important enough for buns.

It wasn't until my mother's sister Suzette got married another year or so later that my dream finally came true. Hanli and I were flower girls in long turquoise dresses with high buns. Hanli's dark hair had been cut short by this time and she had to wear a false bun, but I had kept my blond hair long, perhaps only from the sustained hope that I would one day be a flower girl with a bun.

For two nights after the wedding I slept sitting up to preserve the magnificent construction on my head for as long as possible. By Monday morning the bun had collapsed over one ear, which made me look like an underage whore with a hangover, and Ma declared that I couldn't go to school with my hair in such a mess. I cried while she combed out my hair and put it in the same two boring fat koeksister plaits as always.

The least predictable consequence of my glory day as flower girl was that I was put off any appearances at the altar for the rest of my life. While I stood next to the bridal couple throughout the long wedding service, the eyes of everyone in the church upon us, my legs started shaking uncontrollably. From exhaustion, I thought, because it felt like we'd been standing there for hours, but maybe it was nerves and emotion. All I knew was that I didn't dare faint, because that would ruin my aunt's wedding ceremony.

And then no one would ask me to be a flower girl ever again!

By the time we could walk out of the church at last, I was *hoping* that no one would ever ask me again.

I decided that I would rather not stand at an altar ever again.

I managed to get married twice without going near an altar. The first time I did it right there in my living room in Cape Town, and the second time in a French magistrate's office, as required by French law. Some of my French acquaintances hold a second wedding (with the same person) because they fancy standing in front of an altar, but I was very relieved that I didn't have to do that.

Something else happened early in my school career that I deliberately forgot about for decades. When I was finally brave enough to crack open the door to my pitch-dark subconscious, I wrote a short story about it. The title is 'Tree of Knowledge' and it starts like this:

For years now, the scent of green figs has made me gag in inexplicable revulsion.

It was one of those things you bury so deeply within yourself that it disappears from conscious memory. Selective memory loss as a form of self-defence. But the senses are mightier than the mind. My nose remembered what my brain had tried to forget.

While a friend who lived in the neighbourhood and I were playing in an old fig tree in their garden, her considerably older brother, who was already out of school, lured me into his bedroom and felt me up. When I came out of the room I overheard his mother, who was probably aware of his paedophilic tendencies, tell my friend that I was too old for her and that it would be better if I didn't come over to play again.

I was eight or nine years old. Nine, I decided a few years ago when I wrote openly about the incident for the first time, for a newspaper article on sexual harassment. Nine is, after all, the age at which a young girl – according to Nabokov's diabolical Humbert Humbert in *Lolita* – becomes a 'nymphet'.

Between the age limits of nine and fourteen there occur maidens who, to certain bewitched travelers, twice or many times older than they, reveal their true nature which is not human, but nymphic (that is, demoniac); and these chosen creatures I propose to designate as 'nymphets'.

My friend's mother's cruel words made me believe that I must be demonic, and that everything that happened in the bedroom had been my own fault. It was such an unbearable burden of guilt that I simply erased the incident, the way I would learn to push the delete button on a computer many years later. But when I finally embarked on that short story and turned my physical experience into fiction – a way of sharing without sharing too much, because it is only words on paper, it is just a story – I began to understand that at least some of my unaccountable 'psychological problems' in primary school derived from this incident.

You were also pestered once by a friend's older brother, a teenage boy with a degree of intellectual disability who tried to molest you. But you didn't subside into shame and silence the way I did back then, you immediately ran home and told your father and me what had happened.

It was traumatic for you nonetheless, and you still sometimes have nightmares about it, but I am deeply grateful that you were able to put it into words right away, that we could reassure you that it hadn't been your fault, that you didn't hide it for decades in the darkest corner of your subconscious.

Despite all the anxiety and tummy aches of my first year at school, despite the fact that I struggled to make friends with the other children and wet myself from sheer nervousness in front of my classmates at least three times during the year, despite everything, the overwhelming victory of my first school year is still that I learnt to read and write.

I was already in love with words when I arrived in Miss Hanekom's class, but it was like having a crush on a mysterious person you heard on the radio. Someone you had never set eyes on. And then one day – oh, what joy! – you literally see the words in front of you. And they somehow look even lovelier than they sound.

I could suddenly see the letters 'S' and 'u' and 's', and string them together to read the word 'Sus'. I could hear 'Daan', and then I would write a 'D' and an 'a' and another 'a' and an 'n', and read what I had just written. Yes, like thousands of other children in the sixties, I too was initiated into the wonderful new world of reading by a silly little book called *Sus en Daan*. There wasn't much of a storyline or gripping dialogue (I remember a bee stinging a donkey, and the donkey crying out: 'Bee is stinging me!') but I could look at the pictures for hours and spell out the letters over and over. As proud as Hillary when he reached the top of Mount Everest.

From this mountain peak I had the first glimpse of the rest of my life and a preview of years of reading pleasure. I could even start to dream that I might one day write words that would provide reading pleasure to others. Because once you can read and write, everything becomes possible.

That I had already heard of Hillary at such a young age, but that no one had ever told me about the Sherpa named Tenzing Norgay who had summitted with him, is just another indictment of where and when – and, above all, how – I'd grown up.

7

GIRL FROM THE SUBURBS

If, in the last half of the previous century, you were raised on a farm or in a small country town in South Africa, you will remember dusty streets and dirt roads and deserted plains with windmills pumping water from dry soil and lonely church steeples pointing heavenward like the Finger of God. The church was often the tallest building in the vicinity, the moral pivot of most white people's lives, which inevitably gave rise to a tangle of hypocrisy.

If you felt slightly more sinful than everyone around you, a little alienated and lonely, perhaps more artistic than sporty, the kind of child who asked questions that the grown-ups couldn't or wouldn't answer, you probably dreamt of the wide world beyond your small town. As Lou Reed sings in 'Smalltown', the only good thing about growing up in a small town is knowing that you want to get out one day. Away from the boredom and the narrow-mindedness and the bullies at school and the neighbours gossiping about you.

That's how it was for many of my friends.

Few of us knew the exciting big city from the inside. Few of us spent our childhood in flats in the centre of Johannesburg or Cape Town, like children in New York or London or other European cities that we sometimes read about in books or saw in movies.

And yet many of us weren't from farms and small towns either. We lived all around the cities, as near to the sinfulness of the city as dammit is to swearing, but sheltered at the same time from its worst excesses. Our suburban existence was a domesticated kind of existence. Like animals in a zoo, we may have given the impression that we were wild, even that we were free, but we were never as free as farm children or as wild as real city kids.

We were the boys and girls from the suburbs.

And in these suburbs, especially in the hundreds of new ones that shot up all over the country during the sixties and seventies as the Afrikaner's urbanisation kept gathering speed, we were quite a confused species. No longer unsophisticated country bumpkins, maybe, but nowhere near streetwise city kids. Caught in the middle between farm and city, never quite certain where we really belonged.

The suburbs where I ended up may not have been in the same *skomgat* category that Anton Goosen sings about in 'Boy van die Suburbs', with garden gnomes and fish tanks in the sitting room and flypaper at the screen door. But still. The 'sub' in the word 'suburb' suggests it's not quite as good as something else, as in substandard.

And we were trapped, as in a prison, in an environment of uniformity. Each house was more or less as big (or as small) as the next one, everyone was working class or lower-middle class in suburbs like Thornton or Maitland where my parents were raised, or aspiring to upper-middle class in the suburbs where my ambitious father wanted his own children to grow up, or already wealthy in the most affluent suburbs like Bishopscourt, Houghton, Waterkloof.

The uniformity of this 'we are all like this' – or sometimes the superiority of the 'we are not all like that' – is so inherent a characteristic of a suburban existence that you don't even notice it until you're forced one day to leave your suburb and go to school in the platteland. Had I not spent my final two school years (entirely against my will) in a boarding school in the platteland, I would never have sat in a class with children from both sides of the proverbial tracks.

The whole point of all the new suburbs in the country was that everyone in every suburb lived on the same side of the tracks. Like seeks like, that was how it was, whether you were common or grand. And, of course, white always seeks white.

Black and coloured, so we were told, seek black and coloured. They did not really want to live 'with us'. 'Separate development was better for everyone.' That was 'the truth' we grew up with in the suburbs.

The Truth and Other Stories is another title I considered for this story. But it, too, has already been used by another writer. My friend Harry Kalmer was clever enough to give this name to his debut collection of short stories in 1989, as if he knew from the start what some of his countrymen continue to deny today. That the truth we grew up with was just another lie.

So, when I ended up in a platteland school in Standard 9, I encountered classmates from a wide social spectrum for the first time, something that had never been possible in my safe suburban schools without hostels. Like my mother, who got to know much richer and even some poorer children during her teenage years at Hoërskool Jan van Riebeeck than would have been possible had she gone to school in Goodwood or Maitland like my father, at Hoërskool Nelspruit I got to know the children of doctors and eminent families as well as children from the poorer parts of town; from wealthy farm children to a species that to me, as a suburban snob, seemed somewhat backward.

It taught me something I would never have learnt in my respectable suburban life: that money can't buy intelligence or sensitivity. It was a lesson I could only hope that my own children would also learn at school in the French countryside.

Had you gone to school in Paris or any other big French city, your friends would have been restricted to a certain *niveau*. The French don't like the word 'class', it reminds them too much of the British class system, but of course France also has different classes or social tiers or *niveaux* or whatever you want to call them. And because the law requires that French children attend the school nearest their home, you inevitably have schools filled with privileged children in safe, wealthy neighbourhoods – and schools filled with struggling children in poverty-stricken neighbourhoods controlled by drug dealers and criminals.

In the countryside, you can still escape this kind of social separation. Here your best friend's older brother can be the dope dealer on the corner and your second-best friend's family can own the château on the hill.

The fact that so many wealthy French still keep their children in state schools, at least for part of their school lives, may be a remnant of the (admittedly shaky) national belief in freedom, equality and brotherhood. It is a motto that I too would like to keep believing in. Perhaps your rural school experience contributed to a greater understanding of the inequality into which people, in reality, are born, and how important it is for precisely that reason that everyone should have equal education opportunities. Or perhaps your forced countryside education was just another example of what Philip Larkin means in 'This Be The Verse' when he says that we are all fucked up by our parents: *They may not mean to, but they do.*

The suburb of Welgemoed was laid out in the fifties on a farm of the same name. Apparently it was planned from the start as a kind of 'Constantia of the northern suburbs', with plots almost three times the size of Boston or Parow, and my upwardly mobile bank-manager father decided that this was where he wanted to raise his children. (At least until his restless nature drove us deeper into the interior, five years later.) What appealed to Pa in particular, when we went to live there early in 1965, was that a kind of pioneering spirit still prevailed there.

It was certainly no Wild West town like in all those cowboy movies we went to see at drive-in bioscopes on Saturday nights, but it felt more like a country town than a suburb. There were few houses and large tracts of veld between the houses, there were a few dams where children could play for hours without parental supervision, and there was a fynbos-covered hill from where you could look out over the Peninsula all the way to Table Mountain and the sea in the distance.

The golf course was already there – it's about the only thing I recognise when driving through Welgemoed these days – but it wasn't a golf estate of the kind you find everywhere these days. No fences or security gates or guards to keep non-residents at bay, no high walls separating the houses from one another. It was the kind of suburb you still sometimes see in American movies, where neighbours can greet each other from their stoeps, where children play in the street outside the houses and walk to school together in the morning.

I was among the first forty pupils of the small school that was started in January 1965. It consisted of two classrooms where everyone from Sub A to Standard 2 were clustered together, with two teachers to hold the fort, and it was the closest I would ever get to an old-fashioned farm school. We didn't even have a uniform to begin with, we went to school barefoot, in the same clothes we would wear to play in the veld in the afternoons.

For the first year or so we did indeed lead a kind of idyllic pioneer life, but during the five years we lived in Welgemoed, the country-side idyll already started to fade. The veld disappeared to make way for new houses that kept getting bigger and more expensive, the dusty streets and dirt roads were tarred, ostentatious gardens were laid out and the drone of lawnmowers became the weekend soundtrack.

One day our parents held a meeting to design our school uniform, a democratic process that got everyone involved. (Except the children, of course, who would probably have preferred to remain uniformless.) The adults chose a maroon school blazer with a cap for the boys and a rock-hard straw boater for the girls, a blue school badge featuring a crested coot and a Latin motto, and suddenly we were 'a proper school'.

After that, we moved from the two temporary classrooms next to the cafe to a brand-new school building across the street, where we would ultimately be able to stay until Standard 5. But our little pioneer group of 1965 would always long for the freedom of those early years.

Forty years after my family went to live in Welgemoed, I wanted to show you and Daniel my childhood home in Van de Graaf Street, but the suburb had grown and changed so much that I could recognise absolutely nothing. (Except the golf course, of course.) I got hopelessly lost, driving up and down streets with names that sounded vaguely familiar but without recognising a single house or garden, and when I realised that you two were hungry and profoundly bored with my Proustian search for a lost time, I gave up and went to buy you hamburgers.

You were too young to remember it anyway, but if you like, I will show you the next time we visit South Africa. Because in the meantime Google Maps and GPS have of course made any quest easier – even one back to the past.

It is always a risk, going to look for a house where you were happy as a child. The chances of your being disappointed are simply too great. It will most probably look completely different from what you remember. Run down and neglected, or 'spruced up', modernised and enlarged beyond recognition. That is, if you can still somehow see the house, because these days most houses in South African suburbs are hidden behind high fences with electronic gates. Safeguarded like fortresses or castles.

That is why I was so astonished when recently – this time with the help of Google Maps – I finally found myself back outside our house in Welgemoed. There was indeed a tall fence surrounding the garden, but when I peeped through a gap between the fence and the gate, it was like stepping into a time machine. The house looked exactly the way we'd left it fifty years ago.

The garden path leading to a small stoep with three steps at the front door, and three windows to the left of the front door. Ma and Pa's bedroom at the far end, Hanli's and my bedroom in the middle, and immediately left of the front door Pa's study and occasionally also the guest room, where Great-grandma Nelie still slept before she went to hospital for the last time and we never saw her again. To the right of the front door, the lounge with the large French window that Ma liked so much, a glass door opening onto a patio and a pergola and a lawn sloping towards the bottom of the garden.

Next to the open front door there was a child's tricycle – just like when we still lived there and regularly raced down the grass slope on my brother's tricycle, without brakes, which meant you had to jump off at the last minute or crash into Ma's flower beds. For us this supplied the sort of adrenaline-packed excitement that bungee jumping from tall bridges would offer to generations that came after us.

I could even picture Ma sitting in a sunny spot on the patio, in one of those wire chairs that was always outside, with her cat-eye sunglasses perched on her nose, paging through the Sunday paper and sneaking a cigarette. Yet another scene that Pa captured for posterity with his little movie camera. Ma quickly dropping the hand with the cigarette when she realises she's being filmed, because Oupa Willie and Ouma Hannah weren't supposed to know that she smoked, and what if they saw the home movie Pa was making.

I stood gazing at my former bedroom window for a long time, through that gap next to the gate, wondering if I dared push the intercom button to ask the people behind the open front door if I could come inside.

But the old willow tree right at the front of the garden – the best climbing tree in the world, with wide branches where we children could play and dream for hours – was no longer there. Instead of the willow there were a few palm trees, each one just a single thin, tall trunk, which no child could ever play in. The height of those palm trees, far above the roof of the house, made me realise how old I had got since I was last in that garden.

I turned away without trying to see inside the house.

It was such a fabulous, unexpected gift to find the exterior unchanged. I decided against pushing my luck any further. I would rather remember the interior the way it was, long ago, when nearly all my earthly adventures took place in and around that house.

Diagonally across the road from us lived an English-speaking family (from the former Rhodesia, I seem to remember) to whom my brother owes his first full sentence in the English language. The son of the house was the owner of a very desirable bicycle, with more gears and a shinier frame than any other bicycle in the street, and because Wiaan at this stage only had that ancient tricycle with no brakes, he soon learnt to say, 'Can I please lend your bike?'

No, Ma said, it's 'may I', not 'can I'. And it's 'borrow', not 'lend'.

Thereafter Wiaan would ask, 'May I please borrow your bike?' virtually every day. And because the kind son generally agreed, my brother literally spent hours riding up and down the street on this fancy bicycle.

I had my own bicycle, thanks to the Save Marita From Thinking Too Much campaign, and rode all over town with my friends on their bicycles. We formed gangs, inspired by Enid Blyton's *Secret Seven* and *Famous Five* books, searching for suspicious-looking adults to stalk and spy on. Any adult we didn't know personally could rouse our suspicions – a builder, a truck driver, the friend of another adult living in the vicinity – and with a bit of imagination we turned them into dangerous bank robbers or intriguing cat burglars.

The minute our victims realised they were being spied on by a bunch of underage detectives on bicycles, generally not in a particularly discreet way, they would chase us away and our game would be over. But a day or so later we would spot the next stranger and swiftly convince ourselves that he looked like someone on the run from the long arm of the law. And then we, with our short children's arms and our heads stuffed full of *Secret Seven* adventures, would consider it our duty to keep an eye on him.

Our gang activities came and went in phases, as unpredictable as the schoolyard crazes for yo-yos or playing elastics. One day there would suddenly be marbles or skipping ropes all over the school grounds at every breaktime, and a few weeks later the marbles or the skipping ropes would be gone just as suddenly.

But by far the best games were those we played in and around our garden in Van de Graaf Street, because there I could really give full rein to my imagination. We seldom played 'ordinary' children's games such as hide-and-seek or tag. We preferred acting out dramatic scripts. The willow tree in the garden, for example, would become an aeroplane that our bunch of barefoot children climbed into (each branch was a seat on the plane) and then the plane would crash and we would drop from the branches screaming, and roll around on the ground injured and dying. Next we would wander around a jungle or a desert for months on end (in circles around and around the house) and some would die along the way (if their mothers called them unexpectedly and they had to leave the game) and everyone would have the most incredible adventures.

If Enid Blyton's innocent detective stories inspired our gang activities, most of the dramas in our garden took their cue from movies. Sometimes it was one of Pa's beloved cowboy movies, and then the suburban garden would turn into the Wild West. Sometimes it snowed in our imagination and we would shiver from the cold (while the sun shone in a cloudless blue sky), and sometimes we would crawl through the dry Kalahari.

During our last year in Welgemoed, when at the age of ten I was starting to question whether I might be getting too big for these kinds of games with the 'little ones', Jamie Uys's movie *Dirkie* made an enormous impression on me. Perhaps only because it was in Afrikaans, perhaps because the poor lost boy's little dog made my sister sob so hard that no one on either side of us in the bioscope could hear the dialogue, perhaps because I was completely transported by Liszt's *Liebesträume* on the soundtrack. Thereafter we spent weeks acting out variations of *Dirkie* in the garden. Dirkie with Shane in the Wild West, Dirkie in the snow in Russia, Dirkie with Tarzan in a jungle.

I usually came up with the storylines. Once, when I went to visit my grandmother for a week and on my return questioned my sister about the games they had played in my absence, she answered, 'Oh, you know, just hide-and-seek and things. You weren't here to make up games for us.'

That was the day I realised that it might be a kind of talent, the ability to invent stories. Like catching balls or singing well – two talents I hadn't been blessed with, to my deep regret. And that I might be able to make something of this talent one day.

In the course of our Welgemoed years Pa resigned from his job at the sober-minded Nederlandse Bank and joined Jan Marais' exciting new Trust Bank. Here all the male bank managers were supposed to drive shiny black cars, and the female subordinates had to be young and pretty and wear the shortest dresses possible. Eye candy, that's what they were, in a way that has become almost unthinkable in the current #MeToo era.

Pa thrived in this macho environment, often partied with wealthy clients, started speculating on the stock market, and bought himself a shiny black Valiant.

The afternoon he brought this car home, he took the whole family for a spin on the national road heading north. 'Pollie, ons gaan Paarl toe', we kids sang in the backseat, and Pa enjoyed the drive so much he might have driven all the way to Pretoria had Ma not remembered she'd left our dinner in the oven.

Ma was also working at this time, although not as a nurse, because the hours were too impractical for a woman with three young children. For a while she did 'market research' because it allowed her to choose her own working hours. She loaded boxes of new food products into her yellow Volkswagen Beetle and went knocking on people's doors to ask them to taste the product, and then she had to ask them a list of questions. Ma wasn't a natural salesperson like Pa, she would have hated peddling anything door to door, but she convinced herself that this was research, not sales. She gave people something for free and then they told her what they thought of it.

But Pa decided she would make more money if she actually sold something, and even more if she was working for herself – or for him, which in his eyes amounted to the same thing, because surely everything that belonged to her also belonged to him? And he had always wanted to start his own business, so why not open a shop 'for her'? He would be the owner and she the manager. Ma let herself be talked into it against her own better judgement, as had happened so often in her life with Pa, and probably thought that if she absolutely had to sell something, then it should at least be something classy. Not secondhand cars or cheap takeaway food.

And that was how they started an 'elegant hat shop' in one of the first malls in Bellville. The Sabel Centre on Voortrekker Road was almost laughably modest compared to the enormous Tyger Valley Shopping Centre that would be built later, but in the sixties it was quite something. It brought a vaguely American sense of modern consumer excess to the dull northern suburbs. But Ma and Pa wanted to be classy, and to them France sounded classier than America, so the hat shop got a French name: Le Chic.

These were the first French words I had to pronounce in my life. And possibly the spark that lit my inexplicable passion for France at an early age.

I can't remember how long the hat shop lasted – probably not too long, because Pa wanted to make money in a hurry and he was starting to get worried about the stock market. It was the first of many businesses Pa would start over the years to make money quickly, and as far as I can tell none of them ever really made money. But at night I fell asleep with a seductive new language on my tongue. Chic and sophisticated, as in Le Chic.

Not quite everything that happened to me between the ages of six and eleven took place in the northern suburbs of Cape Town. Pa liked to go for Sunday-afternoon drives, just for the fun of it, right around the Cape Peninsula. Sometimes in the direction of the beaches at Bloubergstrand for soft-serve cones with Flakes in them, sometimes past Table Mountain and the Twelve Apostles (which we never once called 'Gewelberge', as they're apparently known in Afrikaans for their resemblance to gables), to admire the view over the ocean or to watch the cable car suspended against the blue sky. Without ever getting into the cable car ourselves.

Like many Capetonians in those days, I grew up in the shadow of Table Mountain without ever standing on top of it. It was only after we'd moved to the Transvaal and came to the Cape for holidays that Oupa Corrie accompanied his three grandchildren in the cable car up the mountain. Evidently the sort of thing done by holidaymakers, not by native Capetonians.

Now and again we would drive to DF Malan Airport (it's the one you know as Cape Town International, my darling child), not to meet or greet anyone, because we didn't know anyone who ever flew anywhere, but just because it was such an exciting place, where you could stand on an open deck and watch as airplanes departed for exotic destinations. Remember, if you have never flown, any destination is an exotic destination. Johannesburg was as unreachable as Jakarta.

The very first movie Pa recorded with his new movie camera was on one of these Sunday-afternoon outings. He filmed us three children running around in the playground next to the Promenade in Sea Point. Hanli and I in identical outfits as always, but in different colours, a blue striped jersey to match my blue eyes for me, a brown striped jersey to match her brown hair for her, both with pleated skirts and Alice bands. Swinging on the swings and sliding down the slide, spinning around on the merry-go-round and dangling from the ox wagon climbing frame that is still there today.

Every time I look at this film clip, it strikes me anew how terribly white all the playing children were. A lone black woman is standing to one side, on the pavement rather than on the lawn, probably a domestic helper who had to mind one or several of the white children, while her own children weren't allowed to play there.

I know that many white South Africans are tired of constantly being told how wrong apartheid was. 'Just look at what's become of this country!' they will exclaim in frustration. 'Why can't we just move forward and stop whining about the past?' But that is a yearning you can only have if you find yourself in a place of racialised comfort, as Wilhelm Verwoerd, grandson of former prime minister Hendrik Verwoerd, wrote again recently.

After former president FW de Klerk had denied in a television interview that apartheid was a crime against humanity, Verwoerd declared in a newspaper article that many white people were still unable to grasp the extent of the ongoing trauma caused by apartheid:

Perhaps not only people like former president De Klerk, but also me and my children need to sit for many more hours in deep listening circles with fellow South Africans from different racial backgrounds.

'Also me and my children', Verwoerd says, knowing full well that his children's great-grandfather was considered the 'architect of apartheid'. Also me and my French-Afrikaans children, I say to myself, because while your own ancestors weren't famous politicians in the apartheid years, they nevertheless reaped the sweet fruits of those years. Nothing I can do about it, except to acknowledge it. Every time I watch one of my father's all-white 8-mm movies, every time I remember my all-white schooldays in all-white suburbs, every time I think of everyone who was not part of our movies and our photographs.

Spaces tell stories, Roger Lucey sang in the Struggle years in reference to all the blanked-out spaces in censored newspaper articles. All the gaps in my own story likewise tell a story, and you and Daniel and even your French half-brothers must be aware of that story too, or you will never understand where I come from.

Most Afrikaans children from the suburbs still had family on a farm somewhere. Even if yours was already the second or third generation to grow up in the suburbs, even if they were only relatives by marriage, there was usually still an umbilical cord somewhere that connected you to a farm. One of my father's twin sisters had married a farmer from Porterville, and we had vague ties to a family on a farm near Darling, and my visits to these two farms stand out like sharp mountain peaks in a flat landscape when I think of my childhood.

The excitement would begin even before we arrived there. On the way to Darling we would drive through a long row of bluegum trees on both sides of the road, and then we'd know that we were almost at the first farm gate. We would eagerly jump out of the car to open and close the gates. To us it was no boring everyday task, as it was for the farm children. And oh, how we envied the farm children their rough heels! The soles of their feet were tough as leather, which made it possible for them to walk barefoot through a field of devil's thorn! On the farm in Darling I tried to imitate my friend Marietjie's feet-dragging shuffle, but my soft suburban feet were soon stung raw by the devil's thorn's three sharp spikes, and after an hour or so I usually put my flip-flops back on.

On the Porterville farm with the alluring name of Vergenoeg (so alluring that I used it as the Afrikaans title of my novel *There is a Season* decades later) there was a bumpy dirt road between the farm gate and the farmyard that made the car rise and fall like a boat between waves. Pa always drove it a little too fast, egged on by the chorus of children's voices in the back seat, so your stomach jerked upwards when the car dropped suddenly. The closest we ever came to a roller coaster.

On Vergenoeg we fed the hand-reared lambs milk from brown beer bottles and fetched eggs in the chicken run and played hide-and-seek in the large dark barn. Everything was different from our everyday suburban existence. Every visit was like a movie that had better lighting than the rest of our lives – the sky was bluer and wider, the horizon stretched into all infinity, the storyline was more compelling, even the soundtrack was unforgettable. Roosters crowing at the crack of dawn and windmills creaking like old men's stiff joints and screen doors double-slapping every time someone went in or out the kitchen.

And sometimes the movie shocked us with its cruelty.

The farm was where I first became aware of the bloody cycle of birth and death in which I was trapped, just like the animals around me.

On the Darling farm I joined the farm children on the tin roof of a pigsty to watch a pig being slaughtered. And didn't see a thing, because I squeezed my eyes shut against the horror. I tried to block my ears as well, but it didn't help, I could still hear the pig's screams days later. Another time I watched a sheep being slaughtered, and again squeezed my eyes shut when the blade was pressed against its neck, and covered my ears in anticipation – only to drop my hands in dismay when I realised that the poor victim had barely made a sound.

'Like a lamb to the slaughter.' It was the first time I really understood these words.

On the Porterville farm I kept my eyes open – wide with shock – as a sow ate one of her cute pink newborn piglets. My brain did somersaults, my child's grasp of good and evil faltered. In a world where a mother could devour her own children, any evil was suddenly possible.

On Vergenoeg I also witnessed the birth process for the first time, a cat having kittens, and ran to my mother breathlessly calling, 'Mamma, come look, they're just bubbling out!' My nurse mother, who had been present at many births – and who also knew from her own experience that babies didn't just 'bubble' out effortlessly from any animal mother – was quite amused. But I was too young to be burdened with the awful truth; she refrained from warning me that day that I would also one day give birth to my children with blood and pain.

We had pets in the suburbs too, and a few years later I could watch as one of our house cats had kittens. By then I was older and wiser; the birth did not induce the same breathless excitement, rather a strange sense of wonder. How did the mother cat know what to do? How did she know to eat the afterbirth – without eating the babies as well, like that unforgettable farm pig in Porterville?

And the most terrifying of all my questions was how I myself would know what to do when I gave birth one day.

The death of a beloved pet was of course an entirely different experience than when a farm animal was slaughtered to feed people. There was no blood or human cruelty involved – except if the pet had been knocked down by a car in the street – and we grieved for our dead pets the way we grieved for our dead people.

More than we grieved for most people, because our pets were closer to us than most people.

I have zero recollection, for example, of 6 September 1966 when Hendrik Verwoerd was murdered in Parliament. What I do remember about that year is that our little black-and-tan mongrel died unexpectedly. I was eight years old and the death of a dog touched me far more deeply than the assassination of a head of state.

Most Afrikaans people of my age remember at least something of Verwoerd's death, the headlines in the newspapers, the shocked adults, the funeral that was broadcast on the radio. (There was no television in the country, remember.) I would like to believe that it was because my parents weren't such big fans of Verwoerd that his death didn't hit our household like an earthquake. Pa was apparently shocked that a messenger with a knife could stab the leader of the country in the innermost sanctum of Parliament, but Pa was one of the 'enlightened' Capetonians who believed that the Transvaal leaders of the National Party were wrong to alienate the 'Coloureds' from the 'Europeans'.

'They speak the same language as we do, they worship the same God as we do, they belong with us.' That was Pa's reasoning, and to me it sounded fair.

I didn't notice the enormous gap in the argument. 'The Bantu' or 'Natives' were different from us, they spoke other languages and served other gods, therefore they had to be kept away from us. According to this reasoning, coloured people were in fact only to be used by white people to make the superior numbers of black people less overwhelming.

Spaces tell stories. And this story I would only begin to understand later.

Although I remember nothing about Verwoerd's death, I do imagine that I remember the death of Marilyn Monroe.

Impossible, I know, because she died four years before Verwoerd, when I was barely four years old. And I have already confessed that I find no reliable images of my existence before my fifth birthday in my memory. Perhaps, once again, it was something I heard rather than saw, a conversation among adults, the shocked tone of someone's voice.

I know that Ma and Pa watched Marilyn Monroe's movies before I was born. *Gentlemen Prefer Blondes*, *The Seven Year Itch*, *Niagara*. *Some Like It Hot* probably only later, because it was released in 1959 when I was a baby and Ma was pregnant with the next child, so there wouldn't have been much time to go to the movies.

But I am certain that I remember an article in a Sunday newspaper about the anniversary of the blonde actress's death when I was six or seven.

The only conceivable reason why the death of an American sex bomb would have made a bigger impression on me than that of an Afrikaans head of state is tied up in that three-letter word, 'sex'.

When you're a child, the whole world is one great secret to be discovered. There is so much that is hidden from you – especially if you are growing up in a respectable Afrikaans home – that you are constantly stumbling upon secrets. From the day you take your first step until the day you walk out of your parents' home for the final time.

Sex was certainly the biggest secret for many of us. Sex was that bird inside the cage that is covered with a dark blanket so it doesn't wake up too early. Of course, this enforced darkness only fanned the flames of our curiosity.

But if we should dare to touch ourselves ('down there'), or play doctor with one of the neighbours' children, or discover a magazine with shocking pictures in it at the bottom of someone's dad's wardrobe, we didn't breathe a word about it. It was our secret, ours alone, that the grown-ups couldn't know about.

I was fortunate to have a mother who wasn't prudish about naked bodies. When she bathed she didn't lock the door, because the toilet was also in the bathroom and there was always a child who urgently needed to wee. At times the traffic in the bathroom was so heavy that she complained it was becoming like Cape Town station. But it was a resigned, smiling kind of complaining.

I knew, then, from an early age that my little girl's body would one day look very different from now, that my titties would sway like my mother's and that I would grow hair in entirely unexpected places. I never saw Pa naked, he only allowed my brother into the bathroom, so I had to use my imagination about what a man's body looked like. But I knew very well what little boys looked like, because my sister and I regularly bathed with our brother.

As a matter of fact, I suffered one of the greatest humiliations of my young life in the bath with my siblings.

Ma had opened the medicine cabinet above the basin to take something out, and a little bottle of gentian violet fell out and shattered against the edge of the bath. Right next to my head. The next moment my blonde hair had been dyed dark purple. A few drops splashed onto my sister and brother as well, but my body was in the front line of this unexpected aerial attack, and they were left with only a few tiny purple stains on their fingers or toes. I was stuck with a head of purple hair – even after Ma had washed my head dozens of times with shampoo – and was sent to school the following morning with an old lady's purple rinse.

Ma, as you know, had no patience for weak excuses for staying home from school, and in her eyes the humiliation of purple hair was nowhere near good enough a reason to hide at home.

The purple shall govern.

A quarter of a century later, when the political system in the country was in its final desperate agonies, I participated in the famous Purple Rain Protest, as it was subsequently named in the newspapers. The words of the Freedom Charter (*The people shall govern*) were carried through the streets of Cape Town on a large banner to protest yet another upcoming election that was only intended for white people. It would be the last white election ever, but no one among the thousands of protesters on that Saturday in 1989 could have predicted that.

I was too far back in the crowd to be dyed purple, but it was such an absurd and yet also violent experience that I have described it in fiction on more than one occasion. In *Forget-me-not Blues* there is a whole chapter called 'Purple':

And then, suddenly, the world turns purple. The police turn on a water cannon and start spraying everyone with purple dye. The purple stream is so strong that some of the demonstrators who aren't kneeling yet are knocked off their feet. Some of the demonstrators stay on their knees like statues, others panic and start to run.

I would never forget those kneeling purple statues. The dignity of these people reminded me of my own whining outrage in the bath. I had been just a child, of course, nothing to be ashamed of. And yet.

Everything in my native country acquires a political hue at some point. In Alice Walker's novel *The Color Purple* this colour represents all the good things in life that we are supposed to enjoy, including sex. But in the blues of my own remembering, purple certainly doesn't represent good things alone.

159

Thanks to Ma's nursing training she was also more generous with biological information than many of my friends' mothers. I knew that a baby grew inside its mother's tummy after one of the father's seeds was planted there, and that the baby had to come out 'down there' nine months later. But I didn't have the faintest idea how the father's seed ended up inside the mother's body.

The gruesome details emerged gradually in the schoolyard, in the form of jokes about carrots being planted in gardens, and 'my car being parked inside your garage' – the sort of jokes that made us dissolve in hopeless giggling without us necessarily putting two and two together. Or putting the penis and the vagina together. And even after I started to catch on to the metaphors, I still didn't grasp that this was the *only* way in which babies could be made.

Earlier in this letter I made fun of your Afrikaans oupa's incredible innocence as a young man. Reading what I have written here, my dear girl, I realise that my own childish innocence will probably strike you as no less incredible. You were already paging through *Mummy Laid an Egg* as a toddler and laughing yourself silly at the funny pictures of all the ways in which mommies' and daddies' genitals could fit together. You even met Babette Cole, the British author of this most delightful book about how babies are made, at a book festival in a neighbouring village, and asked her to sign your book.

For you, the bird cage was never as dark as it had been for me. From an early age you could lift a corner of the blanket to see what you were ready to see.

Nothing more than you were ready for, but also nothing less.

The truth finally hit me like an electric shock during one break-time at school. Literally everyone who had children did this ridiculous thing with carrots and gardens. There was no other way. My father and mother did it. The headmaster and his wife did it. The dominee and his wife did it! It was a soul-shattering revelation.

Even more shocking was realising that you didn't have to be married to do this thing. Previously I had vaguely understood that two people got married because they loved each other and then that male seed ended up inside the woman's body more or less automatically. If they kissed each other or something like that. When a young domestic worker in our street became pregnant and I asked Ma how on earth was that possible, she wasn't even married, Ma said oh well, it just works like that with some people.

I thought she meant that coloured people could by some miracle have children without being married, but that white people had to get married first before the miracle could happen. The only exception in the history of mankind was the Lord Jesus's mommy. Who must have been a white person, surely?

After the first shock waves of this new knowledge of good and evil had run through my body, I regarded the adults around me differently. Now I had yet another secret to hide from them. They thought they knew something that I didn't know – but what they didn't know, was that I knew what they knew!

That was what I thought when I was about eight or nine, old enough no longer to believe in fairies or Father Christmas, but young enough to still want to believe in secrets. As if I knew in advance that I would soon have to trade the innocent secrets of my childhood for the far more complicated mystery of adolescence.

8

WORDS OPEN WORLDS

It may only be in our childhood that books can truly change our lives, writes Graham Greene in *The Lost Childhood and Other Essays*.

What do we ever get nowadays from reading to equal the excitement and the revelation in those first fourteen years? It is in those early years that I would look for the crisis, the moment when life took a new slant in its journey towards death.

I would love to believe that we remain susceptible to the influence of books throughout our lives, that the words of some authors can strike our hearts at any age and shake us to the core. But I agree with Greene that those earliest revelations in our lives as budding young readers can have an unrivalled effect. Perhaps our first book loves are as unforgettable as our first flesh-and-blood loves?

In my day the setting for this first great word romance was often a public library. Even if you were lucky enough to have a few shelves with books at home, the library was a sacred pace, a cathedral for readers, a place where the glad tidings brought by the word (with a lowercase 'w') were proclaimed.

For me it was the Bellville municipal library, a shiny new modern building with large glittering windows and a pedestrian bridge across a sparkling pond. That was a half century ago, alas, and the library has long had a different address. But as a primary-school child, that bridge I had to walk across to the entrance was like a little boat in which I could sail towards a world of wonder every other week.

On this side of the water was my mundane everyday life; across the water I was an explorer in terra incognita, an exciting place of freedom and imagination where anything was possible.

In the non-fiction shelves I discovered a heavy set of blue books with the enchanting title *Kinders van die wêreld* (Children of the World), which I just about read to pieces all on my own. Since childhood I have preferred fiction to non-fiction – lies rather than 'true stories' – but in the sixties my Afrikaans environment was so isolated from the outside world, without television or internet or social media, that the lives of children in other countries seemed as mythical as fairy tales.

I remember dozens of books with thousands upon thousands of black-and-white photographs and stories about the lives of children everywhere on earth. Great was my disillusionment when I recently established that there were just eight books in the series. It's like realising, as an adult, how small and shabby that circus tent was that looked so magnificent when you were a child.

To me, *Children of the World* was more exciting than any circus.

The countries included in each volume in the series were not arranged alphabetically or geographically or according to any rational system. It meant that you could jump from Isreal to Canada to Japan in the same book, and then in the next book visit children from Mexico, Portugal and Egypt. Every time you turned the page, you could be surprised.

Hey, suddenly you're in Bulgaria – behind the feared Iron Curtain! And the children truly look just as happy as you and your friends!

And a few pages on you find yourself just as unexpectedly in

Vietnam, where there is a war going on that you are vaguely aware of, but the book shows nothing about *that*, only smiling children with funny triangular hats in rice paddies.

In 2001 Susan Sontag wrote an essay in honour of the American adventurer and travel writer Richard Halliburton (1900–1939), because as a child his books had made her dream of a life of travelling and writing.

Before there was travel – in my life, at least – there were travel books. Books that told you the world was very large but quite encompassable. Full of destinations.

Children of the World was the closest I came to 'travel books' at a very early age. It lit a fire inside me that I could never extinguish. After that, the longing to see foreign places and hear unfamiliar languages and learn more about people who were different from me would always smoulder.

It is one of the reasons why I became a traveller, perhaps even the oldest reason why I live in France today and have a daughter who speaks French.

It is certainly one of the reasons why I went to study journalism, that wanderlust that started with a set of blue books in a library.

The Scottish author Ali Smith's *Public Library and Other Stories* is a fantastic mixture of fiction and non-fiction, a hymn to libraries with a chorus of internationally renowned writers. Like Kate Atkinson, who declares unequivocally: *York City Children's Library made me the writer I am.*

And Emma Wilson, professor in French literature and visual art at the University of Cambridge, who tells of her local library – as a child in England in the seventies – where there'd been a French librarian and a shelf full of French books.

I remember seeing the white and cream spines, the foreign words, lavish sentences, Colette, Duras. I learnt to read these French books. In the library. Here in England.

This was without a doubt where her own moment of exciting revelation in her journey to death took place.

A year or so ago I was invited to talk to a hall filled with library staff from across South Africa, as part of the Wow project at the Stellenbosch Woordfees. ('Wow' stands for 'Words open worlds' and it is aimed at schools, teachers and learners.) While I was preparing my speech, I came across an article that Bettina Wyngaard had published on LitNet a few months earlier. She had asked some fellow writers in Afrikaans to say something about the role that libraries had played in their early lives – and it was clear that this had been a very significant role.

Everyone remembers their first library; some even remember the first librarian's name, what she looked like or smelled like. For Eben Venter it was the English Mrs Slater, a grand hat-wearing lady in the Burgersdorp library. For Anzil Kulsen it was Mevrou Maggerman who installed a 'conversation table' in the library in Keimoes, where children could read and talk about their dreams for the future. Karin Brynard recalled 'the smell of wood polish on the floors' and 'the stiff sword fern on the library tannie's counter' in the library in Boom Street, Britstown. Ronelda S Kamfer had to walk a long way to 'the scheme', the setting for the nearest library in Kleinvlei, and was on her way home from the library the first time she was robbed. She ran home as fast as she could, 'flung myself onto my bed and started reading an old copy of *The Merchant of Venice* that I had borrowed that day and that had survived the robbery with me'.

If you prick us, do we not bleed? If you tickle us, do we not laugh? If you poison us, do we not die?

Every time I hear about someone reading this drama by Shakespeare, I think of Shylock's magnificent monologue. It can be read as a plea for revenge, or as an argument for tolerance. I have always preferred the latter option.

'Children didn't have many choices back then,' Bettina Wyngaard writes, 'but no one questioned our choices in the library. Precisely the reason why for me, to this day, libraries are the ultimate democracy. Everyone is equal. Everyone's choice is respected.'

The other reason why I wanted to study journalism was because I wanted to become a writer, but knew that it wasn't something you could just be from the day you finished school. I would have to find a way to earn my living until I could hopefully, sometime in the distant future, do so by writing books. Journalism was the only profession I could think of that would allow me to write as much as possible while I was learning to write.

The books in the Bellville library aside, there were a few books I discovered at home almost by chance, and which each became a beacon on my road to becoming a writer one day.

Most of these were English books from my mother's childhood. One ancient blue hardcover in particular, *Jane of Lantern Hill*, bore the marks of having been a well-thumbed treasure to my mother long before me. Some of the yellowed pages showed signs of eager fingers that couldn't turn the pages quickly enough, on others there were faded little stains that I would sniff curiously to try and guess what kind of liquid it had been. The coffee Ouma Tina brewed in a flour-sack coffeepot? Or the fine spray of a piece of naartjie peel that the poet DJ Opperman wrote about?

'Sproeireën' was one of those poems from which just about every Afrikaans child of my generation could quote the opening lines, at least. The way you and your friends can all recite a line or two from Cyrano de Bergerac's famous ode to his enormous nose. It was

Opperman's *Scent of a Woman* but instead of violets, candy floss and lemongrass, the women he wrote about gave off scents of naartjie, cinnamon and mysterious aniseed.

Although the scent of whatever it was that stained the pages had long since faded by the time I discovered this blue book. (How wonderful, I find myself thinking now, that blue books have lingered in my memory in this way.) But this was probably where my preference for 'previously loved' books from secondhand shops or flea-market stalls originated. *Jane of Lantern Hill* made me realise that old books often tell more than one story. The official story which you can read in 'black on white' – printed in clear black letters on paper that once upon a time was white – but also the concealed story of the readers who travelled through the book before you.

The secret lives of books, is how I still think of it.

Perhaps no one will read books any more by the time you read these words someday, a teenage character writes to her baby sister in my young-adult novel *Swemlesse vir 'n meermin* (Swimming Lessons for a Mermaid).

I mean books that are made of paper, books that you can read on the beach so that grains of sand stay behind between the pages and years later, when you happen to pick up the book again, a bit of sand slides out into the palm of your hand.

The best books from my childhood were all much more than mere abstract tales. They were solid objects with a distinct appearance, a unique smell, a weight in my hands. How the book looked and felt was as unforgettable as whatever was being told in the pages between the covers.

If I close my eyes now, I can see the hard blue exterior of LM Montgomery's *Jane of Lantern Hill* in front of me. The Canadian author's most famous character was Anne (of Green Gables fame), and once I had made Jane's acquaintance, of course I wanted to get to know Anne as well. And LM Montgomery! I wanted her to adopt me! She was a wizard with words and I wanted her to teach me her spells.

It is perhaps appropriate that it was a Canadian writer who allowed me to dream of authorship at such an early age, because to this day I reserve a special corner of my heart for three great women writers from Canada: Margaret Atwood, Alice Munro, Anne Michaels. All three have initials that consist of an M and an A, with which you can make the word 'ma' in Afrikaans and 'am' in English.

(There is no such thing as useless information, a character in my novel *You Lost Me* insists.)

(I don't know if that's true.)

But then I happened on a book that made me realise that you can conjure with words in Afrikaans as well.

Alba Bouwer's *Stories van Rivierplaas*, which I probably received as a gift, wasn't another of the blue books. The cover was a dun yellow-grey and had one of Katrine Harries's sketches, intricate as spider's web, on it. I know that idyllic farm stories such as these, about white children who are waited on hand and foot, and black labourers who are addressed as 'Outa', make many contemporary readers squirm with discomfort. But the language, oh the language, that was what captivated me from the very first page.

Bouwer's Afrikaans sings with joy, full of fresh metaphors and onomatopoeia and ways of saying things that as a primary school child I had never before read in my mother tongue. If that was how a story could sound in Afrikaans, I realised with amazement, then it might be possible not just to become a writer, but to become an *Afrikaans* writer.

Although the language in this book sounded so surprisingly fresh to me, the disparaging words were neither new nor in any way shocking. That was how everyone around me spoke. It is true that in our house 'ugly' racist words were forbidden when we were referring to people – we were not, for example, allowed to talk about '*kaffers*' or '*meide*' like so many other children – but at the same time pejorative words such as these were already deeply rooted in our language as the names of places or things. You know that a grandfather and grandmother of mine lived in Kafferboom Road in Thornton. The other grandmother and grandfather retired next to the Kafferkuils River in Stilbaai, and the wild watermelon preserve my mother cooked and we feasted on was known in Afrikaans as '*kafferwaatlemoenkonfyt*'.

(Fortunately this wild fruit has now been given a different name, because it remains one of the most delicious and beautiful preserves I know. The almost-transparent, light-green chunks in glossy sugar syrup, like shards of glass in the golden late-afternoon light, the crunchy texture when you bite into it. You also tasted it when you were small, my girl, but as with so many of my favourite childhood treats, like pumpkin fritters and sweet potatoes in syrup and *melkkos* with cinnamon sugar, the taste was just too foreign for you to appreciate.)

This matter of offensive words that were part of my childhood language remains a problem for me as an adult. Especially as a writer, with language as my only tool. Especially when I write fiction about the past and must occasionally put derogatory words into a character's mouth to keep the dialogue authentic and convincing. It happened again recently in *Borderline*, where a racist teenage boy in the seventies declares that he cannot wait to go to the border to go kill '*kaffers*'.

If only you knew how much I agonised over that piece of dialogue. Because I know by now how hurtful it can be to present-day readers. And yet I dare not wrap the past – and the language from my own past – in pretty gift wrap to make it look more acceptable.

In the end, for me honesty remains the greatest test of whatever I write – and self-censorship probably the greatest trap I could fall into. Once you start with self-censorship, that trap soon becomes a bottomless well from which you cannot escape.

And then all honesty is lost anyway.

Yet the pejorative words I agonise about now had little influence on the complicated love–hate relationship I maintained with my mother tongue in my youth. There are after all words like these in every language – including English, which to me had almost always seemed more desirable than Afrikaans.

Especially as a teenager in the Afrikaans suburbs of Pretoria, and later on in the conservative Lowveld, I could compare this relationship to the sentimental storyline of all the Mills & Boon romances that my friends and I loved to read. If the heroine of these stories knew from the start which man was the right one for her, there would be no story. She first had to struggle and suffer and hold out against temptation while the wrong men tried to seduce her.

Afrikaans was manifestly the man for me, but I was in love with a tall, dark and handsome brute called English. In time a foreign rogue also turned up, even further out of reach than English, who seduced me with his wicked tongue. His name was French.

The real hero of the story, a nice guy by the name of Afrikaans, waited patiently while I enjoyed my fling with English and French. He knew that he and I would ultimately – and inevitably – find each other. That is just the way stories like these happen to work.

Yes, in high school I would have loved to have been English, rather. Afrikaans teenagers were called rockspiders by mocking English teenagers who – seemingly effortlessly – managed to look and sound cooler than any of my Afrikaans friends. English teenagers could read marvellous English books in which they saw their own worlds reflected. They could watch English movies that the whole world was crazy about. And, most important of all for a teenager, they could listen to rock music in their own language.

I could find no Afrikaans books about credible modern Afrikaans teenagers. There were no Afrikaans movies that sent a rebellious teenage heart racing. (The only Afrikaans movie from the early seventies that left a lasting dent in my memory was *Siener in die suburbs*, perhaps precisely because its sleazy suburb was entirely different from the respectable suburbs I knew.) And 'Afrikaans rock music' was an oxymoron, a phrase as meaningless as 'living dead'.

There was no rock music in my language, only rockspider music, old-fashioned tunes and mawkish lyrics, an unforgiveable embarrassment for any Afrikaans teenager who liked to listen to music from abroad. Only towards the end of the seventies did the 'Musiek en Liriek' movement bring some improvement, with a new breed of singer-songwriters creating original lyrics that Afrikaners didn't have to be embarrassed by – but it still wasn't rock music. Too little, too late, I thought as a twenty-year-old rebel in 1979. I would rather keep listening to Pink Floyd and The Who instead.

In high school I believed that the simplest solution for shedding my Afrikaner status would be to get married as soon as possible to any man who did not have an Afrikaans surname, so I could rid myself of my boring Afrikaans surname. If only I had an English surname, I thought, then surely I would *feel* more English?

But in the meantime my vague feminist feelings were being stoked by the ever-widening scope of my reading appetites. I was no longer all that eager to rush into marriage, and worse, I was increasingly starting to question why a married woman should adopt her husband's name at all.

When I finally got around to getting married for the first time, after my thirtieth birthday – ironically to a man whose surname was as English as bangers and mash – I had long made peace with my undesirable Afrikaans surname. It no longer really mattered whether

I liked it or not; it was the surname I had lived with from birth, it was my identity, it was me. Why on earth would I suddenly turn into someone else?

So I remained Marita van der Vyver. I have by now been Marita van der Vyver for more than sixty years, after two marriages and countless peregrinations. I am almost ready to declare, like the main character in J van Melle's early Afrikaans novel, 'I was Bart Nel from then, and I am still he.'

It may not square with my feminist convictions to refer to myself as 'he', but if Flaubert could declare, '*Madame Bovary, c'est moi*', then I suppose I can forget about my gender for a moment too. Just long enough to misappropriate Bart Nel's famous statement in a post-modern way.

My dear girl, you do not know who Bart Nel was, (never mind, many young South Africans have also never heard of him), but he was the eponymous protagonist of a book prescribed in Afrikaans high schools for decades. Not for quite as long as Flaubert's *Madame Bovary* has been prescribed for French pupils, it's true, because Afrikaans literature is far younger. *Bart Nel, de opstandeling* only appeared in 1936, and in Dutch, at that, before the Dutch-born writer adapted it into Afrikaans a few years later.

Like Alba Bouwer's children's books from another era, and like so many classical novels in other languages, *Bart Nel* unfortunately also contains words and ideas that might upset present-day readers. The name of Bart's farm is Kafferkraal, and the woman who works in his house, is called '*die meid*'. And yet Bart Nel's obstinate attitude impressed generations of Afrikaans readers. His steadfast pride, his refusal to forget the injustices of the Boer War and forgive the English conquerors, make him a tragic hero who ultimately loses everything – except his name.

Ironically enough, he could also have been a heroic figure to modern black readers who still refuse to forgive white people for the injustices of apartheid – if only he hadn't been portrayed as such a bloody racist.

Meanwhile, this character's declaration of intransigence – which could of course also be construed as a destructive clinging to the past – has become one of the most recognisable phrases in Afrikaans literature.

'And I am still he.'

When I decided in the eighties to remain 'me', simply to keep my own name, I constantly had to explain and defend my 'stubbornness'. Not only to occasionally aggressive civil servants, bean counters and women behind bank counters, but also to kind friends and family who simply couldn't understand why I didn't just do 'what all women do'.

In France, as you know, it hasn't been 'what all women do' for some time. Here, you remain who you are when you get married – if, that is, you bother to get married at all – unless you decide that you want to relinquish your former identity and turn into someone else, with lots of new documents to apply for and a brand-new signature that you have to practice for weeks on end before you can reproduce it with a degree of confidence.

While women in the country of my birth still have to contend with incomprehension and administrative impatience when they don't want to do 'what everyone else does'. In an essay in *Vrye Weekblad*, Ronelda S Kamfer writes about the (female) official at Home Affairs who starts to lecture her (*your generation just want to do your own things*):

By now my eyes have become slits and I'm thinking, jeez, Trudy, it isn't that deep. I have a name and a second name and a surname. I don't feel like changing it. It is oppressive, old-fashioned and too much admin.

When the official haughtily declares that a married women gets her husband's surname, that's just the way things are done, Kamfer tries to explain that she married her husband and not his surname.

She lets out a deep sigh and asks why I don't want my husband's surname. The disappointment in her voice is so severe you would swear it's her own husband's name I don't want. The woman talks about a surname as if it was a Christmas present from a colleague.

Kamfer succeeds in unmasking the absurdity of the tradition with subversive humour. And yet I found her account upsetting to read, because it reminded me of my own similar experiences more than thirty years ago. Some things in the so-called new South Africa are still exactly the same as in the previous South Africa.

Once I was able to claim my Afrikaans name – and all the baggage that came with it – to carry with me for the rest of my life, it gradually became easier to claim my language as well. It's a long time since I have wanted to be English, or even French. I have become unashamedly Afrikaans.

Of course I still feel anger and shame about the racist, reactionary, far-right statements that are made in this language. Especially on social media where the most intolerant Afrikaners are often the weakest spellers, as if they can't muster enough respect for this language they're clinging to so grimly to learn to spell it properly.

But as you know, Mia, I become just as angry and ashamed about the intolerance of some French people.

I have accepted that there will always be Afrikaners who make me ashamed of being Afrikaans. Just like there will always be French people who make me ashamed that I have come to love the French language so much.

But I agree with Azille Coetzee, feminist philosopher of a much younger generation than mine, when she explains that her self-understanding is anchored in her language, that she cannot relinquish being Afrikaans without losing and betraying something fundamental about herself. In her 'travel memoir' *In my vel* (In My Skin), she puts it this way:

But along with the identity, the label, comes a dark past, a terrible reputation, which rattles behind me like a string of tins.

Those tins rattle even more loudly when you are living in another country, as Coetzee also experienced while trying to carve out a new life in the Netherlands. And yet, after more than twenty years in France, I feel more Afrikaans than I ever did when I lived in my native country. During one of the writing workshops that I sometimes present at schools, a teenager from the Cape Flats declared in a poem: 'I am Afrikaans down to my lungs.'

Selah, I can affirm. Afrikaans is my mother tongue, literally, it springs from my womb, from my stomach, my heart and my lungs, from the marrow of my bones. It is the language of my body rather than my mind, as I already warned you at the start of this very long letter, my darling French daughter.

And yet I am overjoyed that, thanks to the miracle of translation, we could both be influenced by some of the same books in our childhoods. The first time either of us read Lewis Carroll's *Alice in Wonderland* and *Alice Through the Looking Glass*, it was not in the original English. You discovered your Alice in a French translation – and immediately declared it to be the best book in the world – while I got to know mine through André P Brink's translation.

And given that my reading tastes were less sophisticated than yours, the book did not strike me like a thunderbolt. (A 'good' thunderbolt, I mean, as in the French phrase for love at first sight: *coup de foudre*.)

I only really began to appreciate Alice later, when I read Carroll's original English words.

I received the Afrikaans translation of *Alice through the Looking Glass* as a gift, from a fake Father Christmas after I had ceased to believe in any 'real' Father Christmas. It was at a Christmas party held for employees' children, although I no longer have any idea who the employer was. I only remember a black-and-white photograph, taken by a professional photographer, of a painfully embarrassed child with a heavy blonde fringe and long white bobby socks up to her knobbly knees standing alongside this make-believe Father Christmas with his long white make-believe beard. It is one of the photographs from my childhood that got lost somewhere along the way because we moved too often. Or perhaps I lost this one on purpose, because I felt uncomfortable every time I looked at it.

Everything in the picture looks fake, not only Father Christmas and his beard and his outfit, but also the child in the stiff pose beside him, too big to clamber onto his lap like the smaller children whose pictures were taken before hers. She is probably about ten years old and holds a gift-wrapped book in one hand. She doesn't yet know that it is *Alice Through the Looking Glass*, but she can tell that it is a book concealed inside the wrapping paper. And that is also strange, because all the other children got toys.

By then Pa was no longer working at the Nederlandse Bank. But it couldn't have been a Trust Bank party, either – it all looks just too demure. Trust Bank parties were wild, notorious gatherings for adults, nothing to do with children. Besides, if Trust Bank ever hosted anything like that it would surely have been an annual event, and I recall just this one instance of intense embarrassment.

Curiouser and curiouser, as the very same Alice of the book would say.

Perhaps Ma chose the book, perhaps the party was held by the company where she worked as a market researcher. 'My mother does market research,' I would answer proudly if anyone asked if my mother worked. The phrase sounded far more important than the work really was. It made me think of scientists in laboratories, of clever guys in white coats who conquered diseases and saved lives, while Ma really just knocked on doors and handed people free jars of Purity to feed to their babies.

So there I am in the photograph, frozen for all eternity in the camera flash, with a fake smile beside a fake Father Christmas. Everything in my attitude shows I that am too old for this game of make-believe. Too old, too, for the book I had received as a gift, I thought when I ripped off the paper. But by now we know what became of Mister Thought, don't we?

I was too young, in fact, for *Alice Through the Looking Glass*. Too ignorant and too unsophisticated to grasp the true value of such an imaginative tale – and the words in which it was told. I preferred to read stories about gangs and boarding school. Enid Blyton's *Secret Seven* series, Topsy Smith's *Trompie* series, the steady stream of *Maasdorp* books that Stella Blakemore churned out over four decades, from 1932 right up until the early seventies.

Maasdorp's Kobie Malan, the little tease with her golden curls and her mischievous dimples, was the girl I yearned to be. I would happily have died, with no complaints, if it meant I could come back to earth as Kobie.

Many Afrikaans readers of my generation still cherish memories of Kobie and her irresistible dimples, and of Breggie and her other friends, or of the characters in the *Keurboslaan* series written by one Theunis Krogh from 1941 onwards. I didn't realise until much later that Krogh had just been Stella Blakemore in a different guise, a male nom de plume she had to use because these boarding-school tales were primarily aimed at boys, and boys wouldn't read books that had been written by a woman.

177

The only way I can explain the enchantment of these boarding-school series to you and your brothers is by comparing them to JK Rowling's *Harry Potter* series. (And believe me, it is no coincidence that Rowling uses her initials rather than her full name. When she wrote the first book in the nineties, boys were still reluctant to read books by an unknown woman.) But Maasdorp and Keurboslaan were the Hogwarts of my generation of Afrikaans kids. Kobie was our Hermione, the headmaster Dr Roelof Serfontein was our Dumbledore.

Yes, pity us. We were really used to having nothing.

When in 2004 the *Maasdorp* books were re-issued under the banner 'Retro Series', I bought a couple, with the vague idea of reading them aloud to you one day. I knew the real reason was my own nostalgic yearning for a storybook world from long ago. But I still couldn't believe how poorly written they were when I tried to read them again.

Even the rose-tinted glasses of nostalgia couldn't make *Maasdorp* appeal to me as an adult. I realised, with regret, that I would not be able to share it with my French daughter. Just another in a long list of experiences from my youth that I will never be able to share with my children.

I have since read a magazine article in which Stella Blakemore confessed that she'd intensely disliked her own experience of boarding school. 'There is no more terrifying existence for a child,' she once said. When I read those revealing words, and realised that her boarding-school stories consisted of almost as much wishful thinking and fantasy as JK Rowling's *Harry Potter* stories, I forgave her on the spot for all the years she had made me dream of mischief and midnight feasts in imaginary school hostels.

Because eventually, when I ended up in a school hostel myself, it was without a doubt a more terrifying experience than anything the *Maasdorp* books had prepared me for.

But everything I read in my childhood, from Enid Blyton to Lewis Carroll, from Stella Blakemore to Alba Bouwer – and, of course, the unsurpassed *Children of the World* – were cobblestones in a road that I was building. It was the road that would lead me to authorship, and it was as wonderful as the Yellow Brick Road that had to lead Dorothy to Oz.

A writer is always first a reader, Susan Sontag claims, *a reader gone berserk*. A writer like me is a reader who is so swept away by other writers' words that I cannot but try to sweep readers away too. I am a lifelong reader who has gone berserk. Or as Margaret Atwood puts it in a recent reissue of *The Handmaid's Tale*: *That is how we writers all started: by reading. We heard the voice of a book speaking to us.*

I often want to paraphrase my Protestant ancestor Martin Luther's famous words, 'Here I stand, I can do no other'. My declaration would be: Here I sit and write, I can do no other.

Words open worlds. I still feel more at home in the first world to which words led me than I feel in any other world. It is the world of literature, the never-ending joy of reading, of books, stories, true stories and made-up stories, fiction and non-fiction.

But the world of reading inevitably leads to other worlds. If you study the heavens, you will keep discovering new stars. That is what happens to readers. Through words on paper we become aware of a cultural universe that expands endlessly. Words also lead us to worlds that have little to do with words, the world of visual art, the planets of music and dance, the star of food as art, of sex as liberation, of sensuality without guilt.

Granted, words can only take you so far if you want to explore these worlds (especially when it comes to food or sex), but for many of us readers the voyage of discovery starts with words.

I was twenty-one years old the first time I stood inside an art museum – and what a breathtaking experience it was. It was the Galleria degli Uffizi in Florence, a gallery I had read about in books so often that it felt more 'familiar' than the Union Buildings in Pretoria. I was on my Grand Voyage, like so many characters in so many stories I could recall, a year-long voyage of discovery through Europe. Mine had started in Israel, for the simple reason that it was the cheapest way to get to Europe.

I flew from Cape Town to Tel Aviv with El Al and travelled from Israel to Greece by sleeping on the deck of a ferry with other backpackers. From there, with more guts than experience (or money), I had to find my way through Europe from east to west, from Greece to Italy to France, as well as the north and south of the continent, until I finally ended up on a group of islands off the northwestern coast of Europe. These islands seemed more familiar to me than any other country I'd travelled through, simply because since childhood I had read more books by British authors than those of any other country (including South African and Afrikaans authors).

When by the end of this year of travelling I found myself in the National Gallery in London, I was already a habituée of art museums. I had visited all the most famous ones on the continent, the Louvre in Paris, the Prado in Madrid, the Rijksmuseum in Amsterdam, and dozens of smaller museums dedicated to the work of specific artists. Picasso, Van Gogh, Rembrandt, Rodin and many more. And then there were the world-famous artworks I had contemplated in churches and cathedrals, in parks and on piazzas, as well as all the famous buildings and monuments that had themselves become works of art. Europe was one enormous art museum for an unsophisticated girl from Africa.

Your own experience was, once again, entirely different from mine. You were taken along to art museums and exhibitions when you were still a baby. You did not need words in books to lead you to art, you were surrounded by art, you only had to look around you.

Although as a toddler you were, for the most part, bored in art museums, you did have a breakthrough when you were barely five years old. We were at the famous Edinburgh Festival in Scotland, dragging you along to several art exhibitions, including the biggest one ever held of Andy Warhol's work. I didn't feel any particular affinity for Warhol, but it was an absorbing experience seeing so much of his work in one place, from his earliest sketches and paintings to his famous repetitions of Campbell's tomato soup cans and Marilyn Monroe's face in various colours.

In one hall there were tiny paintings he had made of toys from his childhood – and the curator had had the brilliant idea to hang these 'children's works' on the walls at child height. At the age of five, then, you could see a famous artist's work at eye level for the first time, instead of inaccessibly high up against a wall. While all the adults in the hall had to shuffle from painting to painting with comically bent knees and backs.

I was suddenly alerted by my own body to how inaccessible most art museums were for children – no matter how eager their well-intentioned parents were to expose them to art.

It was a Damascus moment in my life.

I was suddenly almost grateful that my parents had never taken me to an art museum or an exhibition as a child. That gave me the chance to discover art primarily through words and pictures in books. Until I was literally big enough to look the Mona Lisa in the eye the day I first stood in front of her painting in the Louvre.

That wasn't the reason, of course, why Ma and Pa never took me to art museums. It was more a question of a lack of opportunities. The few art museums that were available in Cape Town or Pretoria fell outside of our suburban frame of reference.

But for you that Warhol exhibition instantly opened the door to a wider world. That same week, still at the Edinburgh Festival, we ended up at a far smaller exhibition of William Kentridge's black-and-white artworks in a modest little gallery. Your father and I looked at each other in amazement when you exclaimed that you loved these pictures.

'Must be because the artist is South African,' I teased your father.

When at the age of sixteen you announced that you really liked Camus's *L'Étranger* – even though you didn't really 'understand' it at all – I thought back to your instinctive response to Kentridge's work. There are art experts who say we should be suspicious of any kind of art that we 'understand' right away.

Of course, this didn't mean that you were suddenly crazy about every art museum we took you to. Sometimes we missed the mark altogether, like the time I took you along to a magnificent exhibition of Lucien Freud's paintings in the Pompidou Centre in Paris. You were in no mood for looking at dead art, you wanted to go see the live animals in the Jardin des Plantes next to the Seine instead. I promised I would come with you to look at the live animals if you came with me to look at the dead art.

This is the kind of compromise that parenting truly involves, no matter what educationists say.

Freud's famous larger-than-life paintings of naked bodies, fat bodies and old bodies, young bodies, ugly bodies, might have been quite a shock for a child who'd never seen a nude. You had already been in so many museums that you weren't shocked, but within five minutes you were bored to death with the excess of pink flesh. A matter of perspective once again, I realised after another five minutes. Your head was quite simply too low to view the whole huge painted body, even if you took a few steps backwards like the adults around you. All that was really visible at your eye level was an incredible variety of genitalia, often pink and shrivelled, somewhat pathetic.

Boring indeed.

It all comes down to *Ways of Seeing*, to quote John Berger's eloquent book title. On the cover of my weathered Penguin edition I read:

Seeing comes before words. The child looks and recognizes before it can speak.

Even a child like me, who grew up without great artworks at home or visits to art museums, was influenced by the 'art' that I did see around me. Much of it was kitsch, fantastic kitsch, like Tretchikoff's prints. Even though there wasn't a Tretchikoff in our house (which I rather regretted when the artist went on to acquire an ironic popularity among a younger generation), I was nevertheless surrounded by a laager of Tretchikoffs in my childhood. In Ouma Tina's house the reddish-brown poinsettias hung above the sofa. In a friend's house the Asian woman with the blue-green face glared at me from the passage. In the OK Bazaars in Cape Town there was a whole row of the wilted rose that had fallen out of the water glass, all offered for sale to people who wanted to have 'art' in their homes but who had no frame of reference for it.

Almost as popular as Tretchikoff in many homes in the sixties were prints of melancholy children with impossibly large eyes, the kind that Margaret Keane painted in America. Although I have only become aware of Keane's name in the past decade – thanks to Tim Burton's biopic *Big Eyes* – those heartrending saucer eyes were one of the strongest visual components of what I got to know as 'art' as a child.

Tretchikoff and Keane were the 'modern' artists of the suburbs, but in farmhouses and old people's houses in the platteland an earlier kind of Boere kitsch was ubiquitous. These were pictures that honoured the Voortrekkers as heroes. The Battle of Blood River was probably the best-known of the lot. In who knows how many houses I stared at the hordes of dead Zulus and the small band of brave white people in a laager of ox wagons, as if everything would become clear to me if I would only look at the picture for long enough.

There were many others as well, depictions of ox wagons being hauled up cliffs, women with bonnets and men with hats, all of them white, of course. If they were white they were painted with their clothes on. If they were black their depictions were as naked as possible and preferably also as dead as possible. And gradually I began to understand the message in all these pictures in all these houses. 'We are a tiny minority of brave whites in this country, surrounded by hordes of uncivilised blacks, but the Lord is on our side.'

Something like that.

Meanwhile these Voortrekker pictures have also become sardonic collectors' pieces in some Afrikaans homes. I took you and your French-Afrikaans brother to Evita se Perron in the village of Darling (near one of the farms I used to visit as a child) to show you Pieter-Dirk Uys's impressive collection. You were initially uncertain of how to react. Was it okay to laugh or should you be upset because your poor mother had been exposed to this throughout her childhood?

By the time we were walking through the garden called Boerassic Park, filled with *Whites Only* signs and other horrors from long ago, you were starting to grasp the satirical spirit of this monument to Boere kitsch. Mocking, yet also disquieting, as the best satire must unavoidably be. Definitely not politically correct.

Back in the car your brother looked at me as if I were a character in Steven Spielberg's *Jurassic Park* who had managed to escape from the claws of the dinosaurs, with something like admiration in his eyes.

I don't know if I will ever really escape from the strange little

Afrikaans world where I was born. It seems to me like a process that is still ongoing, and which will continue for the rest of my life. But I suspect that I took my first cautious steps to freedom when I discovered a set of blue books about the children of the world in the library in Bellville.

9

A COTTAGE AT THE SEA

'My name is Marita and I am a writer.' If you knew how many years it took me to say such a simple little sentence out loud – without touching my nose in discomfort, or drilling a toe into the ground like the sweet little fictional witch Liewe Heksie would do whenever she was embarrassed – you would be amazed. But perhaps not as amazed as many other people. After all, you got to know me as your mother, not as a writer. For you writing is just one of the things I do, not the definition of what I am.

I have been writing books full-time for three decades, to survive literally and figuratively, literally to earn my living and figuratively to cheat death, like Scheherazade who would be beheaded the next morning if she failed to enthral the king with her stories every night. And yet only recently could I start calling myself an author without feeling like an impostor who was going to lose her head.

Mind you, an author, not an authoress, please. In France I am forced to say '*une écrivaine*' rather than '*un écrivain*' because every single word in this language is burdened to death by gender. Which makes me all the more determined to exploit the freedom of my mother tongue and to be simply an author in Afrikaans, as in English.

But the reason I struggled for so long to get the word to cross my lips in reference to myself was the hero-worship I nurtured for so many authors. Continue to nurture, I should probably add.

When I was growing up, writers seemed creatures no less miraculous than unicorns. I had heard that they existed, I had seen pictures of them, but I battled to believe it, because I had never seen one in the flesh.

Until the unforgettable day when I spotted not one but two of these rare creatures together, through the branches of a milkwood tree in Franskraal, and curiosity drew me nearer. And that wasn't the only miracle that took place in Franskraal.

In the sixties, perfectly ordinary middle-class Afrikaans families could still afford holiday houses. Our entire political system was based on race rather than class. As long as you were white, you were encouraged to strive and prosper. A second car, a second home, a garden with a lawn and a swimming pool, these were all within reach of an ambitious middle-class man like my father.

We were a herd of snow-white sheep in a beautiful meadow, our shepherds were Verwoerd and Vorster, our president's name was Blackie Swart (no one noticed the irony in the name), we felt safe and lived well.

I am acutely aware that irony can be a dangerous tool in the hands of an Afrikaans writer who wants to turn the past into a story. There is always the risk that someone from another culture or era might read my words out of context, misunderstand them and conclude that I am reflecting uncritically on the days when I was a little white lamb in a herd of white sheep.

But you, my girl, you know me well enough to recognise that I will always choose irony and humour, sometimes pitch-black humour, over rage when I am trying to make a point. You are from another culture and another generation, but I still prefer an ironic tone when I whisper parts of my story into your ear. I can only hope that my words will not arrive at other readers completely twisted, as in that Chinese whispers game of old.

Fasten your seatbelt, as Bette Davis said in *All About Eve*, because things could get bumpy up ahead.

Or as we used to say in Afrikaans fairy tales: *Golden calf, here follows the second half*.

The modest timber cottage Pa built for us in Franskraal had a name, like any proper Afrikaans beach house in those days. Pa fixed a wooden oar sideways on top of a pair of posts and painted *Vyvers-rus* on it. It made us feel terribly important, as if we owned a whole farm rather than a sandy plot with a timber cottage and an oar.

You and your brothers were amazed the first time you drove through the streets of a South African coastal town and noticed all the strange names outside the holiday houses. It probably had something to do with the hankering Afrikaners had for their farming background, I tried to explain, aware that this was yet another thing I could never really explain to my children. Long before Afrikaans TV viewers became unhealthily obsessed with *Boer soek 'n vrou*, the local version of *Farmer Wants a Wife* or the French *L'amour est dans le pré*, my people already had an obsession that we could call 'Boer seeks a name for his beach house'.

We spent almost every weekend and all our school holidays in our little house at the sea. When the dominee of the Dutch Reformed congregation in Vredelust complained about our godless upbringing because he never saw us children in church on Sundays any more, Pa took us to Sunday School in Gansbaai. Sitting in a church hall with the local fishermen's children every Sunday taught me more swearwords than Bible knowledge – but I wasn't complaining.

Gansbaai was an exciting new planet for a young explorer from the suburbs of Cape Town. On Saturday nights my respectable bank manager father partied with the roughest fishermen in the Gansbaai Otel. (It was a hotel that had lost its only star, so they painted out the H and turned it into an Otel.) One of Pa's new buddies had a party trick that entailed biting into his glass – with his remaining teeth – and then chewing the glass shards.

It was a wild and savage, rough-and-ready place. Absolutely irresistible to an obedient child from Welgemoed.

Those weekends in Gansbaai and Franskraal not only enriched my vocabulary considerably – surely an advantage for a future writer – but also offered the opportunity to observe two writing legends up close. The poet DJ Opperman and the journalist Schalk Pienaar also had holiday homes in Franskraal, next door to each other, diagonally in front of our timber cottage. Pa wasn't exactly a man for poetry, but he spoke of DJ Opperman with great respect and harboured endless admiration for Schalk Pienaar, in those days the editor of the Afrikaans Sunday paper, *Die Beeld*. Every time I wanted to go for a swim in the nearest rocky inlet, I'd take a shortcut through a clump of milkwood trees, along a footpath that ran directly past their houses. Then I'd spy on them through the milkwood trees like an overseas tourist getting her first glimpse of two rare rhinoceroses.

So *that* was what writers looked like! And how they sounded! And what they did!

What they did, as far as I could tell, was talk and drink. I never saw them without a glass in hand. The warped lesson that I took from this was that bank managers and fishermen and 'ordinary people' could only get drunk on Saturday nights in the Gansbaai Otel, but writers were free to start drinking at ten in the morning.

Writers didn't have to concern themselves with ordinary people's rules.

I knew, then, for certain that I also wanted to be a writer one day.

By this time I had already written my first story. From the minute Miss Hanekom in Sub A taught my clumsy fingers to form letters on paper, the letters became words and, before I knew it, the words turned into stories.

At seven I was ambitious enough to attempt my first love story. It was a hospital story, inspired by the forbidden photo books that

I secretly read in our domestic helper Dolly Titus's room. *Dokter Conrad Brand. Saal 10.* I also remember a *Suster Elsie*, but given that I can find no proof of her existence, she may only have lived in my imagination – a nursing-sister version of the voluptuous *Tessa*, another photo-book heroine who seldom wore much more than a crocheted bikini. Dolly preferred this kind of story to the action adventures of *Mark Condor* or *Die Ruiter in Swart*. And my mother's romantic memories of her days as a nurse certainly influenced both Dolly and me.

I even briefly considered becoming a nurse, until I realised it was more fun to write about a hospital than to work in one.

The main characters in my first love story, therefore, were a devastatingly attractive doctor and a nurse with the exuberant curves and fleshy lips of *Suster Elsie* – and within a few paragraphs they were locked in a 'passionate embrace'. (I quote my seven-year-old self's words.) Since I had no clue how passionate embraces were supposed to work, let alone what was supposed to happen next, I resorted to the oldest trick in the book. I left the red-hot scene suspended in the air using three ellipsis points – dot, dot, dot – until such time as I might learn more about embraces.

It was more or less at this point – or these three points – that I caught my parents surreptitiously reading my story. I was sorely aggrieved, because they were laughing. Nowadays I know it is far harder to make readers laugh than to make them cry – but that first attempt was definitely not supposed to be funny. It was my first miserable acquaintance with literary criticism and it taught me a very valuable lesson: You cannot be a writer if you cannot handle criticism.

I also learnt that it was better, especially if you were an absolute beginner, to write about something you knew at least *something* about. Or do enough research to ensure that sceptical readers don't laugh at you.

'Cultural appropriation' has become one of the most damning phrases for present-day writers. The dictionary defines it as the inappropriate adoption of the ideas or customs of one group by the members of another, usually more dominant, group. What I did as a seven-year-old wasn't cultural appropriation, then, given that adults were the dominant group in my world.

I understand the frustration of black authors who demand that white authors stop writing stories about black experience. Or Latin American writers' indignation when their stories are 'stolen' by other American writers. Of course, I understand the emotional response on an emotional level.

But – and this is a big but – as a fiction writer my imagination remains my most important gift. This ability to switch perspectives is more important than linguistic skill or stylistic tricks. It is all that distinguishes me from journalists and non-fiction writers, in fact. To see the world through the eyes of a variety of characters. To imagine myself inside someone else's body.

Surely all the greatest literary writers have occupied themselves with cultural appropriation for centuries?

Shakespeare had to be able to imagine that he was a jealous black man to create a protagonist like Othello. Or a vengeful Jewish father in Venice. Or a hopelessly lovestruck teenage girl in Verona. Shakespeare invented a long list of culturally appropriated characters without whom Western literature would be infinitely poorer.

If male writers like Tolstoy and Flaubert hadn't arrogated to themselves the right to create female protagonists – at a time when male dominance was so overriding that precious few women could become writers – we would not be able to read classical novels such as *Anna Karenina* and *Madame Bovary* today. Fortunately, thousands upon thousands of gifted female writers have claimed their place on the literary stage in the past century. Fortunately, women can now tell their own stories.

And fortunately, thankfully, it is still not forbidden for men to tell women's stories.

My most fervent hope is that there will soon also be thousands upon thousands of writers from historically oppressed or colonised groups who will write so many brilliant books that no one will need to feel threatened or angry or indignant when a white writer also tackles a black protagonist.

In the meantime, we ought to be extremely careful of constraining writers' imaginations. Or soon we will no longer have literature, only painfully politically correct 'true stories' about our own tiny islands of experience.

In the sixties Franskraal was part of my tiny island, more a hamlet than a town, almost like a farm by the sea, a place without street lights or electricity in any of the houses. We ate our supper around paraffin lamps and carried candles to bed to read a little before we fell asleep. Once the last candles had been blown out, the night outside was utterly pitch black.

Except for the beam from the lighthouse at Danger Point that swept through the house at regular intervals to illuminate the wall next to my bed for a few moments.

Immediately afterwards everything would be black again.

My greatest fear on these dark nights wasn't intruders, because crime was something that only existed in American movies or in old-fashioned books like *Oliver Twist*. And the latter I got to know as the cheerful musical *Oliver!* (with an exclamation point) long before I read Dickens's book. That was just the way things were on my tiny island.

Instead, I was scared of supernatural phenomena, my imagination stirred up by Oupa Corrie's gripping ghost stories.

But even ghosts couldn't terrify me as much as the possibility of a tsunami.

The more the adults tried to convince me that such monstrous waves had never occurred on the South African coast, the more terrified I became that we would be hit by one as we lay sleeping in our timber cottage right next to the sea. There is a first time for everything, after all – that was my reasoning.

This improbable fear had its origin in a book we read at school, the story of a Japanese child whose home and whole family are washed away by a tidal wave. He or she survives by being able to escape to a steep hill in time. Or perhaps he was already on the hill. The details have long faded from memory. All that is left, to this day, is an irrational fear of tsunamis whenever I sleep near the ocean.

Luckily I can rely on reason to soothe my fear these days, but back in Franskraal I had the most hideous nightmares about flood-waters sweeping everything away. Not only monstrous waves that suddenly rise up from the sea, but any kind of flood, really. And yet again a book is to blame. Two books, in fact. The Bible story of Noah and the flood had made a deep impression on my younger self, but I simply couldn't imagine so much water. Until one day I paged through a book on our coffee table – oddly enough, the only coffee-table book I recall ever being in our house – and came upon terrifying black-and-white photographs of a flood.

The book was a photographic account of the North Sea flood that struck the Netherlands in 1953, when extraordinary ocean storms made the dykes collapse and large parts of the Low Countries were flooded. Presumably it had only ended up on our coffee table be-cause Pa worked at the Nederlandse Bank. There were hundreds of photographs of water, water, water, with only a church steeple or windmill sticking out here and there, and of dumbfounded people fleeing the rising water, in boats and trucks and helicopters, clinging to small bundles containing all their earthly possessions.

I couldn't stop looking. For the very first time I could imagine what the world must have looked like during Noah's flood. (Without the Dutch windmills, of course.) How desperately people were trying to flee. How cruel water could be.

According to most dream interpretations, water symbolises the subconscious, so destructive floodwaters represent displaced negative emotions like rage, grief or fear breaching the surface. Like any sensitive child, I certainly also repressed rage or grief, but I suspect it was mostly fear that I wanted to keep at bay. And given that floodwater was my biggest fear, my flooding nightmares required little by way of interpretation.

And then we ended up experiencing an entirely different kind of natural disaster in Franskraal. On 29 September 1969 the biggest earthquake in South African history struck in the Cape Province. It measured 6.3 on the Richter scale and remains known as the Tulbagh earthquake because it was this Boland town that suffered the most damage. Many of the historical buildings in the main street were left in ruins, as well as buildings in nearby towns like Ceres and Wolseley.

Because tsunamis are usually caused by earthquakes beneath the ocean floor, my fear of flooding would probably have risen sharply – had I not slept through the whole drama.

We three children were with Ma in our cottage at the sea because it was school holidays – poor Pa had to keep working so we could afford both the holiday and the cottage – and the combination of fresh sea air and pitch-dark nights ensured that we were fast asleep by early evening. When the earth started shaking a few minutes after ten on this particular Monday night, not one of us children was woken.

Oupa Corrie and Ouma Tina had come on holiday with us. Ouma Tina believed that the day of judgement had arrived, as many apparently did, and waited in fear and trembling to go to heaven or hell. But Oupa Corrie possessed an ancient wisdom when it came to nature, perhaps the genetic legacy of generations of fishermen who had been forced to live close to it. Although he had never experienced an earthquake himself, he immediately knew what it was. He calmed Ouma Tina and comforted Ma and decided it wasn't necessary to wake the children.

He stayed up with Ma for the rest of the night in any event, just in case the earth started shaking again, so we could flee in time if we needed to. There was no telephone in the house, so they couldn't phone Pa or anyone else to find out what was going on. Perhaps they managed to pick up a station on the old wireless, a crackling news report that could confirm the earthquake, the sound turned down low enough to not disturb the sleeping children.

It was only over the next few days that the photographs in the newspapers of ruined buildings in several Boland towns showed us how bad the earthquake had been. I was quite disappointed that the adults hadn't woken me up. Now I would feel left out having to listen to all my friends' juicy tales of survival when school started again. All I would be able to say, if someone asked me what I remembered of the historic earthquake, was that I had slept through it all.

It is still all I can say.

I even missed out on the many aftershocks that rolled across the country in the months that followed. Once I was in a car on the highway between Bellville and Cape Town; shortly afterwards someone told me you couldn't feel such light aftershocks in moving vehicles. Another time my head was underwater, in the sea or in a swimming pool, and apparently you don't feel aftershocks underwater either.

I was starting to fear that the universe was conspiring to keep the experience of an earthquake away from me. And for a child who was starved for any kind of experience that could be turned into a story, it felt like an unusually cruel punishment.

In Philip Roth's autobiography with the sober (and possibly contestable) title *The Facts*, he focuses on those episodes in his life that he has several times turned into fiction. The idea is to offer the curious reader a glimpse of 'the true facts' behind the fiction – but in typical Roth style he lets Nathan Zuckerman, his alter ego in many books, have the last word. This fictional character writes a letter to 'Dear Roth' with a point-by-point critique of his creator's autobiographical effort.

One of the most significant charges against Roth is that he twists literally everything that happens to him into something he can exploit as a fiction writer. This, of course, is one of the oldest accusations against any fiction writer – and it remains one of the hardest ones to dispute. *Maybe this is the difference between a writer's life and an ordinary life*, Zuckerman speculates, this *relentlessly coherent narrative*.

All I'm wondering is, hasn't anything ever happened to him that he couldn't make sense of? Because ninety-nine percent of the things that happen to me I can't make sense of.

I reread Zuckerman's letter before I started writing this very long letter to you, my darling girl. Characters are often cleverer than the writers who create them, and here Zuckerman's words strike me as truer than anything Roth said about himself.

I resolved to tell you not only about the experiences I have already turned into fiction or that I can 'make sense of' as a writer. To leave room, too, for hit-or-miss, for randomness, which in my dictionary appears directly above 'randy', for which the Afrikaans translation is the playful word *katools*. Another word that you, my daughter, have probably never heard. Random information, right?

The Tulbagh earthquake taught me no life lessons, it was simply one among the random facts of my childhood.

Or perhaps it taught me to use my imagination when I want to describe something I cannot remember? (Sorry, Zuckerman, I can't help myself.)

Our lives at the seaside heeded a completely different rhythm to that of the northern suburbs of Cape Town. In Franskraal there was no school, no extramural activities to keep us occupied, no friends we could play with in the street at a certain time of day; even our mealtimes were more irregular than at home.

Our meals were simpler – mainly, perhaps, because Dolly Titus wasn't there to help Ma cook and wash dishes. We ate lots of fresh fish and seafood, often cooked outside on the fire, as well as braaivleis and braaibroodjies. When we children were hungry – and because we spent so much time outside in the sea air, we were constantly hungry – we spread peanut butter and golden syrup on thick slices of white bread and ate it standing up. Without bothering with plates, untroubled by crumbs falling onto the floor. Dolly wasn't there to reprimand us, Ma pretended not to notice because she wanted to carry on reading.

At home in Welgemoed, Ma and Dolly both made sure that we ate enough vegetables every day, usually in the form of plain, boring stews or soup. Green bean stew, tomato stew, pea soup. Food I ate without enthusiasm but that has now become the most delicious comfort food on earth. I sometimes suspect that we are all doomed to fail to appreciate our mothers' cooking until they are no longer there to cook for us. Then we yearn for it and we try to emulate it and we feast on it. But it never tastes quite as good as when Ma made it.

No, Mia, this isn't emotional blackmail to force you to devour your mother's food. I'm just saying.

From the start your own choice of food was far wider than mine had been. I thought I was doing my children a favour by exposing them to an international culinary culture, probably a reaction to all the dull and boring stews I'd had to eat. Moroccan and Mexican, Spanish and Greek, Japanese and Chinese, that is how we have always eaten in our multicultural household. Until the day when you were already in high school and called me to say that you wanted to invite a friend for supper – but first wanted to check that we wouldn't be eating 'weird food' again.

'What weird food?' I wanted to know, taken aback.

'All that food from other countries, Ma,' was your reply. 'All my friends just eat ordinary French food at home.'

By 'French food' you weren't referring to the world-famous highlights of French cuisine. What you friends ate at home, I discovered when I questioned you further, was *poulet-frites* (fried chicken with chips) and pizza and pasta. And it was no use objecting that pizza and pasta weren't French. It was the 'ordinary food' that 'ordinary' French children apparently ate at home.

To me it sounded just about as bland as my mother's vegetable stews back then.

In our suburban home, time-saving newfangled meals also started to make an appearance, though. Recipes made with tinned food and soup powder and jelly powder, ingredients that nowadays would make discerning home cooks shudder. It is sometimes extolled – ironically, of course – as Crimplene food, because in the sixties Crimplene was one of the new synthetic miracles that wrinkle-free clothing was made of. The kind of clothing you didn't have to iron, as time-saving as soup powder and instant coffee.

Forget-me-not Blues is a novel about three generations of women – a grandmother, her daughter and her granddaughter – and because the daughter was more or less my contemporary, she was the one I could write about with the least effort. Unlike for the grandmother, who was born in the early thirties, or the granddaughter, who was only born towards the end of the twentieth century, I didn't need much research to describe Nandi's experiences. I could rely chiefly on my own memories. We experienced many of the same things at the same age. Cocktails were among these things.

As a little girl, Nandi watched *Mommy, Daddy and Ouma drinking funny-coloured drinks before dinner, things with names like Pink Squirrel and Screwdriver and Greyhound. Cocktails, Ouma Lizzie calls them. Skemerkelkies, Oupa Willie says, just another pretentious American habit.*

Most of the fads and fancies of my childhood blew in from America. Ma and Pa sometimes held cheese and wine parties, featuring a tray with three kinds of cheese surrounded like prisoners of war by a mob of savoury biscuits, cubes of Cheddar wedged between green and red pickled onions on toothpicks, and a few interesting dips for the chips, for those guests who as yet lacked the sophistication to appreciate cheese. Dave Brubeck's 'Take Five' was the background music on the turntable. Or Trini Lopez's 'Lemon Tree'.

It was the high point of Afrikaans suburban hospitality in the sixties.

When fondue dinners became popular (imported via America from Switzerland), a copper fondue pot acquired pride of place on our dining room table.

Long after fondues had gone out of style again, when nearly all the fondue forks had disappeared without a trace (except for one that lingered reproachfully in the kitchen drawer), the copper pot endured as an ornament in our dining room.

A reminder of all the disposable fashions of that time.

But in Franskraal things were different. There, the sea wind blew all the fads and pretension away. The plates and glasses and cutlery didn't always match, because they were surplus from our 'real home'. There was no background music, except now and again the jingle of a radio show. The rest of the time we listened to the rushing of the waves.

In this atmosphere of unbridled freedom I could also give free rein to my imagination. The seclusion and solitude encouraged me to travel further than ever in my mind. While walking by the sea, on the dirt roads through the town or on the beach that stretches out to Uilkraalmond, or all along the rocks towards Kleinbaai and Danger Point, I conjured up other worlds for myself and populated them with all sorts of characters of my own invention.

That was where my love of walking really started to flourish.

I was never really a sporty child. I took part in sport because I had to, not because I wanted to. I had no physical impediments, just a complete lack of interest. I would always prefer reading a good book to chasing after a ball. And given that most team sports revolved around balls, team sports left me cold from the start.

To this day I struggle with the suspension of disbelief that is necessary to cheer on a national rugby team or soccer team, to transform the fifteen or eleven players on the field into an all-encompassing 'we', as in 'Wow, we played really well today!'

What do you mean, 'we', I am usually tempted to ask when one of my sports-mad friends or family members makes such statements.

But I was also blessed from childhood with a well-made, mostly healthy body (despite all my psychosomatic pains and psychological ailments) and an abundance of energy that had to be expended in some or other physical way. I was no fragile and sheltered hothouse orchid, nor a blushing English rose or a pretty Dutch tulip that could be picked and pushed into an arrangement along with other flowers. No, I felt more like an indigenous wildflower, like the sour figs that grew near the sea in Franskraal, the kind of plant that could be left outside untended.

Walking fulfilled all my physical and spiritual needs. I could be outside on my own wearing out my body while my thoughts flew about freely, no rules to follow or balls to catch, no one to compete against, nothing to win or lose.

Franskraal was where I became a lifelong walker. To this day I would rather walk beside the sea or up a mountain than in the city, but when I do find myself in a foreign city, I would rather explore it on foot than in any other way. My need for walking is spurred on by my constant wanderlust, and my wanderlust is in turn fuelled by my never-ending need for walking. It is probably no coincidence that wanderlust, the internationally understood word for the desire to travel, is derived from *wandern*, the German word for 'walking'.

In modern German, wanderlust is usually replaced with *Fernweh*, which can be literally translated as a 'longing for far-off places', the opposite of *Heimweh* or 'longing for home'.

And yet you can suffer from these two conditions simultaneously. Just ask me.

I am a traveller who has carried two heavy suitcases with me for decades. In one hand I carry a suitcase that is stuffed full of *Fernweh*, in the other hand a suitcase filled with *Heimweh*. The desire to keep travelling is always there. But because I live so far away from the country of my birth, the longing for home never quite disappears.

The British writer Deborah Levy – who, like me, was born in South Africa towards the end of the fifties – unlike me had to leave the country when she was still a child because her father was a political prisoner. In her novel *Swallowing Geography* there is a fascinating female protagonist, JK, who, like her male namesake Jack Kerouac, is always 'on the road'. Even when she is having sex, she keeps her shoes on – so that she can walk away more easily.

The American writer Lauren Elkin uses a quote from *Swallowing Geography* as the motto for her walking memoir, *Flâneuse*. This book – *an intense meditation on what it means to be a woman and walk out in the world*, according to *New Statesman* – critiques the canon of male writer-walkers in a fresh and entertaining way. (*As if a penis were a requisite walking appendage, like a cane.*) Elkin traces the footsteps of famous female writer-walkers such as Virginia Woolf and George Sand through cities like London and Paris, and leaves irresistible literary crumbs for readers to pursue in turn.

It is the kind of book that travelling, reading, walking women share with one another like an extraordinary secret. I got my copy as a gift from a friend, and I hope one day to pass it on to you, my girl, because you have also walked with me since your childhood.

During one of our South African holidays I wanted to show you that timber cottage in Franskraal, the fynbosveld on the mountainside where we children acted in our own cowboy movies, the tall dunes at Uilkraalmond where a lovely blond boy gave me one of the best kisses of my life. (But that is another story for later. We are still only in my more innocent childhood years, when the mere thought of kisses from boys gave me the creeps.)

I couldn't find the timber cottage. I knew the wooden oar with *Vyversrus* would be long gone from the front yard, but I hoped that something in the yard, at least, would look familiar. Or the milkwood trees diagonally opposite it, or the fynbosveld behind it. But the street had been tarred and was completely built up with unrecognisable houses. The milkwood trees and the fynbosveld were all gone. And the timber cottage had undergone such drastic renovation that there was no sign left of the original building. Perhaps it had been demolished for a grander holiday house to be built in its place.

You were still small, Mia, so you may not remember how disappointed I was.

I took you down to the rocks beside the sea instead, where I used to dream my days away. If I couldn't show you the beach house of

202

my childhood, I at least wanted to show you the castle I built in my imagination while playing on those rocks.

'Look, there was my bedroom,' I pointed out to you, 'the tallest rock over there. That long flat stone was my canopy bed. And that piece of rock jutting out above the waves was my balcony, do you see it? The ballroom was over on this side . . .'

'And here is the dining hall!' you exclaimed. 'Just look at the long table! Do you see?'

'I see it, my love.' My heart wanted to burst with joy. I had always thought that no one but me would ever be able to see this miracle of a castle.

'*Le château de ma mère*,' you declared with pride. My mother's castle, the title of Pagnol's famous story; you saw the film version when you had barely started school.

Your mother will never have a *château* in France, that you must know by now, but on that day in Franskraal I could show you that, as a child, I had owned a castle in Africa. And unlike the timber cottage with the wooden oar, this home would never disappear. For as long as we can use our imagination, we will always find it again.

10

THE BEGINNING OF THE END

The end of my childhood years in Welgemoed arrived with a mighty bang. A supernatural roar from the sky that for a few moments made me fear that judgement day had arrived.

Just like my anxious grandmother during the earthquake in Franskraal.

We were playing in the neighbours' garden across the street when a lightning bolt suddenly cast everything around us in bright white light. Everyone froze, like startled rabbits caught in the headlights of an oncoming car. Before we could regain our composure, the heavens roared directly above us. With my overripe imagination I thought it was the Lord wanting to talk to us from somewhere behind a cloud.

It turned out to be nothing more than a completely unexpected thunderstorm, a natural phenomenon that was so rare in the Western Cape that I couldn't recall a single other one in my first eleven years on earth.

As a student I got to know a girl who'd grown up in the driest part of the country, near Alexander Bay in Namaqualand, and who at the age of ten felt rain on her skin for the first time. She jumped around outside, mad with joy, until she was soaked to the skin.

You never forget first experiences like these ones.

A decade later, I was working as a dishwasher in London, and one afternoon while I was scrubbing dirty saucepans in the basement of an office building I saw, through the pavement-level window, that something resembling white foam was floating down from the sky. Far whiter than the soap suds in the basin in front of me.

'Look, it's snowing!' someone exclaimed, another South African who had been in England for much longer than me, but who still got excited about snow.

(Our British co-workers didn't even glance up.)

'I've never touched snow!' I yelled at the supervisor, as I tore off my overall coat and rushed past her to get outside. I knew she could fire me because I'd abandoned my post, in which case I wouldn't have enough money to return to my family in South Africa by Christmas, but at that moment it didn't bother me at all. All that mattered was my desire to feel snow on my skin for the first time.

Standing on that London pavement, marvelling at the snow-flakes clinging to my eyelashes, an experience that Julie Andrews had made me dream of when I was small every time she sang 'My Favourite Things' (*Girls in white dresses with blue satin sashes / Snowflakes that stay on my nose and eyelashes*), I remembered my student friend jumping around in the rain. The only thing that prevented me from frolicking about myself was knowing that the Britons around me wouldn't share my excitement. They would just look away in characteristic British style, pretend they didn't see the crazy frolicker in the snow, and walk on briskly.

I went back inside to carry on washing dishes. The supervisor didn't fire me. She had decided to look away, like all the other Brits, and simply ignore my silly behaviour. When my shift ended a few hours later, the pure-white snow had already turned into brown mush on the pavements. My joyful amazement was soon replaced by irritation and frustration because my cheap South African shoes couldn't protect my feet against the unfamiliar cold.

By Christmas I was back home.

But because first experiences like these are so unforgettable, this one would also find its way into a story at some point. In *Forget-me-not Blues* the character Colette is also in London when she touches snow for the first time. She rushes outside in her dressing gown and slippers and stands on the pavement with her head thrown back, her mouth open and her arms spread out, like a statue that will gradually be covered in snow, while the pedestrians all ignore her.

It had been her frozen toes inside her thin slippers, rather than any passer-by's reaction, that had driven her back inside after a short while. She had never realised snow was so cold.

Soon after my first encounter with thunder and lightning in the neighbours' garden, Pa announced that we were moving to the Transvaal. The news was more terrifying than any lightning bolt.

On the long journey to our new home in the northern part of the country we experienced our first Highveld thunderstorm, a spectacle of light and sound that made that version in Welgemoed seem like an amateur play by comparison. And within weeks in Pretoria I had got so used to the wild summer storms that hit the city almost every afternoon that I'd barely glance up from my book when the clouds started to rumble.

But I remember the thunderclap in the neighbours' garden as a gong that signalled something. Not the end of my childhood, not for a long time yet, but the beginning of the end. Of many other things too.

It was the year Pa lost a lot of money on the stock market. He sold our house and resigned from his job at the bank and decided to start his own business, do some speculating in the property market. You can make money much faster if you're your own boss, Pa believed. You can also lose money much faster, we would all soon learn.

The collapse of the Johannesburg Stock Exchange at the end of the sixties certainly doesn't rank among the Big Five of international financial disasters. It wasn't nearly as serious as the Wall Street Crash of 1929 that lead to the worldwide Great Depression. In the more recent past, other American recessions and disasters have also caused hardship on a grander scale. But in the thriving white Republic of South Africa a shiny bubble of optimism burst in May 1969. The Johannesburg Stock Exchange would fall by more than sixty per cent over the next two years and only recover in the eighties.

As a child I was blissfully unaware of all this economic turbulence. It wasn't 'the market' that had collapsed, it was my own safe little world. Pa decided to trade our sleepy Cape Town existence for the exciting moneymaking opportunities of the Transvaal. Like the brave pioneers venturing into the Wild West in the cowboy movies we saw at the drive-in bioscope on Saturday nights, that was how Pa would venture into the Unknown North. That was where the money was, that was where he and his family had to be.

Go West, young man, the newspaper editor Horace Greeley supposedly wrote in the nineteenth century because he believed in the 'manifest destiny' of the American people. My father simply changed the phrase to 'Go North, young man'. He was still in his thirties, he felt young and energetic, and he was convinced of his own manifest destiny.

If not in the north of the country, then 'somewhere over the rainbow', as Ma liked to sing along with Judy Garland.

The year 1969, then, became an earth-shattering year for me – not only because the earth literally shook in September. It marked the end of a time in my life that within a few short years I would remember with nostalgia. It was also the end of a decade, the mythical Sixties that shook all of mankind in so many ways.

Not that it seemed mythical while it was in progress. Even Susan Sontag, whose collection of essays *Against Interpretation* is considered one of the fundamental texts of the sixties, objected to the *omnipresent convention of packaging one's life . . . in decades.* Back then it wasn't 'the Sixties', she wrote thirty years later, for her it had chiefly been the period in which she had written her first novel and started to unload a cargo of ideas about art and culture because these ideas distracted her from the fiction she really wanted to write.

I'd been a child right through the mythical Sixties, too young to be aware of all the political and moral revolutions, the Prague Spring, the French student uprising of May 1968, the growing American protest against the war in Vietnam, not to mention the sexual revolution. One of the things I will probably always regret when I look back on my life is that I was too young for the Woodstock Festival. In August 1969, when half a million hippies descended on a dairy farm in the state of New York for three days of 'Peace and Love' that would change the history of rock music, I was in Standard 4 at Welgemoed Primary School, reading a *Maasdorp* book.

It wasn't until a few years later that my older second cousin Leon played me the double album of Woodstock in his bedroom in Pretoria. It was love at first hearing. I wanted to listen to it so incessantly that in the end he gave it to me, and then I carried on listening until the cover tore and I could sing along to the lyrics of every single song. I could even recite by heart the spontaneous bits of dialogue among the musicians, most of them sky-high on drugs, between the music. (Crosby, Stills and Nash's legendary 'This is the second time we've ever played in front of people, man, we're scared shitless.') It was Woodstock, more than anything else, that made me aware of the war in Vietnam, especially the crowd that roared along with Country Joe and the Fish: *And it's one, two, three, what are we fighting for? Don't ask me, I don't give a damn, next stop is Vietnam . . .*

In 1969 my music tastes were still as unformed as my body. Some of the girls in my class at school were already developing breasts, some even wore bras. But I was young for my class, and my body was even younger than my mind. Under the influence of more worldly-wise friends, mostly those with older brothers and sisters, I became interested in pop music. At the age of eleven I liked innocent songs with upbeat tunes, the kind that could be played on conservative South African radio stations.

I was about to tell you about the first seven single I bought with my own pocket money, when it occurred to me that while you do know vinyl LPs – you stuck your father's old records on your bedroom walls like posters – you might not know what a seven single is. They were 'little records', sweetheart, short-playing records with a single song on each side, which turned on the record player at a higher speed. That was how most of us graduated to the 'big records' back then – by buying the cheaper 'little records' first.

Mine was a local cover of Skeeter Davis's 'Sunglasses' (*Sunglasses mhm to hide behind, sunglasses mhm to cry behind, sunglasses mhm to die behind*). And although dying behind a pair of sunglasses may sound a little depressing, the song was light years away from the psychedelic rhythms and subversive lyrics that reverberated at rock festivals like Woodstock that year.

In the meantime, my reading tastes had also progressed to 'adult books', after I had run through all the most desirable children's books in the Bellville library, but these weren't literary masterpieces that would pollute my young mind. My preference was for soppy love stories by Ela Spence and Dricky Beukes that Ma borrowed from the library on Dolly's behalf, and which Dolly and I then devoured together.

Ma had to take books out for Dolly because Dolly wasn't allowed in the library.

Libraries, like churches, schools, beaches, sports fields and all other places where people could gather, were strictly segregated according to race.

I wish it wasn't necessary to keep providing this background information. But even young people who grew up in the heart of South Africa struggle to understand how divided the country was in my youth. If I told my story to you, my French children, without reminding you about its background, I would be like an actor standing stage front in a spotlight saying my words in front of a closed curtain. When the curtain rises and the audience sees the scenery behind it, my words immediately become easier to understand because they are heard in the right context.

All I really want to do is apply Cicero's rhetorical technique of '*occupatio*'. (Which I'd know nothing about had I not come across it in Philip Roth's autobiography.) As Roth puts it:

'*Let us not speak of the wealth of the Roman Empire, let us not speak of the majesty of the invading troops, et cetera,' and by not speaking about it you're speaking about it.*

Every time I refer, then, to Dolly Titus or to the books Ma had to take out for her or even simply the fact that, at the age of eleven, I was reading the same books as our adult domestic helper, I want you to remember than I am talking about much more than I'm talking about. I am talking about a political system that made people sleep in outside rooms because they were not allowed to sleep in the same house as people from another race, that kept them out of libraries and universities, that forced them to leave school early because they had to go out to work – and for the work they could get, they wouldn't need an education anyway.

I talk about everything that has to be talked about if you want to understand my story. By not talking about it.

I got to know Ela Spence through her children's books, especially the popular *Soekie* series, about the clergyman's daughter Soekie

Rossouw and her impossible twin brothers. They were terribly respectable stories – because I was a terribly respectable child – and there was nothing in the author's 'stories for grown-ups' that could shock an eleven-year-old. When I went to search for Ela Spence on Google just now, I saw that she was 111 years old. (Evidently a mistake, because in fact she died in the nineties, but it probably shows that there aren't enough people who still remember her name to ensure that the records stay up to date.) And yet in the course of half a century, from 1946 onwards, she wrote more than two hundred books that entertained thousands upon thousands of readers for hours.

Her early love stories often feature heart-rending main characters with physical disabilities or illnesses. In *Die uitdraaipad* a girl goes blind soon after her boyfriend declares his eternal love and we are left holding our breath about how long this eternal love will last. In *Goudgeel kappertjies* a girl gets polio and her boyfriend marries her sister. In *Die blinde orrelis* there is, well, a blind organist.

Irresistible stories that made Dolly and me shed tears in equal measure.

Dolly and I got to know Dricky Beukes together through her radio serials. *Die indringer* (which always opened with the phrase 'A story that will touch every mother's heart') was the most popular daytime show on Springbok Radio throughout the sixties. Dolly and my sister and I regularly listened to radio serials together in the kitchen in the afternoons, Dolly while she was ironing or cooking and us while pretending to do our homework.

And from Dricky Beukes's radio stories we progressed to her love stories, books with titles such as *Ryp vrugte* (Ripe Fruit), *Verbode paradys* (Forbidden Paradise), *Verlore liefde* (Lost Love) and *Gebarste mure* (Burst Walls). I don't need to add that the endings were always happy.

If I learnt one thing from all the soppy love stories I read in primary school, it is not to turn my nose up at other people's reading tastes.

Everyone has to start reading somewhere, and some readers discover so much pleasure in the books they start with that they are never tempted to keep searching. Other readers' tastes change, they progress to other genres, they read more widely, their curiosity grows, they discover the great literature of the world. Until one day they find it's impossible to return to the books with which they started. As I discovered when I wanted to reread the *Maasdorp* series with my daughter.

But this doesn't mean that I look down on other adults who want to read *Maasdorp* books or Ela Spence's love stories. Each to his own, and any kind of reading pleasure is to my mind still preferable to sports pleasures or braai pleasures or most other pleasures.

I found *The World According to Garp* an unforgettably enjoyable reading experience. And when I consider the readers around me, I suspect that we all have our own reading manifesto: *The World According to Me*. Mine will probably be in Afrikaans: *Die wêreld volgens Marita*.

Yours, my daughter, will be in French: *Le monde selon Mia*.

As long as we keep on reading.

A few other 'adult books' managed to seduce me in my childhood. Like the flowers that Little Red Riding Hood saw beside the path to her grandmother's house – and found so alluring that she strayed from the path to go and pick some of them – these books showed me that there were other reading paths besides the wide, easy road of love stories. One of them was a collection of travel essays by Audrey Blignault, *Die verlange loop ver* (Longing Goes a Long Way), that I received as a prize at school at the end of Standard 3 or 4.

Yes, in those days the school year concluded with a prize-giving ceremony where clever children were rewarded with books. Something else that you and your brothers don't know because in France it has long been considered politically incorrect to single out clever children. Everyone is supposed to be equal, no one may receive special treatment.

I don't know whether I would be able to defend those old-fashioned prize-givings in a debate with you – but I am grateful nonetheless that I was considered clever enough to get a book prize every year. Sometimes the book was specifically chosen for the child who received it. Sometimes the right book reached the right child at the right time by sheer coincidence. Several of my prize books helped steer my reading tastes in new directions.

Audrey Blignault's collection was a step in exactly the right direction to reignite the curiosity that had been lit by *Children of the World*. This time it wasn't just factual information about strangers in foreign lands, it was an adult from my own country who described her own experiences of other countries in an entertaining, gripping way. With her personal background woven into the narratives. A pilgrimage to Ireland, where her mother's ancestors were from, or a melancholy visit to the island of Bermuda, where a paternal uncle was buried as a Boer prisoner of war.

It allowed me to understand that there were different ways to write about journeys, even if it was only a 'journey' to the nearest park, and to write about yourself, too, in the process. Without really writing about yourself. Cicero's '*occupatio*'. It renewed my determination to travel and to write one day.

The year 1969 was also the beginning of the end of my political innocence. Or perhaps it had already started the year before, when I blithely asked Ma why South Africa was not allowed to take part in the Olympic Games in Mexico City.

It was because the other countries didn't like our politics, Ma tried to answer as diplomatically as possible.

'So our politics are different from other countries'?' I asked, surprised.

Yes, said Ma, we were the only country with a policy of 'separate development'.

'The only country in the whole wide world?'

Yes, said Ma. Of course there was also racism in other countries, but we were the only country with an official policy of racism. (Well, she may not have phrased it exactly like that, but that was the message that reached me.)

I couldn't believe my ears. There I'd been thinking that everything I saw around me was perfectly normal. White people and black people were separated, everywhere on earth, because like seeks like? And now Ma was telling me that ours was the only country in the whole wide world that followed this policy. Then surely everything around me was abnormal?

It is a terrible shock to realise for the first time that you live in an abnormal environment.

'It doesn't mean that we are wrong and all the other countries are right,' one of my friends countered when I dared to share this shocking news with her. But even at the age of barely ten I couldn't quite believe that my country was the only one on earth that was right.

That the 'bad' countries like Soviet Russia and China were wrong, that I could well believe. I was, after all, growing up during the Cold War. I had been brainwashed against Communism from birth. But the 'good' countries like England and France and America? Weren't they supposed to be on our side in the fight against Communism? And now I was told that they did not support our political policy either.

My world wasn't shattered right away. At the age of ten I was too young for a political conversion. But all sorts of uncomfortable questions were starting to simmer inside me. At some point it would all have to boil over.

And then, in 1969, Ma took us children to a bioscope in Parow to watch a matinee screening of Jans Rautenbach's *Katrina*. It is the story of a coloured woman (Katrina September) who pretends to be white and calls herself Catherine Winters, until she is inevitably caught out. The part of the coloured woman was played by a white woman – just like Shakespeare's Othello was performed by white actors for centuries – or it would not have been possible to make the movie in South Africa. But it turned up the heat in my head and caused all the political questions of the previous year to simmer a bit faster.

Why Ma took us to see this particular movie is itself a question that has been simmering in my thoughts for a while.

With Pa we watched almost exclusively Westerns at the drive-in, and with Ma nearly always musicals and child-friendly Disney films in bioscopes. The musicals I remember best are all the international hits of the sixties. *The Sound of Music, Mary Poppins, My Fair Lady, Camelot, Oliver!, Paint Your Wagon, Dr Dolittle, Chitty Chitty Bang Bang, Thoroughly Modern Millie*. Disney's animated musical *The Jungle Book* stands out from the rest, perhaps only because I had never heard jazz music in an animation movie before, and to this day it remains one of my favourites in this genre.

But as was fitting for an exemplary Afrikaans parent, Ma probably also wanted to support the fledgling Afrikaans movie industry. That was how we children ended up at Jamie Uys's heart-rending *Dirkie*, and at the equally heart-rending *Hoor my lied* (Hear My Song), with Gé Korsten playing a singing doctor who was going blind. On top of that, the singing, almost-blind doctor had a paralysed little girl . . .

As Oscar Wilde remarked about a sentimental death scene in Dickens's *The Old Curiosity Shop*: *One must have a heart of stone to read the death of Little Nell without laughing*. I was still too young for Wilde's brand of cynicism when I watched *Hoor my lied* and other Afrikaans tearjerkers. I cried until the popcorn that I liked to eat during movies turned so salty and soggy from all my tears that I had to throw it away.

Other movies like *Die professor en die prikkelpop* (The Professor and the Pin-up) were silly and light and sweet as candyfloss. But among all these tearjerkers and candyfloss movies, we went with Ma to see Jans Rautenbach's *Die kandidaat* (The Candidate) in 1968. It was an altogether different kind of Afrikaans film, cautiously critical of the apartheid system, from which the almighty Publications Control Board cut almost a full minute. In the deleted scene it was apparently speculated whether coloured people had the right to be called Afrikaners.

But that I wouldn't discover until many years later, in an article that compared the groundbreaking influence of *Die kandidaat* on the South African film industry with what Orson Welles's *Citizen Kane* accomplished in Hollywood.

I wonder, now, if there was no age restriction, or if Ma took only me and left the younger children at home?

Or perhaps the Publications Control Board assumed that the political message would be lost on children anyway and figured that it probably wasn't the kind of movie parents would drag their children off to see.

It was, indeed, lost on me. I don't remember the story, just a few vague images.

But *Katrina* I remember. Perhaps because by 1969 I was a year older, perhaps only because Jill Kirkland in the title role sings a terribly sad song while strumming a guitar. *Lost is the girl*, is how the chorus goes, *lost is the girl* . . . The song was not a tearjerker, it didn't make me cry during the movie, but it lingered in my head as a melancholy sound in the background for weeks afterwards. *Lost is the girl*. It may have been the first time that I understood the difference between sentimentality and melancholy.

On the way home from the bioscope we children talked about the movie in the back of the car. Ma sat listening behind the wheel without our realising that she was listening. It is a spying tactic that I would perfect as a mother myself, decades later. While I was playing taxi driver for you and your brothers and your friends, you would sometimes forget my presence when you were chatting. If I managed to stay silent for long enough, I would discover many things without your realising that I was discovering anything.

(It sounds complicated, but any mother will instantly grasp what I mean.)

Maybe there were other children in the car with us. (Back then, adults would easily pack as many as six children without seatbelts into the backseat.) Because I battle to believe that at such a young age I could conduct an interesting political conversation with my even younger brother and sister.

And yet that was exactly what I heard Ma tell someone a short while later. That she'd been quite surprised by the critical questions we'd asked each other. And by the insight that had shone through.

I can't imagine who Ma would have told something like that. Not Pa, surely? Perhaps it was her English friend Rose, who worked in a bookshop and was married to a musician. Rose le Roux was certainly no communist or socialist or anything else that might have scared my parents off, but she was slightly more openly critical of the government's policy than anyone else in their circle of friends.

But it doesn't actually matter who she told, or even what she said, exactly. What matters, what I remember, is that she sounded proud.

I only realised years later that the pride in Ma's voice probably meant that she too had critical questions about our country's policy. Which she could not share with her children.

And that probably also answers the question about why she took us to see *Katrina*.

The biggest revelation of the mythical year of 1969, though, was sexual in nature. Quite appropriate, if you keep in mind that 'sixty-nine' also has a sexual connotation. (Which I was far too young and innocent to understand.)

It's not as if I developed a rampant interest in sex overnight. On the contrary, I was quite slow, a late bloomer rather than one of those soon-ripe-soon-rotten fruits that the older generation was constantly warning us about. But I became aware of things that were starting to happen to my body, and to my friends' bodies, and it made me feel as lost in the girl in *Katrina*'s theme song.

In the course of this year I was invited to my first evening party – a gathering of girls *and* boys – about which our little bunch of invitees were outrageously excited. I knew it would be different from the all-girl parties with cake and balloons that I had attended until then. But I wasn't at all prepared for kissing games.

The party was held in the Duvenhages' house on the corner, one of the most intriguing houses in the neighbourhood because they were a large family with some older children of relatives also living with them. For me as naive eldest child it was irresistible to spend time in a house where teenage hormones reigned supreme and loud rock music boomed out of bedrooms and even the children still in primary school looked like they knew things that I had yet to learn.

There were other intriguing houses in the street, for other reasons. The former Springbok rugby player Ryk van Schoor lived just a few houses away from us, and my rugby-mad father spoke of him with such veneration that I was dying of curiosity to see what his house looked like from the inside. His son and namesake was in my class at school, but that didn't help me get inside his house. Although all the children in the street played outside together often, the girls and boys didn't really visit one another's homes.

Ryk's house remained a mystery.

Another Springbok rugby hero I did occasionally have the opportunity to observe in the flesh, not in Welgemoed but on the beach in Stilbaai when we visited Ouma and Oupa. Jannie Engelbrecht was a good-looking man – even a child could see that – and on top of that he was married to a former Miss South Africa. They were a celebrity couple long before the concept existed in Afrikaans. It was as if they gave off a golden glow when they strolled along the beach, smiling, Jannie with a bare bronzed torso and Ellen in a white bikini, while everyone on the beach gazed at them with yearning. Two gods beyond the reach of earthly desires.

I studied these golden gods, but also the reactions of the people around me, the mixture of desire, envy, admiration, resentment and who knows what else the strolling couple elicited. I was in the process of becoming a writer, I was constantly watching people, but as yet lacked the words to describe my conclusions.

There was also a real, live writer in our neighbourhood, a woman who may have been a better role model than the drinking poet I'd spied on through the milkwood trees in Franskraal. Unfortunately, I only became aware of her writing after we had moved away from Welgemoed. Esme Mittner wrote novels with interesting titles such as *En doef! val die avokadopeer* – imagine, the sound of a falling avocado in the title of a book – and when fifteen years later I started working at *Sarie* as a young journalist, she was the magazine's fiction editor. We ended up in the same office and became good friends.

It was the first time I realised that I could be friends with someone who was older than my mother.

But in Welgemoed I only knew her as 'Hedda's mom'. I had never heard of Ibsen's *Hedda Gabler*, but Hedda was such an unusual name in an Afrikaans suburb that I was impressed. By the time I joined *Sarie*, I knew that an Afrikaans author who had named her daughter after a wilful protagonist in a Norwegian drama – a protofeminist who vainly strove for freedom – was the kind of woman I wanted to know better.

When you are invited to an evening party for the first time, you pay more attention than usual to your appearance. Some of the girls wore fashionable bellbottoms, or short skirts with knee-high lace-up white boots like the supermodel Twiggy in the fashion magazines. I was also crazy about Twiggy; two years earlier her famous boy's haircut had even inspired me to have my own hair cut short. But in the meantime my hair had grown again, and that evening I looked more like Alice in Wonderland than Twiggy. I wore an Alice band, of course, to keep my hair neatly away from my face, and a dress of midnight-blue velvet that Ma had specially made for me for the grand occasion of my first evening party, about which Ma was almost as excited as I was. The dress had a white lace collar, and I wore it with white tights and strappy shoes.

'Little Lord Fauntleroy!' Ma exclaimed when I came out of my room.

I wasn't sure who this little Fauntleroy was, because I hadn't read Frances Hodgson Burnett's children's book, but I knew he had made a big impression on Ma. She often referred to him, and on this evening she sounded so pleased that I couldn't bring myself to tell her that turning up at my first evening party as Little Lord Fauntleroy might not be a good idea.

And it wasn't.

The minute I walked into the party and saw the other children in their casual bellbottoms and boots, I started feeling out of place.

Not long ago, in Tarantino's *Once Upon a Time in Hollywood* I saw that the actor who played Roman Polanski in 1969 wore a velvet jacket over a dashing white lace collar, which consoled me that at least my velvet dress and lace collar had been part of the zeitgeist. Just a pity this zeitgeist hadn't reached primary school children in the northern suburbs of Cape Town yet.

I was overdressed compared to the other guests. At that insecure age when you absolutely do not want to feel different from your contemporaries, this was enough in itself to ruin the whole evening. But then it got worse.

Most of the children went to sit in a circle on the sitting room carpet, eager to play 'Spin the bottle' and to be obliged, giggling and grimacing, to kiss one another. When I protested, along with a few other spoilsports, we were ignored, so we marched indignantly out to the stoep. We knew about the sport boycott against our country that our dads complained about so bitterly. We decided to boycott 'Spin the bottle'.

But while we sat on the stoep in our own little circle assuring one another that it was ridiculous to have to kiss members of the opposite sex, we could hear the jeering and cheering in the sitting room with each new kiss. We were probably all sorry that we had reacted so hastily, but too proud to crawl back, tails between our legs, to ask if we could join in.

It could even be that one or two in our little group of protesters were potentially homosexual – for some of us, perhaps, it wouldn't have been nearly as creepy if we could kiss someone of the same sex – but that was not a possibility that occurred to me that evening.

We spent the rest of the evening sulking outside.

After this groundbreaking event it became almost obligatory to play kissing games whenever we held parties, even in broad daylight. Because I was scared to death of being excluded from future parties, I meekly started playing along. Once or twice I even felt a pleasant tickling sensation in my body when a cute boy gave me a chaste, closed-mouth kiss, the other children screaming with delight.

The tickling was a warning that my body was changing, but I ignored it.

Until one hot summer's day towards the end of the year I saw the shocking evidence of this change with my own eyes.

It was breaktime at school, and I was sitting in a sheltered, sunny spot with a couple of girlfriends, our backs against a wall and our lunchboxes in our laps, comparing our sandwiches and our suntans.

I was still the only one in my family who couldn't achieve a desirable sun-bronzed hue. Every summer I would only add more freckles, or end up bright-red and whining in a vinegar bath ('to draw out the burn', Ma claimed) and afterwards my skin would peel and I'd once again be as pale as before.

What if I took a scrubbing brush, I had asked my mother in despair a few years earlier, and scrubbed and scrubbed until all my skin peeled off? Wouldn't it be possible for my new skin to come our darker? More like Hanli's and Wiaan's skin which, even in winter, looked beautifully suntanned?

But I was what they called 'the milkman's child' back then, and that was that. The pale one among darker family members.

For this very reason I was exceptionally keen to show my friends my tan this breaktime, and because my pale legs definitely did not look suntanned I lifted up my maroon school dress and tugged at the bottom elastic of my maroon school panty to show them that the skin beneath my clothes was even whiter than my legs. And there, in the mercilessly bright sunlight, I caught sight for the first time of two or three longish, blackish hairs against my pale skin. Hair that looked completely different from the blond down on my legs.

I blushed red-hot and yanked my school dress back down before my friends could see anything. Fortunately they were so busy admiring their own (far browner) legs that they hadn't noticed. But I was numb with shock.

Hair like this could surely not appear overnight – or could it? I couldn't understand why I had never noticed them before. Perhaps because the light in our bathroom was too dim. Perhaps just because I had never really studied my lower half. In those days girls were certainly not encouraged to get to know their 'private parts'.

I felt like my body had turned against me, betraying me, doing all sorts of things without asking my permission.

Pa sometimes told an insipid little joke around the braai, about a man who holds his arms open and encourages his frightened child to jump from a height into his arms. When the child finally jumps, he deliberately fails to catch him and says: 'It is a wise child who knows his own father.'

I never found it funny.

When I told a friend about this joke the other day, he admonished me to not underestimate my father. The punchline is presumably a twist on Shakespeare's words, *It is a wise father that knows his own child*, from *The Merchant of Venice*.

Although Pa probably didn't know that.

In a world that was becoming more confusing every day, I at least wanted to know that I could count on my mother, my father and my own body. Now my body had betrayed me by growing pubic hair, and my father by deciding to move to Pretoria, and my mother . . .

It was probably only a matter of time before Ma would betray me too, I speculated at the end of 1969, shortly before we moved away from Welgemoed.

If I'd had to move to a new school in a new city at any other age, it would still have been horrible, because I was an introverted bookworm who struggled to make friends. But sending me to an unknown school in my final year at primary school felt almost de-liberately cruel. Had I been allowed to remain in Standard 5 at the same school I'd been in since Sub B, I would certainly have become a prefect, like all the clever, best-behaved children in Standard 5. Perhaps even head girl, I allowed myself to dream, like my dearly beloved Kobie Malan in the *Maasdorp* books. Or deputy head girl. Why not? I was one of the pioneers at this school after all, among the very first group of pupils.

But then Pa dragged me to Pretoria.

In January 1970 I had to take on my final primary-school year in a school where I knew no one – by Standard 5, most children had chosen their friends years ago – and where all the clever and best-behaved children in my class had already been crowned prefects at the end of the previous year.

The ship had sailed for my becoming head girl, prefect or even just a modest class captain.

Once this cruel truth finally dawned on me, I couldn't help wondering why I had been so well-behaved and obedient through all my primary school years. If I wasn't going to be 'rewarded' with the honour of at least becoming a prefect in my final year, I might just as well have been naughty and had much more fun. I had long since begun to suspect that life was easier for rebellious children, disobedient children, children who did not do their homework or study hard for tests.

The end of the mythical Sixties was therefore also the end of my exemplary childhood. In the seventies I became a teenager, which changed everything. 'The Times They Are A-Changin'' by Bob Dylan became my theme song.

11

A STRANGE, STRANGE WORLD

My darling daughter, when I started writing this very long letter many months ago I knew that, if I wanted to turn it into a book one day, I would have to place myself in isolation. As I do every time I try to complete a book.

What I didn't know, what I could never have imagined, was that this time all of humanity would be living in isolation with me.

When I started writing, the COVID-19 virus didn't yet exist. It was a different world. Now, after many weeks of house arrest in France, I suspect that the world will never be the same again. My most fervent hope is that our existence will once again seem more 'normal' by the time these words can be read in a book. But I think that our idea of 'normal' will change forever.

Normal people scare me. Do you remember the *cri de coeur* you painted on your bedroom door as a young teenager? Now 'normal' has become so strange – masked people scurrying around supermarkets like rats to get their hands on food, the absurd regulations about what we can and cannot buy, the deserted streets and beaches, the bookshops, museums and theatres that need to stay closed for who knows how long – that everything 'normal' also really scares me.

And yet I know that as a writer I am better equipped than most people to handle this lockdown state of silence and solitude. Precisely because it is part of what it means to write. By the way, James

Joyce never said that all any writer needed was silence, exile and cunning. What he did say was more subtle – and more radical:

I will not serve that in which I no longer believe, whether it calls it-self my home, my fatherland, or my church: and I will try to express myself in some mode of life or art as freely as I can and as wholly as I can, using for my defense the only arms I allow myself to use – silence, exile, and cunning.

Every writer chooses her own weapons. Most of us are fortunately not forced to live in exile. But most of us must have at least one or two of Joyce's weapons in our arsenal. For me, cunning has often been more important than silence over the past couple of decades – or, rather, the cunning I needed to create a degree of silence in the midst of a large and noisy household.

When I am well into the writing of a new book, it becomes difficult to fall asleep and my dreams become stranger and stranger and I battle with anxiety and uncertainty and I struggle to concentrate on all my 'ordinary' activities. This is apparently the state in which millions of people all over the world have found themselves in recent months. As if we have all turned into anxious writers who must complete an impossible story in unbearable circumstances.

And it is no consolation whatsoever that I am no longer living alone in my usual writing state of seclusion and confinement.

I had thought that it would require less effort to write about my memories than to create fiction. Now I wake up every morning exhausted, worn out from dreaming, but lacking the focus to remember my dreams. All that lingers are upsetting, absurd images I cannot capture.

I realise for the first time how hard the work of recalling memories can be: sorting through the chaos, deciding what can be recycled, what can go to the compost heap to nourish future fiction and what should preferably be discarded. Long ago, when I read what Susan Sontag wrote about memory I thought I understood what she meant. Now, I suspect that I am only just starting to understand:

Memory is inventive. Memory is a performance. Memory invites itself, and is hard to turn away.

Thank heavens I am not struggling to read, like many others in this worldwide state of emergency. Reading has always been my lifeline in stormy waters. These days it is a survival strategy more than ever before, one of the few 'normal' activities that are left to us in abnormal times.

Or perhaps reading has always been an 'abnormal' activity, something done at home in solitude and seclusion, in contrast to all the other things we do in social herds.

My reading pattern has changed, though. I am reading more biographies and autobiographies and non-fiction than before, not only because I am writing an autobiographical book myself but also because fiction feels insufficient, to me, in a world that has so quickly become stranger than any fiction.

I never believed I would admit *this* one day. Not that reality can be stranger than fiction, I have long been convinced of that, but that fiction can no longer keep up with this reality. I am certain that I will return to fiction, but it's as if I need to catch my breath first. As if I have to take a break while I read non-fiction.

One of the autobiographical collections I went to look for on my bookshelves to reread is Bessie Head's *A Woman Alone*. Perhaps only because the title has become irresistible in lockdown. These days, the earth is fuller than ever of women who are alone.

And yet I have also felt a special connection with Bessie Head ever since I participated in the University of Iowa's International Writing Program in 1997 and heard that she had also been there, in 1977. I don't know whether any other women of South African birth were involved in this program in the twenty years between her sojourn and my own sojourn in the Mayfair student residence. I was a single mother, just like Bessie, when I was in Iowa; indeed, my son was still so young that I had to take him with me when I was invited to take part in the program. It may have been the first time a five-year-old child had lived in the Mayfair with his mother – which inevitably made me stand out among the thirty-odd writers from all over the world who were in Iowa that year.

Bessie Head was probably the kind of woman who couldn't help standing out no matter where she was. Several lecturers and staff members still remembered her and asked me about her, as if I must have known her from childhood simply because we were born in the same country. The sad truth is that I didn't know about Bessie Head when she left for political exile in Botswana in the sixties – and not only because I was still a primary-school child. Even if I had been twenty years older, the chances are slim that I would have been aware of her. We never really lived in the 'same country'.

I was white and Afrikaans, a member of the group that controlled the country, the descendants of the Voortrekkers, whom Bessie Head despised. In her preface to a new edition of Sol Plaatje's *Native Life in South Africa*, which was first published in 1915, she quotes this groundbreaking author:

The northward march of the Voortrekkers was a gigantic plundering raid. They swept like a desolating pestilence through the land, blasting everything in their path and pitilessly laughing at ravages from which the native races have not yet recovered.

Even though I cannot find a Voortrekker among my direct ancestors, I have reaped the fruits of this 'gigantic plundering raid' since childhood.

By contrast, Bessie Head was born in a psychiatric hospital in Pietermaritzburg, because her mother was a white woman from a wealthy family and her father a black labourer. Her mother, Bessie Emery, was declared insane and placed in an institution for the mentally ill by her family while she was pregnant. The baby was classified as 'coloured', and grew up in foster care and orphanages. The mother spent the rest of her life in the institution.

That was what shaped Bessie Head's adult personality, these *myriad dark, inchoate childhood experiences*, to quote Craig MacKenzie, editor of *A Woman Alone*.

No, I had to keep explaining to the kind people in Iowa. Bessie Head and I may have been born in the same geographical territory, within the borders of the same country, but we were raised in different worlds.

When in 1970 I started a new chapter in my young life in the unknown city of Pretoria, I had never heard of Bessie Head. A few months later, when my new school arranged a tour that traced the footsteps of the Voortrekkers in Natal and I set foot in Pietermaritzburg for the first time, I did not know it was the city where Bessie Head was born.

All they really wanted to show our bunch of Afrikaans schoolchildren in Pietermaritzburg was the Church of the Covenant. A modest little white building that had been erected because, shortly before the Battle of Blood River, the Voortrekkers had promised God that they would build 'a house in His honour' if He helped them defeat the enemy. On 16 December 1838, the enemy suffered a spectacular defeat. Not one of the fewer than five hundred Voortrekkers inside the laager of ox wagons died, while thousands of the approximately twenty thousand attacking Zulu warriors lost their lives.

The Covenant of Blood River became one of the founding myths of the Afrikaner nation, incontrovertible proof that there was an

Afrikaans Supreme Being who was on 'our side', even though Afrikaners had always been only a tiny percentage of the country's population.

It is a bloodbath that is commemorated in many of the paintings of ox wagons and dead Zulus that we saw at Evita se Perron, remember, Mia?

This myth, these kinds of paintings, these kinds of school tours to the sacred beacons of a chosen people were part of the *dark, inchoate childhood experiences* that shaped your mother's adult personality.

During the Natal school tour we also visited the monument that commemorates the Battle of Blood River, naturally. Back then the present-day laager of bronze ox wagons had not yet been installed; the only sight for visitors was a lonely granite ox wagon by the sculptor Coert Steynberg on a deserted plain. There was no gift shop or picnic site or even public toilets. It looked like the scene hadn't changed much since the Voortrekkers pitched camp there. Except that there were no Zulus, dead or alive, in sight.

And there, one of the greatest scandals of my young life befell me. Shortly before we had to get back into the school bus, I realised that I urgently needed to wee and that I would definitely not be able to hold out until our next stop. Because I had already wet my pants in front of all my classmates in Sub A, the risk of doing it again in Standard 5 was enough to make me break out in a cold sweat.

And because there was no toilet, not even a tree I could hide behind, I did the unthinkable. I slipped behind Coert Steynberg's granite ox wagon, pulled down my panties, squatted and peed on the hallowed ground of the Battle of Blood River. Scared to death that the Afrikaans Supreme Being would strike me dead with a thunderbolt before I could pull my panties back up. And so ashamed and guilty about my lack of respect that I promised myself I would never, ever, tell anyone about this misdeed.

And I didn't.

This is the first time I have confessed to my own Vow of Blood River, half a century after it happened.

Which just goes to show once more how the dark experiences of our childhood become baggage that we carry around with us for a lifetime, sometimes for no reason.

My new life in Pretoria began in a hotel. I tried to romanticise the situation by imagining that I was Eloise, the young heroine of a series of children's books that Kay Thompson wrote in the fifties. Eloise lived in a hotel permanently, while my own hotel existence only lasted a week or three before we could move into our new home. And Eloise lived 'on the tippity-top floor' of the famous Plaza Hotel in New York – an architectural landmark inspired by a château in the French Renaissance style – something altogether different from my ordinary Pretoria hotel with a name I can no longer even remember.

Years later I read that Kay Thompson may have based her little Eloise on her godchild, Liza Minnelli, who spent a large part of her childhood in grand hotels with her mother, Judy Garland. And that Lena Dunham from the controversial TV series *Girls* has a picture of Eloise tattooed somewhere on her body. I was evidently not the only girl who was enchanted by this fictional hotel resident.

Before we moved to Pretoria, I had never spent even a single night in a hotel. I was so unsophisticated that everything struck me as strange. Sometimes it was exotically strange, like the sound of the gong that a dignified black man beat every evening to announce dinnertime. Or the black waiters who served out food. In Cape Town I'd had almost no contact with black people.

And sometimes it was nerve-wrackingly strange. In the dining room, we three children quickly had to learn to use more than one knife and fork per meal. And to not place our neatly folded napkins on our heads like paper hats from Christmas crackers just to be funny.

The food was probably as unremarkable as the hotel rooms, because I can recall no other details, just the general atmosphere of strangeness.

This strangeness followed me when we moved to a brand-new flat-roofed face-brick house in the new suburb of Lynnwood Manor. This house in Dorking Road, across from an open stretch of veld that my mischievous brother would soon set on fire accidentally when he and a neighbour's boy were playing with matches, was the most spacious, most modern and grandest house we had ever lived in. There was even a swimming pool in the garden. I was happy about the swimming pool, of course, but it didn't compensate for the strangeness.

I was also glad to have my own bedroom for the first time in my life, which I could decorate myself the way I wanted to, with floral curtains that I chose myself and pictures of briefly famous pop stars that I cut out of teen magazines like the British *Jackie* and the Afrikaans *Tina* to paste on my door. At night I was lulled to sleep by David Cassidy's boyish grin or David Essex's dreamy blue eyes behind my door.

My door. My bedroom. I sometimes inserted these words deliberately and unnecessarily into sentences, just to hear what they sounded like. When a decade later I read Virginia Woolf's *A Room of One's Own*, I realised just how privileged I had been to be able to say these words as soon as my twelfth year.

My sister chose more colourful curtains to hang in her own room next to mine, and bolder rock stars such as Marc Bolan of T. Rex to stick on her door.

But as always, our little brother in his bedroom across the passage was the most daring of all. He didn't pay much attention to pop stars at that stage – he kept live snakes in a bread bin under his bed.

From time to time the snakes would escape, and I'd be terrified for days that I'd find one in my bed. Sometimes he took the snakes out on purpose, to terrorise his sisters and the girls in the neighbourhood. The only solution, I soon learnt, was to pretend I wasn't scared at all. Then he would lose interest and go taunt other girls. I forced myself to stop recoiling and screaming when I saw him approach with a snake. I even put out my hand and allowed the snake to glide up my arm, surprised by the velvet softness of such a frightening reptile's skin.

It taught me a valuable lesson for the rest of my life. If you can pretend convincingly enough that you are not scared of something, you sometimes manage to convince even yourself. When I became a writer, I had to pretend for years that I wasn't afraid of talking about my books in public – until one day I realised that I really was no longer afraid of doing it.

In my new school, Lynnwood Primary, I had to hide my fear for months. I was terribly shy, terribly lonely, scared to death that I wouldn't make friends. I wasn't good enough at sport to command the other children's admiration. I couldn't sing well enough to win a sought-after place in the school choir. All I had previously been able to count on to impress anyone was my intelligence and my imagination. But here, on top of everything, I felt stupid for the first time in my life.

Sums and numbers had always been my Achilles heel, and here I realised to my horror that the Cape maths syllabus was miles behind the Transvaal syllabus. It was a deficit I would battle to erase for the rest of my school years. Pa insisted that I take maths up to matric, no matter how I pleaded with him to let me do art or anything else (except domestic science) instead. Pa was adamant that maths would teach me to think logically. I don't know if that ever happened. I only know that I liked maths less with each passing year, and that, the moment after writing my matric exam, I flushed the whole store of mathematical knowledge from my head with enormous relief.

Which probably cannot be described as logical behaviour. Sorry, Pa.

Another one of my numerous failings in my new environment was my handwriting. Previously I had been under the impression that I wrote quite neatly. I even won an Eisteddfod certificate for penmanship once. (Unthinkable, isn't it, if you look at my illegible scrawl now.) But in my new school I heard that my cursive writing ('longhand' as it was called) left much to be desired. Apparently I had learnt to form certain letters the wrong way from the start – and now, alas, it was too late to unlearn my mistakes.

I began to avoid cursive writing like a contagious disease. My schoolbooks were like hospital wards where I was forced to live with the disease. But for all writing outside of school I wrote in block letters, from when I was twelve right up to this day. And I was doing more and more writing that had nothing to do with school. Letters, journals, stories, the beginnings of dozens of 'great novels' that were never completed.

Afrikaans and English were about the only subjects I wasn't afraid of in my new environment. I knew I had a 'knack for languages', of course. Language was my dessert among all those boring subjects that were dished up to us.

But the Afrikaans I spoke to my new classmates was not quite the same language they spoke to each other. They found my Cape pronunciation funny, and I rattled my words off faster than anyone else. To this day I have a tendency to sound like an auctioneer on cocaine when I am excited or nervous. In my defence, I sometimes joke that I'm still trying to catch up on all the hours of talking I lost during my first few years. Because, according to my family, up until the age of about four I spoke painfully slowly.

Pa often teased me with a story about how, as a three-year-old in church, I pointed at a bald man in the next row and asked loudly and clearly: 'Why (pause) does that (pause) uncle (suspenseful pause) have no hair?' By the time I got to the end of the sentence, the entire congregation (except for the bald man) were snorting with laughter.

But by Standard 5 I would have rattled off such a sentence in a single breath – 'Whydoesthatunclehavenohair?' – and I certainly wouldn't have asked it out loud in church. I was far too self-conscious to draw everyone's attention to myself.

It wasn't only speed and pronunciation that tripped me up. Even my vocabulary caused problems. Every time I wanted to take a textbook out of my 'suitcase', I was laughed at. In the Cape I went to school carrying my books in a suitcase, or *koffer*. In Pretoria I soon learnt that the same thing was called a bag, or *tas*.

Fortunately children are endlessly adaptable. Long before President PW Botha said 'adapt or die', I knew that adapting everything, including my language, to my new environment was a matter of survival. Soon I was broadening my e's and rounding my a's like a local. No longer saying '*Ek praat Afrikaans*,' but '*Ack prot Afrikons*.'

In my first year at university, a formidable speech lecturer in the drama department ensured that I was soon rid of these little habits again, until in the end I spoke an acceptable 'standard' Afrikaans.

Another hurdle on my journey to acceptance among both teachers and classmates was my habit of dreaming in class in broad daylight. A rabbit sleeping with its eyes open is what I must have looked like to them. In my previous school everyone knew me and knew that my results would be good enough, even if it looked like I was paying no attention at all. Now I was constantly in trouble for my 'lack of attention'.

There was one teacher, though – the middle-aged Mr Botha –

who understood my dreaminess. When my eyes glazed over he would smile and say: 'Marita, come back to Sorrento.' And then he would whistle the tune of Dean Martin's song about Sorrento. It always worked.

And I kept thinking of Sorrento with an inexplicable yearning until at last, by my sixtieth birthday, I made it to the Bay of Naples and could see the peninsula of Sorrento calling to me across the water.

If Mr Botha had still been alive, I would've liked to have let him know that I did come back to Sorrento in the end.

Because I was so desperate to fit in, I managed to befriend the most popular group of girls in the school. These were the girls who were both clever and pretty, because just clever or just pretty was never quite good enough. Clever girls could easily be dismissed as nerds, pretty girls as dumb blondes. Especially if they were really blonde, like me.

If you were a boy, it was fine to be both ugly and stupid, for as long as you excelled at sport, there would be room for you in the social hierarchy. Girls always had to be more versatile to climb the popularity ladder. If, over and above your intellect and your appearance, you could pride yourself on your sporting talent, you were a queen bee. As desirable as Kobie from *Maasdorp*.

That was why I took part in sport throughout my school years. Not because I was particularly good at it or found it particularly enjoyable, simply because that was what you had to do to climb the social ladder.

Among the multitude of photographs on the cork board above my desk, there is one of Lynnwood Primary's Standard 5 netball team. (Presumably the B team, because the true stars I remember from the netball court are not in the picture.) I am dead centre of a row of seven girls who'd been lined up from shortest to tallest.

It is a surprising position, because I have become a tall woman, but at the age of twelve only my big feet predicted my future height. What further surprises me is that I see, now, that I was a pretty girl. Back then I only saw flaws every time I looked in the mirror. I would have given anything to have fewer freckles, a browner skin, a finer nose, prettier teeth, bigger breasts, smaller feet, slimmer fingers . . . A litany of self-pitying yearning that plagued my life for years.

When I look at the photograph now, I think of Rebecca West's poignant words about how little most of us actually like ourselves:

Were it possible for us to wait for ourselves to come into the room, not many of us would find our hearts breaking into flower as we heard the door handle turn.

Over the years I gradually learnt to appreciate myself more, but at the age of twelve my self-worth was wholly dependent on the opinions of others. Especially those of my contemporaries. One of the measures of the kind of popularity I strove for was an autograph book chock-full of compliments from all the most popular girls.

The autograph book, my dear girl, is something else that you and your contemporaries don't know because you dish out compliments to each other on social media, for the whole world to see, rather than in well-thumbed little books kept safe like secret treasures. And the name is misleading, because it was about much more than autographs. The idea was that this little hardcover book, about the size of the palm of a man's hand, was sent around so that each of your friends could draw a picture or write a special message in it.

If you were lucky, your little book would be filled after a few weeks with soppy verses like: *Roses are red, violets are blue, sugar is sweet, and so are you.* Or silly rhymes such as: *Beware of boys with eyes of brown, they kiss you once and let you down. Beware of boys with eyes of grey, they kiss you once and run away. Beware of boys with eyes of blue, they kiss you once and ask for two!*

No one scored points for poetic originality. Sentiment was all that counted. The sole opportunity for a bit of originality was in the answers you could provide to the lists of questions that were included in some of the books. These were questions such as: *Who is the girl you admire most? What is your favourite pop song? What do you want to be when you grow up?*

I was never brave enough to answer that I wanted to become a writer.

And I don't recall that my name was ever mentioned as the girl in the class who was admired most. A petite redhead nicknamed Tone or Toontjies (Toes or Little Toes) was frequently mentioned, but she was so amiable that I couldn't even be jealous. I simply joined in with the chorus of admirers and started to praise Tone.

Because I so desperately longed to be popular, I sometimes agonised about my answers for hours, convinced that a single wrong answer would jeopardise my precarious place in this fragile web of social acceptance. Once, for example, I evaded the question about my favourite song by asking Dolly Titus what was number one on Springbok Radio's weekly hit parade. 'Venus', she replied, and I wrote down Venice. Blissfully unaware that I had confused the goddess of love with a city, because at that point I had never really listened to the lyrics of Shocking Blue's song.

I just wanted it to look like I listened to the hit parade every Friday night. I wanted to convince my new friends that I was 'with it'; that was all that mattered.

Yes, Dolly moved to Pretoria with us, for which I was terribly grateful. Everything was so overwhelmingly strange, not just the new school and the new friends, but also the unfamiliar trees and plants in the gardens, the thunderstorms in the summer and the frost on the ground in the early morning in winter, the unimpressive hills on the horizon that people described as 'mountains', the fact that I lived too far from the sea ever to hear a seagull cry. But the knowledge that Dolly would be waiting for me in the kitchen every day after school, dressed in her pink overall with a pink headscarf worn low over her forehead, gave me renewed hope every morning.

Dolly became the symbol of everything I'd had to leave behind in the Cape, even my way of speaking.

It didn't occur to be that she must have felt even stranger and lonelier than I did. She was the only coloured domestic helper in the neighbourhood. She couldn't understand the indigenous languages spoken by the black women who worked in the other houses. She could barely speak English; she was a child of the rural Northern Cape.

One of the ways she devised to vent her bottled-up frustration was to rearrange all the furniture in the house, frequently. In the Cape she never did it, but in Pretoria it drove me demented when I would walk into my bedroom in the afternoon after school to find that my bed was no longer where I'd left it when I'd walked out of the room that morning. But if I complained to Ma, she just said: 'Leave Dolly alone. It's her house too.'

After another month or so Dolly would move all the furniture around again. Just as I was getting used to my bed's new position. I realised that, if I waited patiently, my bed would eventually end up back in its original spot. There are only so many possibilities when you rearrange furniture in a smallish room, after all.

It was thanks to Dolly that, at some point in the next year, I would experience a moment of political awakening that shook me to my core. I wanted her to do something she wasn't keen on. It was something trivial, I don't even remember what, but her reaction has stayed with me. We started arguing and she demanded to know why she had to do it. My unforgivable reply was: 'Because you're our maid!'

I had never before – or since – seen her shudder with such rage. She literally started trembling, and snarled: 'I work for you, but that doesn't give you the right to talk to me like that!'

I was initially numb with shock. I honestly couldn't understand why she was 'overreacting' in such a way. But the more I thought about it – and I couldn't stop thinking about it – the more I wondered what it meant to be a 'maid'. I tried putting myself in Dolly Titus's shoes for the first time – and it was such an uncomfortable experience that I immediately kicked those metaphorical shoes off again.

But something in our relationship had shifted. It's not as if I'd grasped the wounding weight of a word like 'maid' overnight. I'd simply taken a teeny, tiny step towards comprehension.

In more or less the same period, perhaps a year later, yet another incident unleashed a multitude of questions. It was on a scorching summer's day at an interschool athletics meeting at the Pilditch Stadium and I was one of thousands of children in uniform who had come to cheer on our respective schools' athletes. Everyone on the track and everyone in the stands was white, but behind the stands, black ice cream vendors peddled their wares from iceboxes on bicycles.

I waited in line to buy an ice cream, sweating in my school uniform, my mouth watering at the prospect of that icy refreshment on a stick, when a young man at the front of the queue started hurling abuse at the considerably older vendor. About what I don't know. I remember only his contemptuous tone and the thought that ran through my body like fire: *As if he were speaking to a dog.*

The ice cream vendor dropped his head and endured the verbal abuse in silence.

Like a dog being kicked by its owner.

I turned around and fled, without an ice cream, burning with shame. I was too scared of what I might see in that black man's eyes if he were to glance up to hand me my ice cream.

My head was a jumble of questions that I couldn't ask out loud. 'That doesn't give you the right to talk to me like that!' Dolly had exclaimed. What, I wondered, gave anyone the right to talk to an older person like that? Hadn't we been taught from an early age to respect older people?

Did the rules of respect not apply to older people of a different race at all?

That weekend in church the questions continued to multiply. The abusive young man was probably also a good Christian, like all the Afrikaners I knew. Was it possible to be an Afrikaner without being a good Christian? And what did being a good Christian mean in a country where most people were routinely treated like dogs?

The minister's sermon gave no answers. Nor the school principal's prayer in assembly the following morning. I started to wonder whether ministers and school principals, teachers and other figures of authority – yes, even my parents – would ever be able to answer my questions.

Towards the end of my primary school years, the song 'Master Jack' by a South African group with the amusing name Four Jacks and a Jill was frequently heard on the radio. I wouldn't have cited it as my favourite song in any of my new friends' autograph books, because it was already a few years old by then and not 'with it' enough to impress anyone. And yet the lyrics captured my confused state far better than love songs such as 'Venus'/'Venice' about burning desires, of which I understood absolutely nothing yet.

It's a strange, strange world we live in, Master Jack . . .
I saw right through the way you started teachin' me now
So someday soon you could get to use me somehow

Over the past few weeks this song has played inside my head day in and day out, for the first time in decades, probably because this COVID-19 virus has made the world seem stranger than ever.

12

THE FIRST TIME THAT . . .

In my first year at high school our family befriended a cold-blooded murderer who was hanged in Pretoria Central the following year.

And now that I have caught your attention with that sentence, my darling girl, let me start by telling you about the more commonplace experiences of my thirteenth year.

By 'more commonplace' I simply mean the things that hit most teenagers for the first time at high school. Because I know that every single first experience during those exciting and terrifying years seems absolutely unique to each of us while we are experiencing it.

Like my first 'tongue kiss', which I got in the same week I went with Ma to buy my first bra. It was during a close dance towards the end of a dimly lit garage party, the last song before I had to flee like Cinderella because I had to be home by twelve.

I had just turned thirteen and was inordinately proud of my new bra, which was clearly visible underneath my T-shirt, thanks to the ultraviolet lights that made our white underwear and our teeth glow in the dark. Swaying in the arms of an unknown older boy who was wearing a tie-dye vest. When I felt him slip his tongue between my lips, I meekly opened my mouth and wondered what I was supposed to do with my own tongue. 'Let it be,' the Beatles sang over the speakers, and I listened to them and allowed my tongue just to lie there while enjoying it more and more.

I was so overwhelmed that I clean forgot to ask his name. And because it was so dark in the garage, except for the ultraviolet lights, I couldn't recognise him at school on Monday.

Which didn't stop me from bragging to my girlfriends that I, too, had – finally! – joined the exclusive club of French Kissers. And since I was a future writer, I had no difficulty coming up with a name for the new character in my story. I christened him Vestie. Because of his tie-dye vest, which had made almost a bigger impression on me than his kiss.

A couple of months later I also started 'going steady' (very briefly) with a boy in Standard 8 who visited me at home and was glared at by Pa like something the cat had dragged in. (That may have been one of the reasons why the affair only lasted a few weeks.) The official reason for the breakdown of the relationship was that a rumour reached me one Monday morning at school that Sonny Boy had been the recipient of an enormous blueish-purple love bite from one of the 'wild girls'.

Let's call her Aileen. Sonny Boy's name was also not really Sonny Boy; it was something equally unlikely that today would sound like it belonged in a Tarantino movie. Until now I have been able to tell my story without concealing anyone's name, because the most important characters were mostly family. From my teenage years onwards, the cast of characters keeps expanding because people outside my family become more and more important in my story, and to some of these characters I would rather give story names.

Aileen always wore a thick layer of stage make-up because she was trying to hide an acne problem. Together with her school uniform, the unnaturally pale face made her look as strange as Bette Davis in *What Ever Happened to Baby Jane*. She was in the class for children who struggled academically, not the kind of girl whom 'good boys' like Sonny Boy would date openly, but she allegedly excelled at love bites and other sexual acts of which 'good girls' like me were barely cognisant. So, boys like Sonny Boy secretly hung out with Aileen on weekends – and had far more fun than with good girls like me.

That was the unpleasant conclusion to which my first broken relationship led me.

Fortunately my heart didn't break along with the relationship. That kind of wretchedness would only hit me at university. During my early teenage years my heart bounced from one boy to the next like a ball, like a game where the ball isn't supposed to stay in any single player's possession for too long. I was still no good at ball games, but I was fast becoming skilled at games of the heart.

And at the end of a year chock-full of unforgettable firsts, I enjoyed my first holiday romance at the seaside. My partner in crime was an impossibly attractive boy with a blond fringe and blue eyes and a dimple in his square chin. The very same one I referred to earlier when I told you about our cottage at the sea.

I'm not making it up, my precious. On the cork board above my desk there is still a black-and-white snapshot of me sitting in the arms of the adorable Erik, with my fingers in my mouth like a starstruck groupie. He remains a feast for the eye even now, with muscular shoulders and a glimpse of washboard stomach above his swimsuit. I am wearing a beach cover-up over my bikini. Perhaps I am holding my hand in front of my mouth because by then my lips had been kissed sore. Behind us is the white sand of the Franskraal dunes, where I quickly learnt that my tongue didn't have to lie in my mouth like a sleeping dog while I was being kissed.

On the contrary.

'Heaven, I'm in heaven,' I felt like humming along with Ella Fitzgerald and Satchmo that whole summer holiday. Despite the fact that it was an 'old-fashioned' song that Ma and Pa liked to listen to.

It was also the year I discovered Bob Dylan and my musical tastes veered dramatically from innocent radio tunes.

Among all these perfectly ordinary and yet unique first experiences of a budding teenager, there were also a few I did not share with my peers. Shortly before my thirteenth birthday I received my first payment for words I had written – a story that was read aloud on the radio – and suddenly my dream to become a writer one day didn't seem quite so far-fetched. But I still didn't tell my friends about it.

My most pressing need was still to be accepted by the cool kids in the school, and because none of them were writing stories, I preferred to keep my writing secret. It is possible, of course, that one or two of my contemporaries may also have been secret writers – but there was no way of establishing that without admitting that I was one too. And I was still nowhere near brave enough for that.

It was almost as unthinkable as confessing that I still sometimes played with paper dolls.

I would only commit this secret sin on those rare school days when I could convince Ma that I was sick enough to stay at home. When I was certain that none of my schoolmates could turn up unexpectedly and catch me at my scandalous regression, I would take Ouma Tina's box with the irresistible 'cut-outs' out from its hiding place at the bottom of my wardrobe. I would spread the cardboard dolls, with their broken bodies and their breathtaking outfits, out on my sickbed and spend hours making up life stories for them.

By the time my siblings would come home from school, or Ma from work, the box would already be safely back in its hiding place and I would pretend I had spent the whole day reading.

The only living soul who knew my secret was Dolly Titus. Sometimes she even came to sit on the bed beside me, between washing and ironing and cleaning and all her other tasks, to admire the paper dolls and their clothes with me for a while.

Today I know that teenagers often hide things from their peers because they are afraid of being mocked. Any sheep who behaves differently from the rest could be driven from the herd.

So it has always been, and so it will probably always be.

But that is just another reason why I am proud of you, my dear girl, because you were able to escape from this kind of typical teenage peer pressure at a much younger age than I was. Perhaps your revolt was encouraged by stories with unpopular outsiders as main characters, young adult books such as *The Perks of Being a Wallflower* and cult movies such as *Ghost World* and *Napoleon Dynamite*. In stories like these, a few sympathetic 'losers' typically band together – the overweight girls and the gay boys and the nerds who are both too shy and too clever – against the conceited cool kids who discover that they can't always win at everything.

If books like these had been available in Afrikaans when I was a teenager, I may not have taken so long to learn that the most popular children at school weren't necessarily going to be my friends for life. I may have discovered sooner that the accursed Kobie Malan of *Maasdorp*, the most popular, prettiest and most mischievous girl in the school, wasn't really part of my tribe.

But that I would only realise many years later.

When you were fourteen years old, I wrote a young-adult novel with the title *Swimming Lessons for a Mermaid* because I wanted to give readers the kind of advice I had needed so badly when I was a teenager. Whenever I visit Afrikaans schools to talk about books, I realise how many teenagers still need it.

One of the characters in this book is Groucho, a boy who is exceptionally clever and exceptionally funny, but because he is also exceptionally ugly he's not admitted to the clique of the best-looking, wealthiest, most popular 'winners' in the school. Groucho consoles himself – and his friends, who are social outsiders like him – when he declares:

'*We know some of the others regard us as losers . . . They don't know they're losers, they'll only discover that later in life . . . And*

I don't know about you, but I'd rather be a loser for a few years at high school than for the rest of my life.'

Groucho predicts that, when a school reunion is held in thirty years' time, everyone will be able to see who the real winners are in life after school.

I never made it to such a reunion myself, probably because directly after matric I fled back to the Cape to study and work there while nearly all my high school friends stayed behind in the north of the country. Within a few years I had lost contact with almost everyone. And thirty or forty years later, at the age when most people become nostalgic about their school days and start organising reunions left, right and centre, I had already been living in France for a long time.

But I have listened to enough of my adult friends' anecdotes about their own school reunions to know that Groucho's words were true.

I wrote my first 'professional' story, *Die hartseer bus*, in Standard 6 for the children's programme *Siembamba* on an Afrikaans radio station. I cannot remember what the bus in the title was sad about, but I wanted to leap out of my skin with joy when I received a letter on the official letterhead of the SABC informing me that my story would be broadcast.

Because *Siembamba* was a morning programme, I pleaded with Ma to let me stay home that morning so I could hear my name being announced on the radio. But Ma packed me off to school as resolutely as on any other morning. A radio story wasn't an excuse to miss school. Finish and *klaar*. That was what she always said, and then you knew there was no point in arguing. So off I went to school, sulking.

She did promise to ask someone to record the broadcast with a tape recorder – and when, a few days later, I could finally listen to the tape, I shivered with delight. Not because my story impressed me all that much, but because the presenter (blissfully unaware that I was only twelve years old), introduced me to the young listeners as 'Tannie Marita'.

Later in life I would come to despise this overly familiar 'tannie', or auntie, almost as much as being addressed as 'lady', but on that first occasion – yet another first in a year of firsts! – it was as exciting as suddenly being called 'Your Majesty'.

And all because I'd written a story about a bus.

This was my first tentative step on a path that other women writers had cleared ahead of me. I have already told you about my grand-mothers and my female ancestors, Mia, but I must also tell you about my literary ancestors. Or at least single out a few names on the long list of formidable women without whose stories my own story would not have been possible. Nor yours.

As Virginia Woolf writes in *A Room of One's Own*, behind every single woman's voice are the echoes of a chorus of women's voices:

Jane Austen should have laid a wreath upon the grave of Fanny Burney, and . . . all women together ought to let flowers fall upon the tomb of Aphra Behn, for it was she who earned them the right to speak their minds.

Aphra Behn (1640–1689) was indeed the first woman to become a professional writer in the English language. The first, according to Angeline Goreau in *Feminist Theorists*:

. . . to leave aside the claim that she merely scribbled to amuse her-self in private hours, and insist upon a literary identity of her own.

I only became aware of her in the eighties, when in search of my own 'literary identity' I embarked on a master's degree in journalism about the role of women in the Afrikaans media. It was soon clear that I couldn't write about South African media without also researching the international historical background, because every one of the remarkable trailblazers who wrote in my mother tongue was following a path that other women in other languages had also had to clear. And Aphra Behn preceded us all.

Thirty years before Daniel Defoe's *Robinson Crusoe* was designated the first novel in the English language, she had already published thirteen novels. She wrote seventeen plays in seventeen years, and also had several translations and poetry collections appear in print. The life led by this adventurous woman would be considered exceptional even today. In the seventeenth century it was downright astonishing. She travelled all over the world, she was involved in slave revolts, she was thrown into prison for debt. She was a passionate champion of women's rights to receive the same education as men, to marry whomever they wanted – or to remain unmarried if they preferred – and to above all enjoy the same sexual freedom as men.

She was way, way ahead of her time.

Like some Afrikaans women, too, in the early history of the language. I was amazed to learn of Totius's sister, Marié du Toit, who in 1921 used the word 'feminist' in Afrikaans for the first time – in her book, whose title translates as *Woman and Feminist, or Something about the Women's Issue.*

You don't know who the 'people's poet' Totius was, and even the older generation of Afrikaners who still remember him have often not heard of his rebellious sister. She was a different animal from her famous brother; he was a rather sober stable horse, she a wild mare who galloped away from the national stable. Her rebellion included trading the uncomfortable Victorian women's outfits of the time for practical men's suits, as the French authors George Sand and Colette had done before her. Naturally, the conservative Afrikaner nation was even more shocked than the French by such scandalous behaviour.

The opening chapter of *Forget-me-not Blues* takes place on 'Dingaan's Day', 1938, when the selfsame Totius gave a speech at the stone-laying of the future Voortrekker Monument in Pretoria. His words were broadcast on radio for the whole country to hear, delivered in a thin and trembling voice and in the melodramatic, declamatory style of those days, which now sounds laughable.

This is the yeaaar of our Looord nineteen-hundred-and-thirty-eight. Now we will ceeelebrate . . . But our meeerciful Father didn't give a celebration but a reviiival . . .

In the course of my research I came across old newsreels and radio recordings that helped me hear Totius clearly. Therefore I could imagine sitting beside the wireless with a fictional Cape family to listen to 'a nation's awakening'. 'There were no Voortrekkers on my side of the family,' the doctor's wife says indignantly, and the six-year-old child wonders 'how she manages to almost make Voortrekkers sound like a swearword'.

I would love to know what Marié du Toit sounded like, but I could find no visual footage or sound recordings of her. Although she had been a trailblazer, she failed to make it into the history books. If anyone still remembers her today, it is as 'Totius's sister'.

It is depressing to think of all the exceptional women who, for centuries, have been remembered as merely the sister or daughter or mother or wife of a famous man. 'Behind every successful man is a woman.' All those misguided sayings that women were raised with so that they would be content to live in a man's shadow. To not claim their own place in the sun.

My wish for you, my girl, is for the sun to shine upon your whole body.

I was a Voortrekker in my early years at high school. Menlopark was the kind of school where even the cool kids were Voortrekkers, and if the cool kids were doing it, then I wanted to do it too. We were six girlfriends in a team called the Dubbeltjies, the Afrikaans word for 'devil's thorn' and a name that therefore elicited a string of prick jokes from the boys. At first we were too naive to catch the jokes, afterwards we just grinned and joined in the banter. Voortrekker camps were an exciting opportunity to be away from home and flirt with boys around the campfire in the evening and lie chatting in our tent deep into the night, mostly about boys and about all the inexplicable things that were happening to our bodies.

We frequently had to sing *Die Lied van jong Suid-Afrika*, a stirring song about the 'mighty roar' of 'a nation's awakening', but for us these lyrics had more to do with biology than with politics. Our version went something like:

It is the song of a body's awakening
Of hormones that tremble and stir.

In those years our hormones were making us tremble all the time. We were endlessly curious about sex, but there was simply no way of discovering more about the subject – besides trying it out in practice ourselves. And most of us weren't quite ready for that. Remember, we couldn't do research on the internet, anything that smacked of "pornography" in movies or books was banned by the censorship board, and overseas magazines such as *Playboy* were as forbidden as Mao's Little Red Book. *Scope* was a local magazine notorious for centre spreads of bare-breasted girls, but none of these pin-ups had nipples. In South Africa you were allowed to see the complete curves of women's breasts, but nipples were Sperrgebiet, like the coast of the former South West Africa that was famous for diamond diving. Any hint of a nipple was covered with a tiny black star. The bigger the nipple, the bigger the star.

And the pubic darkness 'down there' was even more verboten than the Sperrgebiet, whether in photographs or movies or depicted in any other way.

As a result I was 22 years old the first time I saw a nipple on a movie screen. It was during my Big Year Abroad, in a fairly luxurious movie theatre on the Champs Élysées in Paris, where one of the notorious *Emmanuelle* films was being shown. The price of the ticket was the equivalent of three days' food on a modest budget, but I couldn't resist the temptation.

So there I sat in the dark, blushing like a naughty schoolgirl, while Sylvia Kristel's nipples (and the rest of her pale naked body) appeared on the enormous screen a hundred times larger than life. Within half an hour I had reached a state of total nipple saturation.

Can you imagine, my dear girl, how unbelievably ignorant I was in my thirteenth year if I only saw a naked body in a movie after the age of twenty-one?

In biology class a single lesson was devoted to human genitalia and reproduction – one we looked forward to for months with a mixture of daring and fear – but it merely gave the scientific outlines. The rest of the picture we had to colour in using our own imagination.

In the Bible, words such as 'went in' and 'knew' suddenly acquired new meaning. This character 'went in unto' that one, so-and-so 'knew' so-and-so. But once again the details were left to our imagination.

We were so unaccustomed to any descriptions of sex in Afrikaans that even the lamest efforts could make us giggle helplessly. A weathered copy of André P Brink's novel from the sixties, *Die*

Ambassadeur (*The Ambassador*), was passed like a secret baton from one girl to the next to be read surreptitiously at home. We weren't really interested in the story, we just wanted to get to the 'dirty bits'. Any description of a body part that was usually hidden underneath clothing, like Nicolette's small firm breasts, pointing upwards as if two bees sat on it, seemed a piece of irresistible mischief.

All that mattered was that something was going on here that we would never be able to read about in the prim, old-fashioned Afrikaans books that were prescribed for us at school. I realised with amazement that it was actually possible to write about sex in Afrikaans. It was a revelation almost as big as when, at the age of seventeen, in my first year at university, I got my hands on a smuggled copy of Brink's banned novel, *Kennis van die aand* (*Looking on Darkness*), and became aware of political protest in an Afrikaans story.

In one of my early novels two decades later, about a group of white teenagers living in a sultry white fool's paradise in the Lowveld in the seventies, I paid a tongue-in-cheek tribute to Brink because he had showed me and many other young Afrikaans readers that it was possible to write about absolutely anything in Afrikaans.

'Man, André P. Brink is not like other Afrikaans writers.' The way in which she accented the P made the name sound elegant and exotic. 'I'm telling you, it's hot stuff. Nude scenes.'

I didn't want to show any interest. But when my mother took us back to the hostel on the Friday afternoon, after our visit to the Portuguese café, I asked her to stop at the library.

'Have you got Ambassador *by André P. Brink?' I asked the old lady behind the counter.*

'The Ambassador.' She looked at my grey school dress and her heavy eyebrows rose like twin helicopters above her spectacle

254

frames. 'Aren't you a bit young for such a difficult book?'

'It's for my mother.' Without turning a hair. Sometimes I took after my father.

So here I was lying in my holiday bikini next to the swimming pool, sweatily searching for the first nude scene.

But in Pretoria in 1971 my friends and I had neither the knowledge nor the vocabulary to talk about things related to the body with any real candour. The boys would toss words around like 'score' and 'bonk' and 'bone' and 'pork' and 'shaft' when referring to the sex act – references that had more to do with posing than practical experience. And we girls would smother all our anxiety about menstruation beneath euphemisms such as 'the red army arriving' or 'the red tide' we were expecting or 'my grandmother who's visiting'.

Because I was young for my class, and physically a late bloomer on top of that, I completely misunderstood my girlfriends' complaints about their grandmothers in a conversation one breaktime. It was soon after my Ouma Tina had died, and I declared, sighing, that unfortunately I had no grandmother who could visit me. (I opted to conceal my other grandmother's existence, possibly to get more sympathy from my friends.)

'Oh, don't you worry,' one of them remarked, 'she'll be coming soon enough.'

'And once she's there,' a smart-ass joked, 'you'll soon wish she would leave!'

The school bell saved me from betraying my ignorance by blurting out, 'No, you don't understand. My grandmother is *dead*.' It only dawned on me some time later, when grandmothers were once again being complained and boasted about, that they were talking about a different sort of grandmother.

And not long afterwards that grandmother did indeed turn up.

Because Ma had had a hysterectomy at such an early age, 'sanitary pads' weren't on her monthly shopping list, but she kept a pack of Kotex in her wardrobe for the day when her eldest daughter would need it. I would sometimes take a peek inside that pack, and be scared out of my wits every time I'd see those enormous cushions of cotton wool with loops at either end.

How on earth did you hide such a business underneath your clothes? How did you even walk with such an impediment shoved between your legs? These were the worries that kept me awake at night.

And when my grandmother finally did arrive, the Kotex in Ma's wardrobe didn't help me one bit, because disaster struck a long way from home. At least, it felt like a disaster, because it was during the winter holidays after my thirteenth birthday and we were visiting Pa's family on a Free State farm. Not only a long way from home, but a long way from any town with a shop or a pharmacy where one could pop in to buy sanitary pads.

I told Ma, but forbade her to tell anyone else in the house because there were lots of boys in that large family and I would have died of shame had they known. Ma did have to tell the boys' mother, though, so that she could lend me a few sanitary towels – they were far too big to be called 'pads', even bigger than the terrifying Kotex numbers in Ma's wardrobe at home. I waddled around like someone who had spent far too much time astride a horse, convinced that every single soul on the farm could tell at a glance that my grandmother was visiting for the first time.

And just as my girlfriend had predicted, I was already wishing she would leave.

I always found menstruation a pain rather than a pleasure, like most women, I suppose, and for years I was intensely shy about it too. I could never buy sanitary pads in any shop where a high school boy might see me with this product in my hands. If there was a young man behind the till, I died twenty thousand deaths while paying for my scandalous purchases.

My mind had no difficulty convincing me that such shame was truly irrational and ridiculous, but my body still cringed every time I had to buy Kotex or Tampax or whatever. I only managed to shrug off the shame when I read Gloria Steinem's famous satirical essay, 'If Men Could Menstruate', in the eighties.

Steinem helped me understand the reasons why, for centuries, women had felt ashamed about a biological function that makes procreation possible. *Whatever a 'superior' group has will be used to justify its superiority, and whatever an 'inferior' group has will be used to justify its plight.* White people regarded a white skin as a sign of superiority, just like Freud regarded a penis as a sign of superiority, and his widely discussed theory of penis envy was based on that. And if men had been menstruating instead of women, Freud might have invented menstruation envy.

If men could menstruate, Steinem fantasised, they would brag openly about how long and how much they could bleed at a time. Governments would donate money for research about menstrual cramps, and all sanitary products would be available either for free or tax free. Men would convince women that sex was actually more enjoyable during 'that time of the month', and menopause would be celebrated as a positive event, symbolic proof that a man had garnered so many years of cyclical wisdom that he could now do without the cycle.

These are just a few of the clever, funny examples Steinem mentions. The essay concludes with the warning:

The truth is that, if men could menstruate, the power justifications would go on and on.
If we let them.

I thought of this essay involuntarily when you started menstruating a few years ago. Because you never used stupid euphemisms, you talked about your *règles*; you used the French word without any shame, and you were so proud the first time it happened that you couldn't wait to tell your father and all three of your older brothers about it. I wouldn't have been surprised if you announced it on social media.

Sure, you didn't go quite that far. Fortunately, you also understood that one doesn't have to share *everything* with the whole world.

Like your mother and your grandmothers, you don't necessarily like the whole bloody business of menstrual periods, but you are most certainly not ashamed of it.

And that makes me proud, you know? *We've come a long way, baby*, I almost feel like saying to you, as the slogan for your grandmother's 'women's cigarettes' declared long ago. But I suspect you'll tell me, we still have a long way to go, Ma. And you're nobody's baby anyway.

But the most extraordinary event of my life between 1971 and 1972 remains the charming killer who became a family friend. He did become our friend before, not after, he committed cold-blooded murder. (I don't know whether this ought to console me, though.) In any event, it was the kind of experience that would make me look differently at seemingly nice people for the rest of my life.

Pa had opened his own estate agency in Pretoria, to trade in houses and plots, and one of his employees/colleagues, whom we started seeing socially, was a mild-mannered man with a dark fringe and a boyish grin and spectacles that made him look smarter than he probably was. I got to know him as Oom Frans, and I was vaguely aware of there having been some tragedy or other in his past, like the characters in the radio serials I listened to with Dolly in the afternoons.

The mother of his two young daughters was apparently unable to look after them, for a reason that no one shared with me.

Much later I heard that she lived in the psychiatric hospital Weskoppies as a patient with paranoid schizophrenia.

My kind-hearted mother took pity on these two almost-motherless little girls, and on some weekends we'd fetch them from their boarding school quite a way outside of Pretoria to spend a day or two with our 'normal' family.

I know, my child, you're going to remind me now about the ironic postcard that was stuck on our fridge throughout your childhood. A black-and-white snapshot of a prim little family from the fifties, strict father and submissive mother and three frightened little children, with the heading: *One nuclear family ruined my life.*

I still distrust prim little nuclear families, but Oom Frans's daughters could probably have done with a bit of support. To me they seemed like two sweet girls who were trapped in the kind of school to which 'problem children' were typically exiled, away from the city. It was a ghastly place made of ugly brick buildings, with an air of despair that hovered over it like a toxic cloud. Or maybe that was just another invention of my overactive imagination. Still, every time we'd go to fetch them, I'd be grateful that I didn't have to attend that school myself.

Imagine the astonishment of the Van der Vyver nuclear family when we woke up one winter's morning to read on the front page of the newspaper that dear Oom Frans had been taken into custody and was being charged with the murder of his married mistress's husband. We had been blissfully unaware of the mistress – although it may have explained why we had to look after the little girls on those weekends when their father was occupied elsewhere.

Oom Frans's real name was Frans Vontsteen, and his mistress was Sonjia Swanepoel, née Raffanti, the smouldering daughter of an Italian shoemaker. She was married to a former Springbok athlete and policeman, Cois Swanepoel, who was shot dead with his own service revolver in his own bed in the early hours of 4 August 1971. A single shot to the head beside his innocently sleeping wife. Except that within a day or three it became evident that Sonjia may not have been all that innocent. She had waited at least ten minutes after the murder before calling an emergency number for help, and that was just the first of numerous errors she and Frans had made after committing their meticulously planned 'perfect murder'.

It became one of Pretoria's most celebrated murder trials, during which the two lovers repeatedly contradicted and accused each other. Gradually, however, a clearer picture emerged – and it didn't portray either of the two in a good light. Cois's service revolver had disappeared some time before the murder, allegedly stolen by the ideal scapegoat, a nameless 'Bantu' whom Sonjia had spotted in the neighbourhood. In reality Sonjia had furnished Frans with the weapon, and they had agreed that she would leave a window open in the house so that Frans could get inside to shoot the sleeping Cois.

The murder was committed on a night when Frans was staying with relatives outside Pretoria, who were supposed to provide him with an alibi. But the investigating team established that there had been enough time to drive to the Swanepoels' house in the middle of the night (in the relative's car), climb through the open window, shoot the policeman in the head, and be back at his relatives' house in time to be lying apparently innocently in bed the following morning.

I was too young to follow the trial, but I remember how dismayed Pa was two months later when Oom Frans was sentenced to death. 'He looked like the sort of man who wouldn't hurt a fly,' Pa kept muttering. Over and over.

Sonjia Swanepoel was sentenced to fifteen years in prison as an accomplice, but she was released after eight years and later married another man. In the book *Fatal Females: Women Who Kill*, by the world-renowned forensic psychologist and former police profiler Micki Pistorius, it is speculated that Sonjia may have had more of a hand in the murder than the court found. She allegedly told several fellow prisoners that she had been the one who pulled the trigger – although she later denied it. Pistorius even speculates that Frans may only have decided to admit guilt in order to protect Sonjia. Which would be consistent with Pa's view of his colleague as the 'perfect gentleman' who wouldn't even hurt a fly.

When Frans confessed, he said he would 'take the blame upon himself' and reassured Sonjia she had nothing to fear. Was he protecting the woman he loved? If so, he paid the highest price for doing so.

At the crack of dawn on 4 October 1972, in the month declared by the poet Leipoldt as the loveliest of all, when the jacarandas' spring blossoms paint Pretoria purple, Pa and Ma sat bolt upright in bed thinking of Oom Frans, who was taking his final steps towards the gallows.

When a colleague and family friend and someone whose children have played with your children is sent to the gallows, you inevitably start wondering about capital punishment. It didn't turn Pa or Ma against capital punishment, as far as I know. But it did push me to begin questioning it at a young age – again, questions that no one around me could or would answer – and that was how I ended up on a path that would ultimately lead me to the wholehearted rejection of capital punishment.

No matter how, no matter where.

There isn't a 'humane' way to take another human's life. To do it as revenge because that human had behaved inhumanly by taking someone else's life simply means that we descend to a level of inhumanity ourselves.

I know that some of my nearest and dearest, and many of my readers, still support capital punishment, and I learnt a long time ago that, like abortion, it is one of those impossibly emotional topics that people are unable to debate rationally. So, I no longer even try to convince anyone to the contrary. I am just grateful that everyone in our household, at least, holds the same view about this.

There are plenty of topics that we debate enthusiastically and vehemently in this house, but about the most important political and moral issues, like racism, sexism, religious fanaticism, unbridled capitalism, homophobia – and capital punishment, thank heavens we agree.

I wasn't awake when Oom Frans was hanged. I suspect that Ma and Pa deliberately concealed the date from us children so as not to upset us. But after the earthquake two years earlier, I had begun to fear that I was doomed to sleep through all the most newsworthy events in my life. And for someone who was contemplating a career in journalism – at least until she could become a 'real writer' – that was quite a disadvantage.

Besides, the more hours I spent sleeping, the fewer hours I had left for writing. And for reading and living and doing all the other things I still wanted to do before I died.

There was only one solution. I would have to learn to sleep less.

I've tried, really, I have. From my teenage years until now.

In my early twenties I heard that Margaret Thatcher managed with barely four hours' sleep a night. I never admired the Iron Lady's politics, but I was terribly envious of her ability to eschew sleep. Over the years, more and more names were added to my imaginary list of achievers who slept less than most people. In the early nineties it was Cheryl Carolus, rising star of the ANC and among the foremost Codesa negotiators who teamed up to end apartheid. Someone told me that she, too, got by on just a few hours' sleep a night. No wonder she had accomplished so much at such a young age, I thought.

It was becoming increasingly clear that I would never amount to much, given my scandalous need for sleep.

In the same decade I befriended Deon Meyer, long before he became a world-famous writer of crime novels, although I suspected from the start that he was destined to move mountains. Not only because he was an incredibly hard worker, but especially because he could manage on four hours' sleep a night.

As you know, my girl, your mother still needs a good seven hours' sleep a night, even after her sixtieth birthday.

When you were a baby and your brothers still small, I was forced to get the sleep I needed bit by bit rather than all in one go, because an uninterrupted night's rest is a rare luxury for a mother of young children. But if I don't spend at least six out of every twenty-four hours in a state of sleep, even if those six hours are knocked together from several loose chunks of sleep, my brain turns into a computer that is about to crash.

I become a social embarrassment, the kind of woman who would fall asleep face down in a plate of soup. And a danger, too, to myself and others, because I have also dozed off behind a steering wheel.

That is why I had a vital question to put to André P Brink the first time I met him in the flesh, two decades after *The Ambassador* had reduced me and my teenage friends to helpless giggles. The meeting took place soon after my first adult novel had made me an 'overnight sensation' – despite the fact that I had already published three award-winning young-adult novels in the preceding ten years. I was suddenly plucked from the shadows of young-adult fiction and invited to the big kids' playground, where the spotlight was so bright that I understood for the first time why writers like Etienne Leroux constantly wore dark glasses.

So there I was at a glittering literary event at the Lanzerac Hotel in Stellenbosch, seated at the main table next to André P Brink, who by then had already published about sixty books and who knows how many reviews and columns and essays. I was so overwhelmed that I couldn't think of anything to say to him that wouldn't make me sound like a silly blonde groupie. But he managed to put me at ease – possibly because he liked silly blonde groupies – and I blurted out the question that seemed, in that moment, to be the most important question on earth.

How many hours did he sleep at night?

I wasn't looking for serious literary advice, I honestly just wanted to know exactly how little one needed to sleep in order to write so many books.

His reply was unexpectedly encouraging. He needed seven or eight hours' sleep, he confessed. And I decided that, if such an astonishingly prolific writer needed that much sleep, there might be hope for me after all.

I clung to that confession for years, every time I felt guilty about sleeping too much and writing too little.

These days, I no longer feel guilty about my sleep patterns. There are plenty of other things to feel guilty about. These days, I strive for sleep like Hamlet – *to sleep, perchance to dream* – and to dream as much as possible while I still can. *For in that sleep of death what dreams may come?*

13

SNOR CITY

You burst out laughing while paging through a tattered little book with homework assignments and nonsensical phrases scribbled in a childish hand. It is the magazine pictures that are taped over the text every few pages that amuse you in particular. Most are of romantic couples, in the unpardonable outfits of the seventies, gazing longingly into each other's eyes. The women all have too much blush too high on their cheeks and shiny trilobal dresses. The men are in knitted waistcoats and multicoloured shirts with collars as wide as trowels.

One of the men, with a long fringe and a flaccid moustache and the facial expression of a bored civil servant, makes you squeal with delight.

'Did you like men with *moustaches*, Ma?'

No, my darling child, I was thirteen years old and all I liked were schoolboys without any sort of facial hair (it was strictly forbidden with a school uniform), but the fashion magazines from which I cut these pictures were full of such male models with moustaches. And I lived in Pretoria, remember, about which Bernoldus Niemand aka James Phillips would write a satirical song called 'Snor City' a decade later.

Oh save me dear God, from the awful moustache conspiracy, in Pretoooria

If I were a terrorist, I would design a moustache bomb, for Pre-
toooria

The little book that provided you with so much entertainment recently was the 'Werkplan' that every pupil at Hoërskool Menlopark received at the start of the year, with the school song and the
school rules and the names of all the teachers and prefects, and a
calendar where each day's homework had to be dutifully recorded.
I have preserved two of these exhibits of my youthful indiscretions,
for the years 1971 and 1972. I don't know what became of 1973's
Werkplan. Perhaps it was so incriminating that I decided to destroy
it back then already.

Until now I have had to write my story without the aid of any
tangible mementoes – aside from the collection of photographs on
the pinboard above my desk – but from my high school years onwards I started keeping letters and postcards and homework diaries
and later on even journals. That is why, rather reluctantly, I un-
earthed a bundle of these mementoes from the wooden kist at the
foot of my bed.

My reluctance to be confronted with documents from my past
stems from more than just embarrassment over how silly I was. After all, all teenagers are silly; we aren't born wise, and alas some of
us never become wise. It probably also has to do with fearing a kind
of nostalgia that is too comfortable. The older we get, the more we
hanker after 'the good old days' of our youth. There is a growing
temptation to subside into nostalgia, as onto a bed of soft pillows.
And there is certainly nothing wrong with occasionally reclining on
such soft pillows for a while, as long as we remember that pillows
can also suffocate us.

There was a great deal in my youth to be nostalgic about. But
there was also more than enough that nostalgia could stifle.

Besides, I try to live in the moment, and if you look back at the past too often you could turn to stone, like Lot's wife. And then the present would pass you by.

You have probably heard of Lot's wife, my girl, although you may not really know who she was. It is not the sort of knowledge you would pick up in a French school. In my high school's Werkplan, every new week opened with an edifying quote in the top left-hand corner. The first quote of the year was always: 'Fear God and keep his commandments, for this is the whole duty of man.'

That explains everything, doesn't it?

Later on in the year, as we became sillier, we started playing around with these sayings intended for our moral improvement. For example, 'A good name is better than precious ointment' was altered by crossing out 'name' and writing something else over it, such as 'A good boyfriend is better than precious ointment'. Or 'Life is a treasure' was turned into 'Life is a bitch'.

At the end of the first term in Standard 6, below my results for each subject, I had to write down 'My career choices'. Of course, I wouldn't write 'author' or even 'journalist' where my friends' potentially mocking eyes could see it. My career choices were: (1) building castles in the air, (2) unbending bananas, (3) opening gates in the sky for aeroplanes.

Perhaps all three of these ridiculous careers can be considered metaphors for writing fiction.

I kept the homework diaries and other writings in an old school suitcase made of sturdy brown cardboard. (Definitely a Cape 'suitcase' rather than a Transvaal 'bag'.) Decades ago, I had glued some snapshots inside the lid of the suitcase, and also a headline cut out of a magazine: 'Nothing lasts forever', in fat black letters, like a warning from the distant future.

I've already told you that I'd become intensely aware of the transitory nature of everything around me, ever since that day in Ouma

Tina's toilet in Thornton when the realisation of my own inevitable demise had caused me to pray so desperately.

While I was sifting through the contents of the suitcase with mounting disbelief – I even found the first handwritten version of my first radio story about the sad bus – you drew closer, curious, and picked up the homework diaries. A stray Standard-6 report card slipped out from among the pages, a *bulletin* as you call it in French, and you looked at my results, a bit flabbergasted.

'I didn't know you were an *intello*, Ma!' you exclaimed.

Not necessarily with admiration. *Intello* is the French term for what in my school days would have been called an 'academic wreck'. Not usually intended as a compliment back then in South Africa, and still not a compliment among French schoolchildren today.

But let me quickly explain that in South Africa it has always been easier to get the kind of results that in French schools would be truly extraordinary. On this report card of mine, I got above eighty per cent for all my subjects, except for domestic science, which I hated with rancorous hate and at which I definitely didn't excel. I even got A's for maths and science, which borders on miraculous when I recall how little I liked these subjects. To earn results like those in a French school, I would truly have had to be a nerd who devoted more time to schoolwork than to anything else.

You only have to leaf through my messy Werkplan to see right away that parties and friends' birthdays got far more attention than tests or exams.

And matters of the heart were of cardinal importance week in and week out.

'Who was Sonny Boy?' you wanted to know, because his name was spelled out in gigantic letters across several weeks of my Werkplan, one huge capital letter per week. When I add the eight letters in his name together, I get the sum of eight weeks – more or less the length of time we went steady before that tart Aileen gave him a love bite. On one Sunday in the course of those eight weeks I noted, 'To church with Sonny Boy', an outing I can't remember at all, but which probably goes a long way towards explaining why he went chasing after Aileen instead.

I was the sort of girl who Sonny Boy wanted to be seen in church with. Aileen was the sort of girl who showed him things for which he would have gone to hell with a smile on his face.

A year later I was a great deal naughtier, although never in Aileen's league of naughty. By 1972, alongside the romantic couples I had also pasted two pictures of the movie star Steve McQueen and a dozen pictures of bikini girls in my Werkplan. Not the voluptuous pin-up girls reclining in the centre spread in *Scope*, but rather the kind of bikini girl I longed to be, smiling and suntanned with a natural, make-up-free beauty.

'But why are all the girls anorexic?' you wanted to know, paging through my little book.

It is true, my love. Now that I look at them again, I can see that most of them are far too thin. But the fact is that this was the desirable androgynous appearance of the seventies, which I strove for. In primary school I had always been skinny, as you know from photographs, but when in high school I finally started developing curves, long after most of my friends, I instantly desired fewer curves. Within a matter of months I developed the kind of hourglass figure that would have made me very happy had I been a teenager in the fifties, but twenty years on hourglasses had long since gone out of fashion. I didn't want to look like Marilyn Monroe, I longed for Jane Birkin or Ali MacGraw's leggy, flat-chested, boyish look.

By my fourteenth birthday I was on the first of many starvation diets with which I would punish my body for a decade or more in a futile attempt to look like an ironing board instead of an hourglass.

I found Ali MacGraw irresistible in *Love Story*, which I went to see with a group of girlfriends at Sterland to celebrate my thirteenth birthday. Ma packed half a dozen of us, all dressed up in our best bellbottoms and wet-look tops, into her lime-green Ford Capri and carted us to the glittering new bioscope. We walked in giggling with excitement – and two hours later stumbled out as sobbing wrecks. Oh, but it was sad! We wept so bitterly that I couldn't hear half of the dialogue. Several of the most moving scenes between Ali MacGraw and Ryan O'Neal I saw only vaguely through a haze of tears. Like watching a movie from behind a shower curtain.

A year or so later I also read Erich Segal's book with the same title (apparently he wrote the screenplay for the movie first and the book only afterwards) and again wept buckets. Only after matric did it dawn on me that the story was cloyingly sentimental, actually. And the movie was a shameless tearjerker, with its sweeping soundtrack and the poor, beautiful Jenny who is suffering from an unnamed terminal disease but remains absolutely beautiful until she gently breathes her last. In the arms of the attractive Oliver, of course.

No wonder the folk singer Dory Previn wrote a caustic song about this cinematic death, depicted as clean as a washing-powder commercial. These days I can smile nostalgically when I listen to 'The New Enzyme Detergent Demise of Ali MacGraw' (*Mine was a bloodless death . . . Neat and tidy / Not like Christ's on Friday*), but *Love Story* will always hold a special place in my heart. It was the first love story that wounded my tender teenage heart, long before I experienced such wounds on a more personal level.

The Fault in Our Stars was probably a similar experience for you – only perhaps even more heartrending, because the main characters were teenagers, not much older than you were, and the loving couple were actually *both* terminally ill. (This much pathos would have shattered me in my early teens.) Plus you read the book first before you watched the movie – a sequence I always recommend –

and praised it so highly that I became curious enough to read it as well. Afterwards I read a few of John Green's young-adult best-sellers with you, and once again wished that there had been such books in Afrikaans when I was a teenager.

Then *Love Story* wouldn't have made me and my friends grieve so inconsolably, would it.

But *Love Story* is intertwined in my memory with an incident that causes me far greater embarrassment than my sobbing sentimentality. Because on that day I was ashamed of my mother. I am ashamed of myself today when I think of it. I wasn't ashamed of anything she had said or done, but because I thought she was too fat.

As she walked ahead of us to the box office to buy tickets for the movie, I found myself wishing that her bottom wasn't quite so big in the pants she was wearing.

Ma battled with her weight her whole life. Even in her teenage photographs she was already overweight. Never really obese, just mostly bulkier than the norm for female beauty. Like many brides she probably starved herself for months before her wedding, because I remember the incredibly tiny waist of the wedding dress that we children used as a fancy-dress costume for years. After six pregnancies she tried every diet on earth, and Pa willingly paid for all sorts of miracle cures and magic potions because he badly wanted a slimmer wife. In the seventies, with the aid of one Dr Sachs, she lost too much weight in too short a period and for the first time in her life my mother looked almost too thin.

But no one seemed concerned about her health, least of all Ma herself. Everyone encouraged her weight loss and cheered it on. I did too. In those days a thin female body was more valuable than a healthy female body.

Within a year or two she'd picked up all the weight she'd lost on the miracle diet.

That was the other reason for my own obsessive dieting that

started in my teens. Aside from the influence of the zeitgeist and the peer pressure to be thin, I was afraid that I might be genetically doomed to get fat, like my mother. In high school I heard a boy joke that if you wanted to know what a girl would look like in thirty years, you only had to look at her mother. He wasn't talking about my mother in particular, he had never even seen her, but it made me feel paralysed with fear. Please, no. I did *not* want to look like my mother.

Later on I learnt that many women do indeed become more and more like their mothers, myself included, but that it often has nothing to do with their appearance. These days I am proud of most of my mother's traits that I recognise in myself, like her love of reading and her sense of humour and her ability to pretend that everything is fine while her heart is breaking. (Nat King Cole's 'Smile' was her theme song: *Smile through your fear and sorrow . . .*) Sometimes the little habits I've inherited from her would also irritate me, such as constantly talking to myself while I'm cooking. She used to hum as well, especially when she was nervous. If I were better at holding a tune, I would probably hum too.

What I can only see now, when I look at photographs of Ma, is how beautiful she actually was. Big brown eyes and a thin aristocratic nose and a generous full-lipped mouth like Sophia Loren. Ma was blessed with the sort of mouth that women these days try to obtain through expensive injections, and which is often so overdone that it looks like their lips have been stung by a swarm of bees. Ma's lips were as natural as everything else about her body. She never dyed her dark hair, and although quite a lot of it fell out as a result of the chemotherapy she had to endure, there wasn't a grey hair on her head when she died shortly before her 65th birthday.

There is one photograph in particular above my desk that I find myself staring at often. She and Pa were on their way to a smart costume party, dressed up in hired outfits in a style from the seventeen hundreds. She was already a grandmother at that stage, and a grandmother with cancer to boot, but she looks stunning in a pink dress with frills and bows and one of those tall powdered wigs that Marie Antoinette and her courtiers wore. Pa looks dignified beside her, also with a white wig and knickerbockers over ballet tights (which is hilarious if you know Pa), but she is the showstopper in this photograph.

How is it possible, I wonder, that as a child I never noticed her rare beauty.

Among the letters from my grandmothers and my friends that I discover in the brown school suitcase, I also find a postcard from Ma with a picture of Lion's Head and the Twelve Apostles. It was probably the first postcard she ever wrote to me, from the Cape where she had gone to support her younger sister after the birth of her second daughter.

Your new cousin is beautiful! Not red and wrinkly, but a pretty round little face. For now, the little nose has wings just like Ouma Tina's.

She wasn't a travelling mother, so it had never been necessary for her to write to her children before. It was only when I went to university, far from home, that Ma's regular letters and cards became a lifeline I could cling to whenever life threatened to blow me away.

Because I became a travelling mother myself, and because those words in my mother's handwriting meant so much to me, I have always sent you postcards from my travels, my girl. From long before you could read them yourself until long after most people had stopped sending 'old-fashioned' postcards, because nowadays we keep in touch on the internet, obviously. But messages on WhatsApp and social media will never be as special as words in the handwriting of a loved one – even if the handwriting is as messy as mine.

I pasted my postcards to you in 'Mia's book', along with information about your first words and your favourite picture books and your early achievements. (To a proud mother everything that her young child does is an achievement anyway.) Most of my solo travels had to do with my writing, otherwise I took you along when I could. Now this book is bulging with all the postcards to 'Prinses Patat', as your father and I called you from your first moments on earth, because the Afrikaans words for 'princess' and 'sweet potato' both sound the same and mean the same things in your mother's language as *'princesse'* and *'patate'* do in your father's.

From KwaZulu-Natal, where I had to give a lecture to university students at the end of 2000 when you were eleven months old: *This is the first postcard I have ever written to you in my mother tongue. Hopefully there will be many more. Hopefully I can continue to write to you in my mother's language – in your own mother's language. Hopefully I will someday even be able to write to you in flawless French! I dreamed of you all night, my sweetheart.*

A year later, from Cambridge, Britain, a postcard with an aerial photograph of the historic university campus: *In less than a month you'll be two years old – and you have never stopped surprising, amazing and delighting your whole family.*

From Vienna, Austria, where I attended a conference about Afrikaans, I sent you a postcard of the famous opera house – that the neighbours' dog chewed until the ink ran and my words became illegible. From The Hague in the Netherlands, when you were three years old, a postcard with pictures of Dutch cheeses and clogs and tulips, not terribly original, but I was trying to keep things simple: *Today I rode in a tram (like a bus mixed with a train) and saw lots of clogs. They are the funny wooden shoes you can see in the picture.*

Shortly after your sixth birthday, when you could already read yourself, I was at the International Time of the Writer Festival in Durban, where I actually managed to write a whole postcard in

French to *Ma petite Princesse Patate*. Just as I had promised in that first one.

In my teenage years the relationship between Ma and me, like most mother–daughter relationships, was wracked by stormy weather. We were caught in the wild winds of change and resistance, sometimes there were furious lightning bolts and tears that fell like rain, but no lasting damage was done.

The storms between Pa and me were scarcer, but far more destructive.

As in many households, my parents acted out the good cop/bad cop scenario. One parent always had to play the stern policeman, and in most cases that was the father, even if it was only because he was less present than the mother, who usually had to be the caring police officer. I knew a few homes where the father was the 'good' one, but I didn't know a house where both parents were equally strict and uncompromising. Except in storybooks, where anything was possible.

Unlike my naughty brother who regularly got a hiding from the bad cop in our house, and my tomboy sister who often got up to mischief with him and sometimes got spanked along with him, I cannot remember that Pa ever hit me. It wasn't only because up to my teens I tried terribly hard to be the exemplary eldest child. Apparently Pa did spank me once – the fact that I cannot recall it at all may even suggest suppressed shock – but I refused to cry.

That threw Pa completely.

My little brother used the opposite tactic of starting to cry dramatically and lustily even before the first blow fell. By the third or second blow the wailing was so bad that Pa couldn't stand it. Especially as Dolly Titus and the two sisters were usually right outside the closed bathroom door, wringing our hands and pleading for him to stop.

Then Pa usually stopped.

So, when I still hadn't made a sound by the fourth of fifth blow (with his flat hand rather than a cane or a belt), Pa decided that in future this child would have to be punished in a different way.

I never received corporal punishment at home again.

At school it was another story. Errant girls could be hit on the palms of their hands with a ruler or cane, and especially during my final high-school years I was often deemed naughty enough to be humiliated in this way in front of classmates or in the principal's office.

I feel humiliated all over again to be telling you this, my girl. And grateful once again that you could escape any form of corporal punishment, at home or at school.

But precisely because I never got spanked at home, it came as a hell of a shock to me when Ma once slapped my face. Not on purpose – it was closer to an accident, in fact. A slap isn't planned in advance like a hiding, after all; a slap can be considered a 'crime of passion' while a hiding is more like premeditated murder. But the fact that a slap is almost always unexpected only makes it more shocking.

On a perfectly ordinary Sunday I had decided to wake Ma from her afternoon nap (with hindsight it wasn't a good idea) with a mug of steaming hot, milky coffee on a tray. I probably wanted to ask some or other favour and thought that, if I offered coffee, she would be in a good mood. When I bent over her to touch her shoulder, her eyes flew open and her arm shot out and she slapped my face (very hard). Indignant, I stormed out of her bedroom and went to cry next to the swimming pool.

I soon realised that it had been an instinctive reaction – she may have been caught up in a bad dream when I bent over her – but all I was waiting for, there next to the swimming pool, was for her to come and tell me she was sorry. I waited for hours, in vain. When it got dark, I crept back inside. By this time I was no longer angry about the slap, but because she hadn't apologised.

My mother never apologised for that slap – and I never forgot it. A few years before she died I told her how it had always troubled me that she couldn't admit that she had been wrong. Perhaps even then I was hoping to hear that 'sorry' at last, the one I'd waited for for so many decades.

Ma looked at me as if I had sucked this story out of my fertile writer's thumb. She couldn't remember anything about slapping me one Sunday afternoon when I'd brought her coffee in bed. Even less that I'd sat next to the swimming pool for hours waiting for an apology.

Most of our stories don't have the endings we hope for, do they?

Another time, we were having a stormy argument about some trifle or another that seemed crucially important to both of us at that moment when she pierced my heart with a warning: 'One day you'll have a teenage daughter who'll treat you like you're treating me now. *Then* you'll understand!'

It felt like the curse that the uninvited thirteenth fairy pronounced at the feast for the baby girl who would become Sleeping Beauty.

It made me terrified of having a daughter.

And from the moment you were born, my darling Mia, I began to fear your teenage years. That curse of my mother's lingered over my head like a thundercloud. And I couldn't even ask her to retract it, because she died, of course, in the same week you were born.

To make matters worse, when you were barely three years old I watched a terrifying movie titled *Thirteen* that left me even more convinced that your teenage years would be a disaster for our relationship. Holly Hunter received Oscar and Golden Globe nominations for her performance as the struggling single mother of a clever, well-mannered daughter who, at the age of thirteen, under the influence of a far wilder friend, undergoes a complete transformation. The friend leads her into a destructive world of drugs, sex and crime, which causes her to start cutting her arms and rejecting her mother and ultimately failing the school year.

Exactly the kind of movie that would completely freak out a mother who was already anxious about her daughter's teenage years. *Thirteen* gave me nightmares right up to the day of my daughter's thirteenth birthday – and for a long time afterwards.

But now I can finally look back on your teenage years with an enormous sigh of relief. Our relationship didn't just survive it; I can honestly say it wasn't nearly as bad as I had feared.

Perhaps I should encourage all mothers of little girls to watch a scary movie like *Thirteen*. Then whatever happens between you and your daughter will never seem as bad as all the things that could really happen.

My relationship with my mother also survived my adolescent rebelliousness and kept getting stronger over the years. By my twenty-first birthday I could give her a little book that I had written and bound myself to thank her for carrying me that far. It had twelve pages with photographs of her and me at the same age. Her as an infant in the lovely young Ouma Tina's arms, me as a baby in my own mother's arms; her as a teenager with her baby sister and a fancy bow in her dark hair, me as a teenager with a puppy, my blond hair long and loose. Between the pictures I'd written quotations from poems and stories about mothers, ending with Breyten Breytenbach's wonderful wishful thinking in 'Die hand vol vere' (A hand full of feathers):

mammie
I always thought
if I came home someday
that it would be at dusk, unexpectedly

278

with years of hoarded treasure
on the backs of iron cows . . .
mammie
I always thought how we would cry
and drink tea

But just as I am about to suffocate in nostalgia, I discover, in the back of my Werkplan, two full pages of rules and regulations about school uniforms that make all nostalgia disappear instantly. In 1971 we girls had to wear, throughout the year, in winter and in summer, a skirt that had to be purchased at 'official suppliers' such as Uniewinkels in Church Street. *Skirt of charcoal-royal blue fabric (55% terylene and 45% wool). NB: Length is no more than 7 inches above the knee when girl kneels.* With 'black lace-up shoes', NB, not the forbidden buckle-up shoes we found so much more desirable. And long blue socks – *sock length not less than 2 inches below the knee. NB: When socks are purchased, fit to length of leg not size of foot.*

In other words, it didn't matter how uncomfortably the socks fit your feet. All that mattered was that not too much leg was visible between your socks and the hem of your school skirt.

And if a skirt of almost fifty per cent wool worn with long socks and lace-up shoes strikes you as uncomfortably hot for Highveld summer days, well, it was.

In 1972 the skirt still looked the same, but now it had to be made from 'special blue Tetrex fabric', a mixture of polyester and viscose, and suddenly you could show even less leg. *NB: Length is not less than two inches and no more than four inches above the knee when girl kneels.*

Almost fifty years on, some of the ever-changing regulations sound so absurd that I'm not even going to try to explain it to my French children.

When at the age of sixteen Daniel decided to spend three months as an exchange student at Paul Roos Gymnasium in Stellenbosch, he wore a uniform for the first time in his life. He had no idea how to tie the maroon school tie, because he had never needed a tie before. The week before he started there, he asked, in all innocence, whether I agreed it would create a better impression if he removed the stud in his ear and the brand-new stud in his upper lip when wearing the uniform.

I stared at him, speechless.

When I could find the words, I had to deliver the cruel news that he could not even *consider* having studs in his face while he was wearing the uniform of one of the oldest and most respected boys' schools in the country.

In the seventies, uniform rules were even stricter. At our school, regular inspections were held, where girls had to kneel in rows like praying virgins so that a teacher or a prefect could measure your legs with a ruler to ensure that exactly the correct amount of skin was visible between your knee and your skirt.

The boys didn't kneel; they had to stand to attention while the back of their heads were scrutinised from up close. Their necks were measured as relentlessly as the girls' legs. The difference was that with the girls as little skin as possible had to be visible and with the boys as much as possible. Of their necks, at any rate, between their shirt collars and their hair. And the hair had to be cut "in the traditional style". *NB: No deviating haircut is permitted.*

There were a few joyous months of exception when the school decided to stage *Romeo and Juliet*. All the boys who had been cast in the play were allowed to let their hair grow longer. (It was difficult to picture Romeo and his companions with the close-cropped hair of Afrikaans high-school boys.) Never had schoolboys been so eager to act in a Shakespearean drama. Most of them didn't want speaking parts, because they could neither act nor speak English well enough, but they would have killed one another to be chosen as a silent soldier or for any other walk-on part.

Back then, schoolboys would do absolutely anything to have a 'deviating haircut'.

The boys who didn't make the cast of *Romeo and Juliet* invented all sorts of other plans to trick the teachers and prefects. They would borrow their grandfathers' Brylcreem to make their hair look shorter and flatter. (In those days teenage boys didn't put gel in their hair for fun; it was only old men and Elvis Presley who would ruin the natural appearance of a hairstyle with greasy products.) Sometimes they were even desperate enough to use their sisters' hairclips or their mothers' hairspray to hide longer bits of hair underneath the shorter bits.

Such tactics didn't work, of course, when a hair inspection was held unexpectedly and a strict teacher scrutinised your neck at close quarters. They were merely ways to buy a little time before the next inspection, when your cunning plans would inevitably lead to corporal punishment and a forced haircut.

Daniel had fortunately been wearing a buzz cut for some time before he landed up at Paul Roos. I say 'fortunately'– because at least it meant he wasn't forced to remove the studs from his face *and* cut his hair – but I was never happy with that close-cropped head. With my childhood exposure to hair fascism I found it difficult to accept that my teenage son wasn't at all interested in growing his hair.

It simply confirmed once again the perverse effects of having so many rules and regulations. Since your brother had never been forbidden by a French school from having long hair, he could find no reason for wanting long hair.

Another consequence of the endless rules of my teenage years was that, as team leader of the famous Dubbeltjies (the long-suffering targets of prick jokes), I was threatened with expulsion from the

Voortrekkers. During one camp, we six former Drawwertjies were caught on the boys' side of the campfire. (Drawwertjies was the generic term for primary-school girls in the Voortrekkers, my child, so I had been a Drawwertjie before I became a Dubbeltjie. It's no wonder I developed such an aversion to diminutives.)

We hadn't sneaked over to the boys' end of the camp because we wanted to have wild sex or use drugs or commit any kind of sin. We just wanted to visit our classmates in the Knorhane team (I can't remember the team's real name, but it was something fanciful from the animal kingdom) and the fact that it was completely forbidden to be on their side of the campfire at night made it completely irresistible for us to get there.

Once again, the perversity of rules and regulations.

But we were caught while we were drinking coffee and giggling with the Knorhane, and Ingrid and I, deputy team leader and team leader of the Dubbeltjies respectively, had to spend the rest of the camp with a few other errant girls in the 'punishment tent'. This tent was pitched directly next to the parade ground, so that during the daily raising and lowering of the flag everyone would be aware of the sinners incarcerated there. If the officers intended to make a public spectacle of us, it backfired completely.

We lay flat on our stomachs peering out from under the tent flaps at the poor children who had to stand on the parade ground in the hot sun. We pulled faces to make them laugh (parade was a very serious business) and tossed them notes and within hours the punishment tent had turned into a bootleg joint with chocolate and condensed milk and sweets being passed to us under the tent flaps.

It was probably the best Voortrekker camp of my life.

So, when I was subsequently threatened with expulsion unless my parents came to resolve the matter with the officers, I realised that maybe I no longer needed the Voortrekkers in my life. Besides, the older boy with whom I'd recently started going steady wasn't a Voortrekker. Reason enough in itself to remove my pocket knife and rope from my Voortrekker belt and pack away the ugly grey uniform.

The punishment tent episode sank to the ooze at the bottom of my subconscious and only floated back up thirty years later when I started to work on the novel *There is a Season*. I seem to be compelled to poke around in those dark waters every time I write about a character's childhood. Sometimes what I stir up from the bottom genuinely surprises me. Things I hadn't been able to see for who knows how long, because the water was too muddy, suddenly become visible.

And then it becomes fiction.

'Mom, you have no idea how conservative the Voortrekkers are!' *cried San. 'It's unbelievable. It's like . . . like the Hitler Jugend!'*

'Hitler Jugend,' Adèle repeated faintly.

'They caught us with beer and cigarettes.' There was no apology in Bella's husky voice.

. . .

'Were you smoking?'

'No, Mom, we were playing pick-up-sticks with the cigarettes,' *said Bella sarcastically.*

. . .

'And you, San?' Adèle waved her cigarette through the air indignantly, scattering ash over her lap, and frowned angrily at her elder child. 'You make out that Bella is innocent!'

'I never said she was innocent, Mom. It's just, the way Oom Worsie went on, you would swear they were taking LSD and dancing naked round the tent!'

One of the many biographies I've read in recent months, while this long letter to you kept getting longer, was Victoria Glendinning's *Rebecca West: A Life*. West was a British author and journalist who succeeded in almost everything she turned her hand to over the course of her long life (1892–1983) – except for motherhood.

For West, her relationship with her only child, Anthony, was a source of grief and dismay until the day she died. What made it even more complicated was that Anthony West also became a writer (his father was the famous HG Wells), although not as successful a writers as his parents. He created fictional characters who were recognisably based on his mother – depicting her in a far from favourable light – but she believed that he deliberately tried to get at her even in his non-fiction, when writing about female trailblazers such as Madame de Staël or George Sand.

Few things make me as despondent as failed mother-child relationships. When journalists ask me what I regard as my greatest achievement, I don't think of literary awards or a new book that is selling better than I expected, but of my children who are becoming balanced, sensitive, likeable adults. Motherhood is simultaneously the most common and ordinary, as well as the most difficult and daring task I have ever embarked on.

Glendinning also quotes Rebecca West as follows: *If man has a talent, it is for tightrope walking.* She was definitely referring to women as well. Women often become outstanding tightrope walkers out of necessity, burdened in addition with a *distressing multiplicity of characteristics* (West again) that we try to hide from ourselves and others, and of which we want to rid ourselves, like *too much cargo*.

In my mind's eye I see myself at the age of fifteen, carrying a heavy school backpack and an enormous suitcase in each hand and perhaps even a stack of books on my head, balancing on a thin tightrope high above the ground. Advancing inch by careful inch. By Standard 8, four years after I ventured out on my first day in a new school in Pretoria trembling with fear, I had already become a skilful tightrope walker.

I was still shy and self-conscious, I still read far more than most of my friends, I still cherished the apparently impossible dream of one day becoming a writer – but I felt at home among a group of popular girls, with whom I sat chatting in a circle during breaktimes at school and lay tanning next to swimming pools on weekends, or with whom I'd catch the bus to Sunnyside or the Pretoria city centre to listen to the latest records and try on the latest fashions in trendy boutiques. Like them, I yearned for older boys who played in bands (any guy who held a guitar in a sexy way stirred up our hormones) and like them I was invited to the most desirable parties.

By all appearances I was just like them.

Pretty and smiling and a bit rebellious (but not too rebellious) and naughty enough to bunk classes to loaf around at Plankie's house near the school. Smart enough to get good results without turning into a pitiable nerd. I 'made out' with an attractive matric boy who invited me to be his partner at the official farewell at the end of the year. I wore a simple, demure dress printed with tiny dark-blue flowers, which Ma considered suitable for a fifteen-year-old girl – no sequins or bling and not too much exposed flesh. Pierre's younger sister sent the picture of the two of us at his matric dance to a popular teen magazine (without our knowledge), and a few months later we appeared in the pages of *Tina* like some celebrity couple.

I still felt 'different', as if I had to hide parts of myself like pieces of a puzzle because no one would ever appreciate the full picture. But I was also beginning to suspect that if you were a teenager it was normal to feel abnormal.

And pop stars like David Bowie made me realise that there was no shame in being different. *The Rise and Fall of Ziggy Stardust and the Spiders from Mars* was a revelation for a fourteen-year-old schoolgirl from Snor City. A year later his next album, *Aladdin Sane*, hit me like the psychedelic lightning bolt that was painted on his face on the cover. This strange, androgynous creature with feather-cut flaming orange hair and different-coloured eyes instantly made me feel like the most normal person on earth. It wasn't long before I attacked my own hair with scissors and a razor to create a schoolgirl version of Bowie's spiky look. When I heard that *Aladdin Sane* was derived from 'a lad insane', I bought the LP with my limited pocket money and listened to it non-stop for weeks on end.

In that same year I also acquired *Who's Next*, another LP with an unforgettable cover image. The four members of The Who stand in a deserted post-apocalyptic landscape next to an enormous concrete block against which they have apparently just urinated. Three of them are still fiddling with their flies. I only realised much later that the concrete structure was a reference to the monolithic object in Stanley Kubrick's *2001: A Space Odyssey*, but even in my youthful ignorance the cover immediately seduced me. It looked like an obscene gesture beside the naughty-but-decent covers of the popular *Springbok Hit Parade* records, which all featured an iconic illustration of a bare-breasted girl with hair like Rapunzel's.

And that primal scream in "Won't Get Fooled Again" left a lasting impression on me and many of my contemporaries. Late one night in France, at a big feast to celebrate my fiftieth birthday, a bunch of middle-aged formerly rebellious teenagers (both South African and French) screamed uproariously along with Roger Daltrey. When soon afterwards I started planning *Forget-me-not Blues*, the primal scream was still fresh in my memory. It was perhaps inevitable that I would make room for it in a scene about a teenage party that took place in Pretoria in the seventies.

They are holding their breath with mouths wide open, poised to let loose the moment Roger Daltrey concludes the song with a long, blood-curdling scream.

Then she realises that they are not, thank heaven, really yelling at the top of their voices – rather, it is a supressed, fake sort of shriek – and without another thought she too shuts her eyes and opens her mouth wide and feels a reckless cry rise to her throat. She supresses it, just like them, and joins their soundless scream. Whaaaaaaa!

In the next paragraph the young character is reminded of 'a famous painting of a screaming woman on a bridge', a passing reference I had forgotten about until I came upon it recently. But Edvard Munch's screaming woman had turned up in another novel in the meantime. In *Borderline* there is a coffee mug with a picture of Munch's *The Scream*, which shatters in an important scene. When sometime later the protagonist's former husband is bundled into a police van, his eyes 'wide with horror and his screaming mouth . . . like a black cave', the protagonist remembers the shattered coffee mug and wonders how she could not have predicted this ending.

I find it inexplicable why certain cultural landmarks – paintings, music, books – appear in my stories repeatedly, like road signs that time and again help me find my way to a fictional past. While other paintings and music and books, which once upon a time seemed equally important, are completely absent from my fiction. Or perhaps it is just more proof that the roads (and the byways) that lead to fiction have no rational explanation.

It remains a deep and dark pool, one you swim around in underwater when you're creating a story. Maybe anything you discover at the bottom is sheer coincidence.

It is disconcerting to think that my life in France may itself be the consequence of a long series of coincidences. Had Ma not run a hat shop with a French name in the Sabel Centre in Bellville, I might not have become aware so early on of the enchantment of French words. And then I might not have chosen French as one of my subjects in high school. And then I wouldn't have got to know the French teacher who coaxed a fluttering flame of Francophilia until it blazed as inextinguishably as the Olympic flame.

The pretty Miss du Plessis had apparently just returned from her studies in Paris when she blew into my stuffy high-school life like a fresh breeze. I don't know whether she had acquired the famous *je ne sais quoi* of French women along the way, or whether she fascinated me purely because she was conspicuously different from all the other teachers. She wore her dark hair piled on top of her head with careful insouciance, and colourful silky wraps draped around her slim shoulders – at a stage when I believed that only old ladies wore 'shawls'. She played Georges Moustaki's records in class and brought a gas burner to school so we could make crêpes (*kgêp* was how she pronounced it) and one evening she invited the whole class to a French restaurant in the city centre, where I tasted rabbit for the first time.

Before that, I hadn't even realised that it was possible to eat something as exotic as rabbit.

Her companion that evening was a bohemian character with unruly dark hair and a lavish beard whom I thought looked exactly like Moustaki on the cover of one of her records. I almost fancy that he drove an improbably low-slung sports car. But maybe I should rather not let my imagination run.

Still, even without any flights of fancy it was an evening that shook the foundations of my suburban existence. I became convinced that my life would have no purpose if I didn't get to France as soon as possible after school.

After Miss Hanekom in Sub A, Miss du Plessis was probably the teacher who had the greatest influence in my life.

I started confiding to my friends that I was itching to go backpacking through Europe. A few of them admitted that they too were dreaming of such an adventure, and together we speculated about all the faraway and foreign places we would visit.

But the following year my father moved us again and I had to brave a new school again and find new friends again. I kept in touch with some of my friends in Pretoria, and a few of my new friends in Nelspruit were apparently also planning to travel around Europe one day. As soon as we were of age, we promised one another, because we knew perfectly well our parents would never allow it before we turned twenty-one.

In the end, nearly all my friends from Pretoria and Nelspruit went to study at northern universities closer to home. I ended up in Stellenbosch alone, except for a single friend from Pretoria, and soon after graduating I got on a plane to Europe on my own.

Pa could no longer stop me because I was twenty-one. And I was using my own money, which I'd worked hard for while I was studying.

I would definitely have felt less afraid had I been able to tackle this adventure with a friend. But I was so determined to rush to Europe – in case I died young – that I simply couldn't wait until the day when someone else would be ready to go with me. At least I had a student boyfriend who promised to join me in a few months, but I had to clear the way and scout the foreign lands on my own. I had been a Voortrekker, after all. I could use a pen knife and coil a rope, and for the rest I would rely on blind faith as I ventured into the unknown.

I became a solo traveller, not because I wanted to but because I had to, and discovered with wonder that I liked it. Despite some moments of intense existential loneliness during that year of travel, I started to accept my need for solitude.

It became another tightrope I would walk for the rest of my life, this taut wire that still spans solitude and loneliness. During the COVID-19 lockdown of the past several months I came close to losing my balance for the first time in decades. The longing for my children, my family, my friends sometimes became more intense than any consolation that solitude could offer me.

Because solitude is a state you choose, loneliness is something to which you are subjected. Billie Holiday's 'Solitude' always struck me as a lovely song about lost love, while Wordsworth's 'I Wandered Lonely as a Cloud' reminded me of intense loneliness.

Now a worldwide, dangerous virus has whipped loneliness and solitude into a nasty brew that most of us are compelled to swallow.

But as always when I start to waver on my tightrope, I reach for a book to regain my balance. In Tolkien's *The Lord of the Rings*, which you have also started reading recently, my darling girl, Frodo says: '*I wish it need not have happened in my time.*' And Gandalf replies:

'*And so do all who live to see such times. But that is not for them to decide. All we have to decide is what to do with the time that is given us.*'

I know, my love, it is 'just' a fantasy novel. But this is where I have always found the wisest counsel: in fantasy, fairy tales, myths, fiction. Lies grounded on the deepest truth.

14

A FARM IN AFRICA

When I tell my French friends that I have lived on a farm in Africa where there were mambas in the trees and once even a hippopotamus in the swimming pool, they look at me with such amazement that it feels like I am turning into Karen Blixen before their eyes.

That's not a joke, my child. Once, when you were still small, I was indeed mistaken for the Danish author of *Out of Africa*. A local high-school radio station had invited me to talk about my books, and while I was sitting there concentrating incredibly hard on my limited French language abilities, a learner took the wind right out of my sails by asking whether I had met Meryl Streep. Because hadn't she acted in the movie that was based on my book?

Look, people have confused me with other writers before, especially in the early days of my writing career. At a conference of the Afrikaans Writers' Guild in the nineties, an older and more famous Afrikaans writer with a somewhat crazed look in her eyes recited a whole paragraph from someone else's work and told me how she admired me for having been able to create something like that. But I had never before been mistaken for a Danish baroness who had been dead for decades.

'Karen Blixen, *ce n'est pas moi*!' That was all I could yelp. *Karen Blixen isn't me*. A bewildered contradiction of Flaubert's famous *Madame Bovary, c'est moi!*

In truth I am more 'out of Africa', of course, than the grand Baroness Karen von Blixen-Finecke, also known as Isak Dinesen, ever was. I was born in Africa, like nearly all my ancestors for hundreds of years and even further back, thanks to Ouma Saayman's connection to Krotoa of the !Urill'aelona tribe at the southernmost tip of the continent. And when I think back, here in the heart of Europe, on the two years I spent on a farm in the Hazyview district, near the Numbi Gate of one of the biggest game reserves in the world, where we'd often see lions and elephants up close on weekends, I understand how compellingly exotic it must sound to anyone in Europe.

But for much of those two years of sweltering heat and dangerous snakes and fragrant frangipani flowers floating in the swimming pool, I yearned to be elsewhere.

I didn't feel like Blixen in *Out of Africa*, more like Marlow in Joseph Conrad's *Heart of Darkness*, a character who is compelled to journey deep into the interior, becoming more and more disillusioned by everything he discovers along the way.

I was a cosseted little pot plant who'd suddenly been ripped from my small patch of earth, roots and all, and left outside to survive in the wilderness. I was a city girl (a suburban girl, at any rate), a rebellious teenager who had recently discovered rock music and romance, who wanted to hang around in discos and hotels with my friends on weekends. And here was my father dragging our family from the city to the countryside because he wanted to develop a holiday farm in the Lowveld. And then he went and bought a banana farm too, where we could live, because like so many Afrikaans men of his generation Pa yearned for the lost farms of his ancestors.

And as with that 'elegant hat shop' in the Sabel Centre, Ma was once again co-opted into Pa's moneymaking schemes, whether she wanted to be or not. Because Pa would be very busy with the development and marketing of the holiday farm, Ma had to take care of the 'real' farm. And the more she protested that she knew nothing about farming, the more enthusiastically Pa assured her that farming with bananas and avocadoes and mangoes was child's play. Because in such a fertile subtropical landscape everything grew by itself, that was what Pa said, and all Ma would have to do was to ensure that the fruit was delivered to the right places on time.

Besides, there was a 'boss boy' by the name of Never Die (supposedly because he had been bitten by a snake several times without coming to any harm) who would actually be managing the farm. Ma would just have to play 'boss woman' to the 'boss boy'.

Which is not, of course, how it worked out.

And I never got to know Never Die's real name and surname. The only other black farm labourer I remember was John (surely also not the name his parents gave him, but one that white employers could pronounce more easily), a clever young man who initially worked in the garden but whom Pa soon promoted to the role of 'chauffeur', with a smart white cap on his head, like the ones chauffeurs wore in overseas movies. He drove Pa's car on long journeys, although at least Pa didn't sit in the back seat like the important people in overseas movies.

I must confess that my life on a Lowveld farm did not, as one might expect, bring me any closer to my black compatriots. I participated in farm life as little as possible. On weekends I stayed in my bedroom with its midnight-blue walls listening to rock music or reading. (I had wanted to paint the walls black, to make it clear that I was in mourning for my lost city life, but Ma put her foot down. So I chose the darkest shade of blue I could get my hands on.) And during the week I lived in the hostel.

That was the worst of all, even worse than suddenly being trapped on a farm 'in the middle of nowhere' – the area adjoining the Kruger National Park truly did seem like nowhere to me – the fact that I had to go to boarding school for the first time in my life.

By now I was convinced that Pa had a knack for moving me to new schools at the most inconvenient times. It is never easy for a child to adapt to a new school, especially not for an introverted child like me, but it had been particularly distressing to find myself in a new school in my last year at primary school. And then Pa somehow went and did it again in my second-to-last year at high school. At the age of almost sixteen I had to move from a city school to a school in the platteland – and if I thought that Hoërskool Menlopark was strict, I learnt within days of arriving at Nelspruit High that I had no idea what strict meant.

After a week or so in the hostel my perspective shifted yet again. By then the school's day scholars seemed like the happiest, freest children on earth, compared to us boarders who were trapped behind bars.

Two decades later I took on a bildungsroman about a teenage girl from the city who spends her final two school years in a strict Christian National boarding school in the imaginary town of Swartstroom in the Lowveld. Much of what happens in *Childish Things* is pure imagination, but I was able to construct the general background of the story from my own experiences. Especially the horror (and I don't use the word lightly) of that first acquaintance with a hostel.

Since my arrival the previous day, I had felt like a wild animal locked up in a zoo for the first time. Later I realised that an Afrikaans school hostel in a conservative platteland town could, in fact, be described as a kind of zoo. The windows were barred to keep inmates in and outsiders out. There were feeding times and visiting hours and sleeping times and even times when pupils were gated. Sometimes we behaved like animals, too.

Hideous, I'd thought when I first saw the hostel room.

A grey blanket on a grey iron bed, greyish linoleum on the floor and a greyish-white clothes cupboard. Empty, but with a musty smell emanating from its interior. The smell of lost dreams, I thought with the poetic licence of an almost sixteen-year-old. Actually, it was only the smell of stale food, I realised later: of cake and rusks and other edibles hidden behind clothes and gobbled in silence.

Perhaps I had a premonition that it would become the most eventful year of my life when in January 1974 I opened my new journal with a quote from *The Outsider* by Albert Camus. Unlike you at the same age, I had not actually read the book. I didn't even know that the phrase came from *L'Étranger*, which my future French daughter would find so enchanting.

I came upon the quote by chance in a teen movie entitled *Jeremy*, about a shy cello player at a New York arts school who falls in love with a ballerina in a younger class and embarks on an innocent romance with her. Exactly the kind of story that would captivate a shy and artistic child in the seventies.

Today I cannot remember a single scene from the movie. I see on the internet that it won the prize for best debut film at the Cannes Film Festival in 1973, which hopefully means that it wasn't quite as embarrassingly sentimental as *Love Story* and other similar movies that captured my teenage imagination.

But now that I reread Camus's words on the inside cover of my journal, carefully copied out in my handwriting of long ago, I understand why this book by the French philosopher was exactly the right book at the right moment for you:

For the first time, the first, I laid my heart open to the benign indifference of the universe.

My journal was one of those perfectly ordinary little notebooks with a black cardboard cover and a spine of thin red fabric, covered in white paper and decorated with an illustration that was typical of the early seventies. A doll-like figure with enormous eyes and a mop of purple curls, in a short little dress with green and blue flowers and purple boots on her skinny little legs, sitting on a pink stool holding a gift. (Wrapped in pink-and-red paper, with a large yellow bow.) The background is orange and strewn with flowers that float in the air like brightly coloured butterflies. There isn't a colour in the rainbow that you won't find in this picture. If you stare at it for long enough, the colours start to run into one another like in one of those kaleidoscopes we played with when we were small.

I wonder whether I chose this picture because I attached some symbolic significance to the unopened gift. A new journal, a new year, a new home and school (again), new friends (again), an entirely new boarding-school life that lay ahead? Shame, I was trying so hard to stay positive while the world tilted and spun around me.

Influenced, in spite of everything, by Norman Vincent Peale's *The Power of Positive Thinking*, from which Pa had always quoted so liberally.

My family's move to a Lowveld banana farm was a disaster on the scale of the volcanic eruption that had laid Pompeii to ruin. My previous life was destroyed, buried in ash, I would never be able to return to it. That was what I thought when Ma left me behind in a stark hostel room at Nelspruit High School.

There are two banana farms in my past, actually. We lived initially on the one farm, which had a dam rather than a swimming pool, while Pa looked for a 'better farm' (with a swimming pool), which we moved to a few months later.

Both farms were near the town of Hazyview, which struck me as quite a poetic name. Plus it was English, a language I still found more appealing than Afrikaans. And if I absolutely had to live on a farm (which alas I did), I preferred the sound of a farm in Hazyview to one in Pofadder or Koekenaap.

But I cannot for the life of me remember the name of either of our two farms. Which is unforgiveable if you consider how important the names of farms (and holiday houses) have always been to my people. Why would I remember so clearly that wooden oar with 'Vyversrus' painted on it in Franskraal, even though I'd been so much younger, but no name board in Hazyview? Perhaps another case of deliberate amnesia, I speculated, because the names weren't evocative or imaginative enough to fit into my story about my adventurous farm life.

And then this morning I received a message from Pa. As far as he could remember, we had named both farms 'Boland'.

I burst out laughing, because Boland in the Lowveld is about as unexpected as a crocodile in Camps Bay. But then the metaphorical suggestions began to dawn on me. 'Boland', literally meaning higher land, a more elevated place, in contrast with the valleys of the Lowveld. Zeus's Mount Olympus versus Hades' Underworld.

No, I don't believe that Pa regarded the former Lowveld, now part of Mpumalanga, as hell. He quite liked this 'untamed world', as he described it to our relatives in the Cape.

But we all carry our past with us. And Pa's whole past was anchored in the Boland area.

These days, when I talk about my farm years in Hazyview, I don't necessarily explain that there had actually been two farms. 'Don't let facts spoil a good story,' as they say, and factual details like these could slow the pace of my story. Besides, musing like Karen Blixen that 'I had a farm in Africa' (especially in Meryl Streep's fake Scandinavian accent), sounds decidedly more poetic than specifying that in reality I lived on two different farms in the Lowveld.

My Standard 9 journal is smaller than my hand, small enough to tuck into a blazer pocket to hide it in a hurry. Every time I wrote something in it, I felt as if I was committing a secret act of resistance. I was blissfully unaware of the underground activists in the South African Struggle; instead, my role models were the heroes of the

French resistance during the Second World War. Which is just more proof of the kind of fool's paradise I inhabited, blind and deaf to what was happening in my own country and in my own time. But every confession in this little book made me feel brave and daring. The mere thought that someone else could get their hands on it and read my rebellious words sent adrenaline coursing through my body.

In the end I hid it away so thoroughly that I would search for it in vain when I started working on *Childish Things*. I had hoped that these youthful confessions would help me remember what being sixteen felt like, but the little book had disappeared without a trace.

Not until a decade or so after my bildungsroman was published did my sister discover the little book among her own possessions while moving house. Along with a long-lost pale-blue school notebook (Transvaal Department of Education Item No. A25) in which I'd written my adolescent poems. She mailed both books to me in France, in the days when letters from South Africa still reached foreign destinations reliably and fairly quickly, and I had an unsettling reunion with my teenage self.

The little journal was tightly bound with a piece of string that was impossible to untie. I had to cut it like an umbilical cord. When the child I used to be was reborn after so many years, in the pages of a long-lost little book, I was astonished to find that she had written nothing at all about her first impressions of the hostel or the school or the farm. Perhaps it had all been just too upsetting, too complicated or too conflicting to be captured in the vocabulary of a naive teenager.

Perhaps that was the reason I started writing poetry that year, to sneak up on those emotions and experiences via a detour. To lure the awful truth into a lyrical ambush, a way of glorifying the everyday awfulness.

Or perhaps these childish things were like the unripe green avocadoes on our farm that Ma would wrap in newspaper until they were soft enough to eat. Perhaps everything that happened had to be left to ripen for years before I could write about it.

What I did write about in my Standard 9 journal, ad nauseum, were matters of a more physical nature. Matters of the heart and of eating.

I was in love with an ever-changing assortment of boys, often with more than one simultaneously, never truly heartbroken when one relationship didn't work out because I'd usually have my eye on the next one already. *I am so in love with C!* I wrote in my first week in the hostel about a recent holiday romance with a lifeguard on the beach at Franskraal. A few weeks later: *I wonder if I could be falling in love with O.* Then I became involved in a relationship with J, who was at the same school, while on some weekends I flirted with W from Stellenbosch or G from who-knows-where on game farms in the area. *I am so in love with R!* I declared at the end of the year during yet another seaside holiday romance, this time with an English-speaking boy, and barely a week later I was equally in love with both R and B, a surfer-heartbreaker from a previous holiday who had suddenly reappeared. Meanwhile, I wasn't entirely sure that my relationship with J at school was really over, and every time I visited my old friends in Pretoria more names were added, boys with whom there'd been flirting and kissing.

It is a merry-go-round of declarations of love that makes my head spin as I page through my journal.

But even more irritating are the endless diets. The seesaw of binge-eating (common to most boarding-school children), at least, alternating with resolute hunger strikes. *I am on a liquid diet. I have already lost 8 pounds this week, but I am going to carry on until I lose 15 pounds. I just have to do it!* South Africa had switched to the decimal system in the sixties, and when we had to prepare food in the detested domestic science class (which by Standard 9 was fortunately a thing of the past) we measured out the ingredients in grams or litres. But throughout my school days I thought in pounds rather than in kilograms when I thought about my weight.

If my journal is anything to go by, I thought about it far too often.

Between the confessions about matters of the heart and the litanies about having eaten too much or too little, every few pages I also managed to fit in a lament about homework that wasn't done or exams I had to study for. Few other things, whether in my personal life or in the politics of the country, impressed me enough to be recorded. 'Overseas' was no more than the seductive background for movies and books, fantastical destinations that I longed to visit one day. But for the moment it was more important to decide just how little effort I could put into preparing for a history test without getting poor results on my report card, and which lovely young boy I wanted to hook up with next and how much weight I could lose in the next two weeks without fainting from hunger.

In my latest novel I quote snippets from an imaginary teenager's imaginary journal. I didn't reread my own adolescent journal before I wrote it. As I have already explained, I dislike being confronted with the foolishness of my younger self. But as happens every time I write about a fictional character's teenage years, all sorts of displaced 'childish things' floated to the surface again.

I did fear that I may have overdone things a little, though, with all the exclamation marks the teenaged Theresa used to describe her silly crushes and her ridiculous diets. But paging through my own exclamation-riddled journal of 1974 again, I realise I can relax about it. Large parts of this real journal are even more idiotic than Theresa's made-up journal in *Borderline*:

I have to study for exams but I can't concentrate because I am hungry and crazy with excitement because HD spoke to me today!!! He's in matric and he plays in a band and I think he's so gorgeous I

want to cry just looking at him . . . so now I'm not eating anything,
just drinking Ricoffy all the time without milk or sugar, but all the
suffering will be worth it if I can just get ONE CLOSE DANCE
with this guy.

You would never guess from looking at my journal that my two
years on a farm in Africa was the most dramatic period of my life
until then. About the real crises that hit me, the emotional torment
that was far worse than puppy love or exam results, I simply kept
quiet. Or referred to it almost casually in a single paragraph.

Today I know that, if I were to represent my life as a graph, it
could never be an even line. There were always too many highlights
and low points. But two periods in particular would stand out on
any graph. The most traumatic year is still the one between 1989
and 1990 when my eldest child was born with brain damage and
spent ten months in a hospital before he died, while my marriage
was falling apart before my disbelieving eyes and my mother was
diagnosed with terminal cancer.

In the end Ma managed to live with cancer for another decade.
Sometimes I suspect it was sheer willpower that kept her going. She
simply refused to die when her eldest daughter's life had reached
such a low point. Only after my divorce and the birth of another
son, after I had established myself as a writer and met my French
beloved, only when you were finally born – my only daughter and
her only granddaughter – did she allow herself to die.

By now I know that I have inherited my mother's willpower. And
the more you grow up, my girl, the more convinced I become that
you have also inherited it from your grandmother. Perhaps it isn't
even willpower, perhaps it is only an inextinguishable kind of hope,
despite everything, that makes us refuse to accept defeat. Like Scarlett O'Hara declaring at the end of *Gone with the Wind* that tomorrow is another day.

Your grandmother read the book and watched the movie too, and I think it would have saddened her to hear that Margaret Mitchell's saga is also deemed politically suspect these days. Scarlett's family had been slave owners, after all, willing to go to war to retain their privileged social position. But my mother was a good woman, of that I am convinced, even though she liked Scarlett and other spoilt Southern Belles.

I hope you will also be able to say, one day, that your mother had been a more or less good person. Even though I ate meat and helped pollute the atmosphere by flying around far too much and threw away literally hundreds of plastic toothbrushes in my lifetime – and all the other things I did that will probably be regarded as unforgivable sins by future generations.

I hope that my descendants – in the event that there are descendants – will also be charitable enough to judge me in the context of my era.

The year I turned sixteen is the other standout year in my uneven life graph. Although I wasn't confronted with severe illness or the death of a loved one, there were serious accidents and emotional damage. Aside from the painful adjustment to living on a farm and in a hostel, there was friction between Ma and Pa, and my own rebellious relationship with Pa was becoming ever more complicated. My sixteenth birthday was one of the most awful days of my life because Pa and I had one of our ugliest arguments ever. I had actually wanted Ma to stand up to him, because he'd been picking a quarrel with her all day, but like most Afrikaans women Ma had learnt to keep quiet when the man in the house was in a mood.

It was on my sixteenth birthday that I decided to hell with keeping quiet, I would not become one of the multitude of silent and oppressed women, I would open my mouth right now and tell my father what I thought of his domineering behaviour.

It did not go down well.

Back then I had already come across Edmund Burke's famous quote about evil. (*The only thing necessary for the triumph of evil is for good men to do nothing.*) And while nothing happening in my house could really be described as 'evil', although I had yet to learn not to avert my eyes from the true evils in South African society, I was starting to realise that 'good men' (and women, of course) could not do nothing when they encountered unfairness.

That argument with Pa was my trial run. I didn't just open my mouth to speak out, I also took action. When Pa stormed out of the house with the threat that he didn't know if he was ever coming back, I ran ahead to lock the door of his car. (In those days you could lock cars by simply pushing down the button inside the window and slamming the door shut from the outside.) All I wanted to do was buy a little time, to prevent Pa from simply jumping into his car and speeding off. If he had to take the keys out of his pocket to unlock the door before he could start the car, he would hopefully realise that he was overreacting.

So I thought. But you know what I always say about Mister Thought, don't you? My desperate act only made everything worse. When Pa realised that the key was locked inside the car, that he would have to smash the window to open the car because he didn't have a spare key, he went almost mad with rage. Trembling, apparently on the brink of tears, with a bright-red face and his hand clutching his chest like someone who was having a heart attack, he looked up at the sky and called out: 'What have I done to get a family like this!' And, pointing a finger at me: 'You, yes you, you are driving me to my grave!'

This is not what any girl wants to hear from her father on her sixteenth birthday. It is the kind of curse that stays in your memory, that you try to unravel with a psychologist years later.

Or maybe my ill-considered attempt to keep my father with us did help a little. He was so upset that he realised he needed to lie down for a bit. He may have been afraid that he really was going to have a heart attack. And while he lay on the couch, seething, my practical little brother bent a wire coat hanger to push in through the side of the window and unlock the door from the inside.

My sister and I helped him until he got it right.

The three of us could fight like cat and dog. Hanli and Wiaan would literally give each other bloody noses on the long road to our holidays in the Cape. Ma's solution was to make me sit in the middle on long trips, like the Berlin Wall that had to keep two arch-enemies apart. But that didn't keep them from fighting. All that happened was that the Berlin Wall sustained collateral damage. I tried hard to carry on reading while punches and slaps rained down around me, but more than once I got in the way. On those occasions I retaliated. Sometimes the book that was constantly in my hands turned into a handy weapon that I could use to clout an attacker on the head.

But whenever we discerned a threat from outside, we instantly closed ranks. Pa's warning that he would leave us, and his terrible rage, were all it took to make us work together in silence until we could finally unlock the car. That was the miracle of brothers and sisters, I also realised on my sixteenth birthday.

Pa did drive off in the end, after he had calmed down. But by then we knew that he would be back.

If in the course of this eventful year Pa had decided to flee his family – or at least send his eldest daughter packing – none of us would have been really surprised. I truly tried his patience to the limit.

My only defence is that I didn't do it on purpose.

I wasn't deliberately trying to be impossible. I was more like a gambler whose luck had unexpectedly run out. You can't stop gambling because you refuse to believe that your luck won't turn again, and in the meantime your bad luck keeps getting worse. Within a few months I was responsible for two of my father's cars being written off and a third one being badly damaged.

The first accident occurred right after my traumatic sixteenth birthday. Pa had given me a secondhand Beetle, perhaps to compensate for everything that had gone wrong on my birthday. The first time I drove the car further than the farm roads, with no driver's licence or any experience of traffic, I drove into a high pavement way too fast and bent the car's axle. Don't ask me how something like that happens. It was neither the strangest nor the dumbest thing that happened to me that year.

After the accident, the black Beetle, which I had named Julius, was out of action for several months. And before it could be repaired, I caused another accident. This time the damage was greater in every respect. Pa and Ma were away for the weekend, and I didn't have permission to drive our orange farm bakkie. And then I went and rolled it.

It probably wouldn't have happened had Pa and Ma not asked Oom Hans and Tannie Hettie to keep an eye on us three children for the weekend.

Oom Hans was what you would have called a black sheep in the old days. That one member of a respectable Afrikaans family who was trouble from the start. There were other interesting characters, too, among Ouma Hannah's many siblings. I recall a dignified deaf aunt, for example, who was always exquisitely made-up, with her hair in a sumptuous purple-white coiffure, her poodle as perfectly styled and groomed as she was – but Oom Hans was in a different league of interesting.

Oom Hans was a tailor and an incurable womaniser. (That was what I heard Pa call him when I was small, the first time I ever heard that word.) At a time when divorce was still a big scandal he'd been married more than once, and in his later years he no longer even bothered to get married at all. (That was what I heard the family whisper among themselves, never loud enough for other people to hear.) Oom Hans, then, was the first relative I ever met who was living 'in sin' with someone.

That in itself was enough to arouse my curiosity.

In addition, he had a tricky alcohol problem, and at some point in his merry life he went bankrupt – maybe even more than once. The year we moved to the farm, Pa heard that his ageing uncle was stuck in Durban with neither money nor means. Because Pa knew how it felt to lose all your money without expecting it, he took pity on Oom Hans and his companion Tannie Hettie, and soon afterwards he fetched them from Natal to live on the holiday farm in Hazyview for a while.

This jolly couple hit our boring farm life like a whirlwind – and promptly blew away several of my teenage prejudices. I never would have dreamt that old people could be so much fun. Oom Hans always had a tin of snuff handy, from which my brother and sister and I were regularly allowed to take a sniff, and when he was a few drinks strong (which was most of the time) his once-nimble tailor's fingers became so clumsy that half the snuff powder would spill onto his white shirt. His enormous stomach was always sloping to one side, like a lopsided hill, with a trail of brown snuff that you could follow all the way to his nose. A bit of snuff would usually have stayed behind under his nose, like a Chaplin moustache. And his eyes glittered constantly, like Chaplin's when he was full of mischief, or like the naughty schoolboy he must have been very long ago.

When Ma and Pa sometimes went away for a weekend, Oom Hans and Tannie Hettie were supposed to keep an eye on us children. We soon discovered that we could do whatever we liked as long as we kept our congenial minders supplied with drinks. We could also drink and take snuff ourselves, listen to music as loudly as we liked, invite our friends to visit until late at night, and of course drive all the cars in the yard.

Alas, this lawlessness came to an end the weekend I rolled the bakkie down an incline, and it dawned on Pa and Ma that they could no longer set the wolf to keep the sheep. Oom Hans and Tannie Hettie were never asked to watch us again. Pa may also have tried to persuade them to drink a little less – he was concerned about their health, he said – which probably wasn't to their liking. Because a month or so later they disappeared, presumably to stay with other charitable family elsewhere in the country.

You know, Mia, I think of Oom Hans every time someone asks me how I came to be a writer without a day job. How has someone like me, from a perfectly ordinary Afrikaans family of former farmers and labourers, not a scholar or an artist among us, made a living from writing for over thirty years? With no salary, no paid leave or sick leave, and for the past twenty years in a foreign country to boot?

I think a wayward character like Oom Hans made me realise at a young age that you don't have to run with the herd your whole life. That you don't have to march to the same drumbeat as everyone around you. There may be a different tune playing inside your head. Maybe you would rather dance than march.

You have hopefully known this since childhood, my darling girl. You were never really one for marching, anyway, except with your father to the beat of the silly 'Colonel Hathi's March' in *Jungle Book*. And even then you made it look more like dancing than marching.

A few months after I rolled the bakkie, I was involved in yet another serious accident with one of Pa's cars. Thank goodness I wasn't behind the wheel this time, or I would surely have been too traumatised ever to get my driver's license. It was nevertheless my fault, because the driver was my school boyfriend, Jessie, a year older than me, but still too young to have a driver's license. Pa had given him permission to drive our yellow Kombi, perhaps because he figured that as long as I wasn't driving, the vehicle and the passengers would be safe.

Poor Pa.

I know, Mia, it probably sounds to you like your grandfather was irresponsible to hand his car keys over so easily to his children and their friends. But in those days, in that wild world of ours, most white farm children raced around without driver's licences. Pa wasn't less responsible than other parents. Just a lot less lucky.

My school boyfriend somehow went and rolled the Kombi – with me and my sister as passengers – when he took a corner too fast and lost control of the car.

That second experience of being trapped inside a rolling vehicle was even worse than the first time.

It is impossible to describe the feeling of disbelief and unreality that hits you when you are spinning around like laundry inside a tumble dryer, head over heels (remember, no one ever wore seat belts), with the cold, calm knowledge at the same time that these are probably your final moments, that this must be what dying feels like, all in slow motion.

No, I did not see my life flash before me, but those tumbling seconds seemed to last forever, and were the cause of years of anxiety dreams. The terrible calm is what I remember best. It is only once it's over and you realise with amazement that not only did you survive, but that you are also completely unscathed, that the shock and the adrenaline kick in. Only then do you start trembling or crying or laughing hysterically, or however your constitution responds to an enormous shock.

But the first time I had been alone in the vehicle; it was only me who could die or be removed from the wreckage with a broken neck. The second time my stupefaction was mixed with the awful knowledge that there were two other people in this rolling car with me. Someone's knee hit my chin, my fingers grabbed at someone's foot, and I was aware throughout that it was highly unlikely that all three of us would survive this headlong tumble unharmed.

And yet that was exactly what happened.

We three teenagers emerged from the wreckage of Pa's yellow Kombi with no more than a few scratches and helped one another back up the hill that the car had just rolled down.

And as with my previous accident, Pa's relief that no one had been hurt was far greater than his rage about yet another vehicle that had been written off.

In my sixteenth year I survived more car accidents within a few months than in the rest of my life.

It is probably no coincidence. If you have been in three accidents even before you get your driver's licence, you are going to be an exceptionally careful driver for the rest of your life. And because as a writer I cannot help but look for meaning in whatever happens to me – the sin of which Philip Roth is accused by his own fictional character Zuckerman in *The Facts* – I have to invoke Roth yet again and ask: 'Well, what does it signify?'

So many car accidents in such a short time may have made me realise at a young age that we spend our lives on a tightrope between luck and misfortune. Between happiness and unhappiness, between chance and accident.

'Shit happens' has become my motto, in a way. The most unlikely accidents, crises and miseries can strike us at any moment.

This is why John Irving's novel, *The World According to Garp,* fascinated me so much when I read it in my early twenties. The constant sense of catastrophe concealed behind the humour resonated with me straight away, the looming absurdity that can undermine everyday events. The *lunacy and sorrow*, as someone refers to it in the novel, that is an integral part of our lives on earth.

Nothing we can do about it.

There are other reasons why I identified so strongly with this book and with the main character. Garp's mother, Jenny Fields, is a nurse, like mine was; Garp has an idea from childhood that he will die young, an idea that helps him become a writer; and Jenny Fields decides that she wants a child but not a husband.

In Standard 9, several years before I read *The World According to Garp*, I floated Jenny Fields's provocative decision during more than one Sunday lunch, like waving a red flag at a bull. Or throwing down the gauntlet to challenge an opponent to a duel. Both the bull and the opponent were, naturally, my father, and I wasn't really convinced by what I was saying. Part of my teenage heart still yearned for a fairy tale romance, a Prince Charming who would rescue me from my mundane existence and carry me off to his castle where we would live together happily ever after. But I wanted to provoke, shock and upset my father; in short, I wanted to torture him in all the usual ways in which rebellious teenagers torture their long-suffering parents.

At the same time I wasn't the sort of child who would ever really punish my parents by running away from home or becoming addicted to hard drugs or sleeping around left, right and centre or even just getting poor results at school. One of Ma's favourite sayings was, 'You cut off your nose to spite your own face' – and I never wanted to ruin my own face (or my own future). I was far braver in words than in deeds.

I just wanted to argue about all the moral codes in society that I was starting to question – and thank heavens I was raised in a home where it was possible to have arguments like these with my parents.

Pa and Ma may have been morally conservative compared to present-day parents, but they allowed us a great deal more freedom, nonetheless, than many of our friends' parents. Especially the freedom to argue during Sunday lunch – usually the only meal in the week where the whole family was together at the table – when Pa poured out a tiny bit of wine into sherry glasses for us children as well. When there were adult guests at the table, we had to 'know our place' and preferably not talk too much, but we were never expected to be seen and not heard.

And when it was just the five of us eating together, voices were sometimes raised and the arguments became heated. Especially when I declared, after knocking back two sherry glasses of wine, that I wanted to have a child one day without getting married.

I still ask myself whether it might have been a self-fulfilling prophecy. After all I *did* try to do 'the right thing', to get married and have a child the 'decent' way, but the marriage was a fiasco and the child died. After that the whole idea of holy matrimony began to fade.

I became more and more convinced that I could live without being married, even without a male companion in the long run. But I couldn't imagine my life without a child.

In the same year in which I survived three car accidents without any injuries, I did manage to break a bone in my body for the first time. By dancing, believe it or not.

In the winter holiday of that year I attended a weeklong 'charm course' with two of my new hostel friends, Corlia and Elize. It was presented at a school hostel in Brits, of all places, by a grand lady with the nickname Poodle. Don't ask me why we called her Poodle. Perhaps only because, like the British writer Anita Brookner (whom I have always admired), she had a face with poodle-like features. Or perhaps her immaculate hair or her skinny legs reminded us of a poodle that had been groomed in the French style.

I also can't explain why, after struggling for six months to adjust to living in a school hostel (and the struggle was by no means over),

I chose to spend part of the holiday in another school hostel of my own free will. Unless I found the mere thought of three weeks on our banana farm, without any friends or distractions, so unbearable that I would do anything to avoid it.

Or maybe it was just the prospect of an overnight train ride to Pretoria that was appealing enough to justify a week in a hostel.

The train ride with my two friends did turn out to be an exciting adventure, 'lots of fun', according to my journal (where I offered no further details), and from Pretoria we caught a bus to Brits. The mere fact that we were travelling on our own made us feel grown-up and free and exuberantly cheerful. By the time we reached Poodle in Brits, we were like three Duracell bunnies on Ecstasy. Many of the other girls, from towns all over the Transvaal, arrived in the same state of adrenaline-driven excitement.

I don't remember a single charm lesson. I do remember that we had to listen to a dead-boring speech about nature conservation, and visited an aquarium and attended a cheese-and-fruit-juice reception and took part in activities like potato races and three-legged races. And that some of the girls smoked on the sly and apple-pied one another's beds at night (a silly prank where a sheet is folded back on itself halfway down the length of the bed so you can't straighten your legs). I remember above all a general atmosphere of rebelliousness and disobedience.

But I watched most of these activities from the sidelines, not because I wanted to behave like a solitary writer, but because I broke a bone in my foot on the first night and spent the rest of the week limping around like Hopalong Cassidy.

It took me two nights and a whole day in between to realise that I had broken a bone, because it happened in such a silly way that I refused to believe it. I had wanted to show the other girls a movement I had learnt in a modern dance class in Pretoria the previous year, a high jump with both legs extended to one side, and then you kicked your heels together while in the air. But I performed my party trick on an uneven road in the dark, landed awkwardly and hurt my foot badly.

I thought it was a sprained ankle and the matron at the hostel simply wrapped a bandage around the ankle. On the second night I woke up because my whole foot was throbbing with pain, and when I got out of bed to go to the bathroom and put weight on the foot, (which by now looked like a fully inflated blue balloon), I fainted. Another first in my life. When I came round, I dragged myself to the bathroom on my bum and realised I had to get to a doctor.

My brother and sister thought it was hilarious when I got back home. Ma sends me away to a 'charm course', presumably hoping I'll learn to become a little more ladylike, and I come home with half a leg in plaster, burdened with two wooden crutches between which I hang like fish biltong on a drying line. Less ladylike than ever before.

When the cast finally came off six weeks later, another equally improbably accident befell me on the tennis court of the holiday farm. We weren't playing tennis. (I never learnt to play tennis.) We were a bunch of teenagers on the court using old tennis racquets like hockey sticks to dribble the ball to each other. (I couldn't really play hockey either.) Running head down with my eye on the ball in front of my "hockey stick", I crashed into one of the net posts on the side of the court, with catastrophic consequences for my face.

I almost lost a tooth and had to go back to the hostel on the Monday with a badly swollen mouth. Every time I told someone it had been a tennis accident, I got stared at like a woman who is abused by her husband and tells everyone she walked into a door.

Sometimes you really do walk into doors – or run into tennis net posts. But probably only if you're the kind of unlucky fish I was in my sixteenth year.

When I look back at everything that happened during this year 'on a farm in Africa', it all seems just as unreal to me as it sounds to my European friends. The hippopotamus that ended up in our swimming pool and the black caretaker who was called Never Die because he had survived several snake bites and my own incredible ability to survive car accidents unharmed and the lions that roared right outside our rondavel in the game park on weekends and the night safaris in open vehicles that we enjoyed in private game reserves. As if it had happened to a character in a book.

Some of the strangest experiences did eventually get a second life, of course, in books.

Like the time Pa braaied a black mamba on the coals. It may also have been a different kind of snake; I only remember that the creature was exceptionally long and as thick as a man's wrist. We were on our way to a game reserve when the car ahead of us crushed the snake's head. Pa pulled over and put the dead animal in the boot, perhaps only to show our Cape friends in the game reserve that he wasn't exaggerating when he talked about the massive snakes in this part of the world. But that night around the campfire things got out of hand when a few credulous strangers took his boasting seriously. As so often happens, one lie led to another, and soon he had backed himself into a corner.

'Here, a man eats meat,' Pa said. 'Beef, venison, lion . . .'

'Snake?' asked the man from the Cape, who was beginning to grasp the game.

'Snake,' my father said. 'Only last week we had a snake barbeque.'

'No, really, Carl, now you're talking shit.'

'Not so loud, there are children around,' Pa said primly. 'Come and have a piece of sausage meanwhile.'

I adapted the story a little in *Childish Things*, but not much. So much of what happened to us was truly stranger than fiction. Sometimes, when I wanted to turn the facts into fiction, I actually had to dilute them a bit to make everything sound more believable.

Pa got so carried away that night that he told the people we were with that his whole family feasted often on snake meat. Before I knew it, the snake from the boot was being braaied over the coals – and I, along with the rest of the family, had to pretend that I had eaten snake meat many times.

That night around the campfire I could never have dreamt that I would one day sit around a fire with my children in my own house in France and make them laugh with the story about the first (and thank heavens the only) time I had to eat snake meat.

I didn't want to live on a farm in the Lowveld. But if I had spent all of my youth in the prim and proper suburbs of Cape Town, I would have had far fewer stories to tell you and your brothers. Had Pa not decided to move to Pretoria so he could make and lose money faster, had he not subsequently blundered even deeper into the interior because he was determined to own a farm, my childhood would definitely have been more monotonous.

Like the Rolling Stones sang at our teenage parties, 'You Can't Always Get What You Want', but sometimes you get what you need. Today I know that I needed both the Cape suburbs and Sunday school with the children of Gansbaai fishermen, both the Voortrekkers in Snor City and the French teacher at Hoërskool Menlopark. And without question also the two years on two farms in the Lowveld.

(I'm still not convinced about the two years I had to spend at boarding school.)

All these divergent experiences made me who I have become. An Afrikaans writer who is writing a letter to her French daughter because after sixty years she is still trying to answer an all-important question. Because I believe that this question isn't only important for me as a writer, but also for me as a mother and for you as a daughter, for both of us as thinking people who became aware of Camus's *benign indifference of the universe* early on. In the words of the novelist Roth and his fictional character Zuckerman: Well, what does it all *signify*?

15

THE END OF THE BEGINNING

That teenager posing with shy pride in front of a poster for a bull-fight in Lourenço Marques in the seventies doesn't know yet that she is experiencing a *Götterdämmerung*. But it is indeed the twilight of the gods for Portuguese colonialism in Africa.

Soon Lourenço Marques will be known as Maputo, but the only effect this will have on her own life in her final year at school is that LM Radio will no longer exist. And even the end of the beloved radio station won't be a complete disaster for her.

Her school boyfriend Jessie (yes, the same one who rolled her father's yellow Kombi) has a home in Lourenço Marques – where his father works – as do quite a few of the other children staying with her in the hostel at Nelspruit High, because it is the largest Afrikaans school close to the border. Jessie plays in a band (she has always been more attracted to rebellious musicians than to model head boys) and he knows a presenter at LM Radio who gives him stacks of seven singles that they need to get rid of before the proverbial curtain comes down.

JM Coetzee would write *Waiting for the Barbarians* a few years later, but at this point the schoolgirl hasn't heard of Coetzee yet.

She is very pleased when her musician boyfriend brings a pile of these cool records from LM Radio with him when he visits her on the farm in Hazyview on weekends. Sometimes he or his brother even smuggles forbidden music across the border, from the musicals

Hair or *Jesus Christ Superstar*, which makes her feel like a daring, dancing freedom fighter.

She is barely aware of the real freedom struggle being waged around her.

In April 1974 the peaceful Carnation Revolution began in Lisbon, so named because one of the protestors gave a soldier a carnation to put in the barrel of his gun, after which thousands upon thousands of Portuguese protestors took to the streets carrying carnations. The government fell and the Portuguese colonial wars in South Africa's neighbouring states, Angola and Mozambique, came to an end. They were almost immediately replaced by devastating civil wars that lasted for decades, though, spurred on by the Cold War between American capitalism and Russian communism. Of these wars I would become thoroughly aware, because so many boys and young men among my friends and family were drawn into the devastation as conscripts.

My boyfriend's family was fortunate to get out of Mozambique in time, without losing too much. They hadn't been living there for generations. His father went back to work in South Africa and he spent his final school year in Pretoria.

Our romance had blown over by then anyway.

But during the two years I spent on a farm near the Mozambican border, the stream of Portuguese refugees out of that colonial flesh-pot became steadily bigger. About one million *retornados* fled south from Angola and Mozambique. I saw only part of the Mozambican convoy of bewildered people with my own eyes – and mostly from a distance, because the Portuguese weren't 'my people', or so I was informed. The fact that most of the refugees were white did, however, elicit sympathy from my people. Shocking photographic reports in the press showed us that the river of refugees from Angola in the west flowed just as strongly as the eastern stream out of Mozambique.

The news photographs and the dirty, dazed and desolate people I saw in Nelspruit reminded me of that coffee-table book about the North Sea flood of 1953. The book hadn't come to the Transvaal with us, but the black-and-white photographs had evidently left an indelible impression. Especially the bewildered expressions – the shocked eyes and the slumped shoulders of refugees who did not even know the extent of their losses yet – that I saw again among the Mozambican Portuguese. This time in full colour, in the flesh, in my own lifetime.

Which only confirms once again that there's no getting away from disasters and accidents. Whether a flood or a car accident, civil war or a broken bone, the sudden arrival of a communist government or your father going bankrupt again and losing his farm (which would happen to me within the next year), this sense of impending disaster is something I carry with me to this day. A dark cloud waits behind every silver lining. But this hasn't made me a pessimist. On the contrary.

As you know, my girl, I became eternally hopeful *because* I've seen since childhood how often most of us can fall from that tight-rope we keep trying to dance on. Or walk on. Or simply stand on. But after every fall we get back on. If we stumble, we pretend it's part of the dance. Until we tumble down again.

Among the swarms of colonists who fled from the former Portu-guese colonies in my final school year, there were also small groups of Afrikaners who had settled in these countries. Mozambique and Angola had been alluring places where a white man could lead an adventurous pioneer life without the stink of apartheid that clung to South Africa, without the Protestant piety, the forbidden books and movies and music that characterised South Africa, without a slew of laws separating races and keeping everyone in their place. But they were still places where the white man was in command of wealth and political power.

Until 1975, at least.

Until the seventies, colonialism was really just apartheid's more cosmopolitan grandmother. This grandmother was ostensibly kinder, cleverer, better travelled and educated. She spoke many languages – English, Portuguese, German, French, Spanish, Dutch – while her grandchild was a little Afrikaans runt. Unsophisticated, even somewhat backward in the eyes of the outside world.

But as the colonial bubbles in Africa burst one after the other, many of the grandmothers were compelled to seek shelter with the backward grandchild.

In *Borderline* a Cuban character recalls the smell of despair that hung in the air over Luanda in 1975.

'I remember the long convoys that were moving towards the south. To South Africa, the only tierra prometida . . . promised land for white people in Africa. Some of them probably started again from nothing, after they lost everything in Angola. Others just gave up on Africa. They were desilusionado. So they fucked off to Portugal or Brazil or wherever.' He looks up from his wheelchair at Theresa as he continues: 'But I do not have many memories of Luanda, as soon as we arrived we were sent into the bush. To stop the enemy that was coming from the south. Your people.' Again his smile softens his words.

'My people,' Theresa nods.

That was the backdrop, the sets on the stage where I played and danced in my matric year. We weren't entirely carefree, because we had to study for matric exams and make important decisions about the rest of our lives. What we wanted to study, where we wanted to study, for some of us also how to obtain study bursaries. I thought that my father had enough money to pay for my studies, but I had also already learnt that I couldn't rely too much on my father's fluctuating financial status; it was better to have a Plan B . . .

But there were also wild parties and fun picnics on farms, watermelon feasts beside the school swimming pool where the boys smeared the girls' bodies with slices of watermelon (any excuse to touch a girl's body), the excitement of the matric farewell and the boys' hostel dinner. For us girls, the excitement revolved chiefly around our appearance, which dress to choose, what to do with our hair, which colour to paint our nails.

These were difficult choices because there were almost as many rules for our matric farewell as for the rest of our school lives. Your partner had to be someone who was in matric at the same school as you, no outsiders from other schools or (heaven forbid) boyfriends who had already left school. Dancing was strictly forbidden and the girls' dresses had to show as little skin as possible. No bare shoulders, thin straps across the back, lowcut necklines, thigh-high slits or any other enticements.

The boys' hostel dinner fortunately took place in the winter, and although winter in the Lowveld still feels like summer anywhere else, the temptation to expose our bodies was at least considerably less. I circumvented the rules by asking Ma to make me a long hippy-style button-through dress with long sleeves (which I had copied from the fashion pages of the American magazine *Seventeen*) and wore it with a bandana made from the same fabric. Everything was as covered as could be, even my hair was covered by the head wrap, and yet I managed to make a rebellious statement. It wasn't the 'usual' look expected of a matric girl at a hostel dinner.

For the matric dance in the sultry spring I needed a different tactic. Long sleeves and head coverings wouldn't do in the heat. I chose a light-blue dress of chiffon with tiny white flowers and a frill around the shoulders, as pretty and innocent as could be, but there was at least the possibility that later in the evening I could tug the frill down to bare one or even both of my shoulders 'by accident'.

And I painted my nails blue. It was my one essential act of rebellion. With such a prim and proper dress at least something about my appearance had to show that I didn't really want to look like that.

My partner was a good-looking boy with bright brown eyes, my best male friend in matric. His name was Otto, like the lively puppy in the lift-the-flap books I would later buy for you and Daniel – the Afrikaans version of Eric Hill's *Spot* – and something about Otto (the person) always reminded me of a naughty puppy. We had been 'new kids' together, arriving at this school from elsewhere the previous year, and had immediately been attracted to each other, perhaps only because we were both outsiders. We even started a brief romance, but afterwards I started dating other guys and he other girls without spoiling our friendship. I was exceptionally grateful that I could sit next to him during the long and boring farewell dinner (especially since we couldn't do anything but sit), because he could always make me laugh.

Like all the other boys in my matric class, Otto was also called up for military service. He ended up in the air force and a few years later his plane was shot down somewhere across the border. His death shocked me, but by then I was starting to get used to young men in my circle of friends dying in the war or coming back wounded.

My student boyfriend, Johann, had been a paratrooper who'd spent almost a year at 1 Military Hospital in Pretoria after being shot to pieces on the border. We met right after he was discharged from hospital. He had lost part of one leg and had no sensation in his foot and tiny pieces of shrapnel remained under the skin on his back. I often stroked his back in wonder.

My best English-speaking friend, Zelma, whom I had known since childhood because our parents were friends (Rose and George le Roux were my parents' only close English-speaking friends), married a very attractive soldier in the famous 32 Battalion. She went to live with her combat bridegroom in an army settlement on the

322

border of the former South West Africa as a young bride, and experienced far more of the war than any other woman I knew. But her husband died in a skirmish shortly after they were married and she returned to South Africa an exceptionally young widow.

My first husband, David Bishop, was also a conscript in Angola in the seventies and, although he wasn't physically wounded, like many other men he sustained severe emotional damage. You're aware that your half-brother Ian's father spent most of the last quarter of a century of his life in psychiatric hospitals. A few years ago he died in Stikland, in a state of catatonic depression.

And these are just a few of the border-war casualties that touched my life.

After the launch of my most recent novel a grand madam from a book club asked me why I was writing about the border war, of all things. Her tone was lightly accusing, characteristic of the kind of reader who regularly wants to know why we Afrikaans writers carry on so about the horrors of apartheid and the past. Isn't it all history by now? Aren't we living in a democratic country where there are other, newer, horrors to write about?

I suddenly thought of Uys Krige's poem 'Ken jy die see', one of the few 'old-fashioned' Afrikaans poems that impressed me enough when I was at school that I can still recite large parts of it off by heart. A fish vendor tries to convince a complaining buyer that the sea is deadly dangerous, and after every few lines he repeats the refrain 'And then you tell me, sir, that the fish is dear'.

Do you see the bent old woman, Mrs Matthee,
Who keeps gazing out over the sea
She thinks this breeze will bring her sons in time for tea
But they sleep behind the churchyard wall, all three

And then you tell me, sir, that the fish is dear . . .

'Do you know the border war, Madam?' I wanted to ask this book-club woman. 'And then you ask me, Madam, why I write about the border war?'

Just like apartheid, the border war is by no means 'over', because the damage is still noticeable every day. I see it in the men of my generation who have retained visible and invisible wounds – and I include the men from the former 'enemy' here, the freedom fighters of Swapo and uMkhonto we Sizwe and Frelimo, even the Cuban men I also chose to write about in *Borderline*. And I see it in their female family members who are powerless to help them because they are mostly deliberately excluded from the macho experience of the battlefield. I notice it in their children, in an entire younger generation that has suffered under a father's excessive drinking or depression or violent behaviour.

These days, you'll see the consequences of repressed and untreated post-traumatic stress among even the grandchildren of some former conscripts. The sins of the fathers that would be visited upon the children to the third and fourth generation – that was what the Bible taught me when I was small, my girl.

I would so love to believe that I could protect you from this atonement because I raised you in another country. But I know that I brought my baggage along with me into my new life in France. My past still rattles behind me like 'a string of cans' – to quote Azille Coetzee again.

What's past is prologue. This short and powerful quotation from Shakespeare I also encountered in my matric year, in our setwork play, *The Tempest*. Earlier in high school I struggled to get a grip on Shakespeare's complicated language, like all my classmates, probably, but in matric I had two wonderful strokes of luck.

My English teacher was a short, round little woman with snow-white hair who seemed older than my grandmother – and more like a friendly little witch than an educator who would make William Shakespeare's words accessible to me.

Yet that was exactly what she did.

Mrs Davey saw something in me that other teachers may have overlooked. She became excited about my essays and pushed me harder than the other children because she believed I had the ability truly to understand Shakespeare, if I only tried harder. I did – and I did. It was as if she'd given me a key to unlocking Shakespeare's language, and once I started to turn the key, nervous and afraid at first because I didn't know what to expect, I entered a new world.

Words open worlds, it is true.

But the real breakthrough came because she encouraged our whole class to attend a stage production of *The Tempest* in a Johannesburg theatre. Most of us were eager to go, not because of Shakespeare, but because a long bus ride and a night in the big city offered an exciting opportunity to make out, mess about and misbehave.

In the end we got twice the opportunity to misbehave, because on the first occasion the school bus broke down on the way to Johannesburg and by the time it was finally repaired it was too late to get to the show that same night. (No one was exactly heartbroken that we had missed *The Tempest*.) But the next weekend the bus full of horny matric pupils again embarked on the long journey to Johannesburg, and again there was a great deal of messing about in the bus. We made it to the theatre this time, though, exhausted from all our antics.

And there, in the pitch-black darkness of the theatre, in my school uniform among all my uniformed classmates, I saw the light. It was more than the stage lighting that suddenly illuminated Shakespeare for me. Perhaps it was just the final turn of the key I needed; I simply knew that never again did I want to return to the darkness I'd been in before I could understand Shakespeare. That night I reached for every single word of *The Tempest* the way a hungry boarding-school child reaches for the last piece of chicken on the table.

I was besotted with Shakespeare after that. And it wasn't something that would just blow over like all my other crushes at school. It was, as the famous final sentence in the movie *Casablanca* predicts, the beginning of a beautiful friendship.

Maybe not a 'friendship', really, because although Shakespeare's words have meant the world to me, I have never meant anything to Shakespeare. Except maybe to encourage others to read his work too.

As I am doing with you again now, my dear girl.

You were not exposed to Shakespeare in your French schools; you had to study Molière, for which you initially had as little appetite as I once did for The Bard. And there is nothing wrong with Molière (I should hasten to add before I incur all your French teachers' displeasure), but Molière just isn't Shakespeare. Even your French father admits it.

As you know, I keep a weathered green book beside my bed to this day. *The Complete Works of William Shakespeare*, all the dramas and sonnets in one place, printed so fine to fit everything into the same volume that I may soon need a magnifying glass to read it. But I would keep it beside me even if I went blind. Literally within reach in case I have an anxiety attack in the middle of the night. If my eyes ever became too weak to read it, the mere sensation of the well-thumbed book in my hands would hopefully be enough to console me.

So many wise, funny, comforting, heartrending, life-affirming words in a single book remains a miracle for someone who lives on and through words.

From *The Tempest*, which I discovered as a sixteen-year-old schoolgirl, I will always remember this enchanting phrase: *We are such stuff as dreams are made on, and our little life is rounded with a sleep*. And Prospero's magnificent admission about Caliban: *This thing of darkness I acknowledge mine*. It has helped me acknowledge several 'things of darkness' in my own background. But the words that made the greatest impression, especially now as I look back on my youth, remain these: *What's past is prologue*.

Everything that happened in my past was the prologue to my present. Just like everything that has so far happened to you, my beloved daughter, is the prologue to the rest of your life. It isn't as terrifying as it sounds. It's more like Gandalf's advice to Frodo, which I have already shared with you. You cannot always choose what happens to you, but you can choose which story you are going to write about what has happened to you.

Once I got the hang of Shakespeare, my grip inevitably loosened on other books I had enjoyed until then. If you have drunk instant coffee made from chicory your whole life and you taste real coffee made with freshly ground beans from Ethiopia or Vietnam for the first time, you may not stop drinking instant coffee right away, but it will no longer taste as good. You will gradually drink more and more real coffee and less and less instant coffee. Until one day you would go without coffee rather than accept disappointing instant coffee.

It is true that my taste for coffee only developed after school. In matric I was still quite content with a mug of Ricoffy in my bedroom at home. Even the weak hostel coffee with its blue sheen that we had to pour from large steel urns didn't disgust me too much. But my taste in books was already changing. I was reading the poorly written instant books, passed around by the girls in the hostel, with growing reluctance.

It was my own fault that I had become a link in this reading

327

chain. Soon after I arrived in the hostel, a few girls in the same corridor went crazy for some or other Afrikaans love story. Readers who get excited about books make me excited – always did, always will – and these girls sounded so excited that I also wanted to read the book. I wasn't the only nosy parker; there was already a waiting list and I was quite far down the list. While I waited for my turn, everyone around me got swept up in the wave of enthusiasm. Every girl who had read the book before me was apparently crazy about it.

Until at last the coveted book reached me.

I can't tell you what it was called or who wrote it because I honestly cannot remember. I don't remember the storyline or a single character. I remember nothing about the book, except for the incredible disappointment that washed over me, page after page. If this was what everyone was raving about, then surely there had to be something wrong with me? I found it an unremarkable story told in unoriginal language.

This was something I was only able to articulate later, though. Immediately after I had read the book, I knew only that I didn't like it – and that I didn't dare admit this to anyone. I was still new at the school, and I so badly wanted to fit in; I was afraid they would think I was a show-off because I came from the city. I was prepared to lie and pretend I was mad about the book, just like everyone around me, in the hope that they would accept me.

If I had just kept my mouth shut the incident wouldn't have haunted me for the rest of my life. As an adult you learn to keep quiet sometimes to avoid hurting other people's feelings, after all. These days, if someone gives me a book I really don't like, I prefer to say nothing rather than disappoint the giver.

But for an uncertain teenager in a new environment there was too much at stake.

'It's fabulous!' I said. It's smart, I said. It's sharp, I said. All the words we used back then for things that would these days be described as cool.

I was accepted, in the hostel and at school. On weekends I was invited to the best parties and during the week I could sit with the most appealing groups in the playground. A year later I was 'popular' enough to be chosen as a cheerleader for the school's sports day, a secret desire I hadn't dared share with anyone and which I never expected to be fulfilled because I hadn't been at the school for long enough.

Being a happy and silly cheerleader, spending a whole Saturday leaping around in an ugly red-and-black costume (chosen by the other cheerleader's mother) in front of hundreds of singing, cheering, clapping schoolchildren, made me feel like Janis Joplin at Woodstock.

It was the crown on all my efforts to be 'popular'. It was the reward for all the mediocre little books I'd had to read in the hostel while yearning increasingly for 'real books', while writing poetry I didn't dare tell anyone about, while Shakespeare's words were starting to light the darkness around me like bright shining stars.

From then on, I gave myself permission to cut loose. A few weeks later, at the interschool sports day in Belfast, I was no longer a cheerleader. I wasn't even in the stands. I was behind someone's dad's bakkie getting drunk with a group of the naughtiest kids in the school.

It wasn't as bad as it sounds, my love. Or perhaps it was even worse than it sounds.

We were clever enough, so we thought, to make sure that no-one saw us drinking. There were no cellphones or social media to display our reckless behaviour to the rest of the world. Sure, there were a few rumours at school the following week, whispered speculation about who had been part of the group of sinners, but there was no proof. Everyone involved kept dead quiet, because once we sobered up we fully comprehended how stupid we had been. Not for drinking, because that was something most teenagers did anyway at parties on weekends. But getting drunk at an athletics meeting – in your school uniform – was the kind of transgression that could get you expelled on the spot.

But we weren't hooligans or juvenile delinquents. As far as I know, we all became respectable adults. In fact, the reason I don't mention anyone by name is because some among our little group of underage drinkers have now become respectable grandfathers and grandmothers who may not want their grandchildren to hear about their youthful transgressions.

And for me this experience of drunkenness at sixteen had positive consequences. The nausea from drinking too much was so horrible that I never, ever, wanted to experience it again. It may not have made me a teetotaller, but I became a careful drinker for the rest of my life. Just like three car accidents at the age of sixteen didn't deter me from driving, but made me cautious behind a wheel for the rest of my life. I have never in my adult life been so drunk that I've completely lost control, thrown up, passed out or done anything I couldn't remember the next day.

Except for that one time in my twenties, which I will tell you about one day, my girl.

A few years ago, I was sitting around a lunch table with good friends in a garden in Stellenbosch when your sixteen-year-old brother called me from France to confess that he had got completely drunk at a party the previous night for the first time in his life. And that it was such a horrible experience, Ma, that he never wanted to do it again! So I consoled him with the story of my own drunkenness at the age of sixteen.

My friends were surprised and delighted that a teenage boy would call his mother in another country to tell her about his first awful experience of drunkenness. It made me realise, not for the first time, that despite all the things I may have done wrong as a mother, I seem to have got a few things right.

I do not expect my children to tell me everything. We all need our secret gardens, teenagers even more than the rest of humanity. But I am sincerely grateful every time you or your brothers share something with me that I could never have shared with my own parents.

With you, my girl, there were times in your teenage years when I almost wanted to close my ears. I don't have to know *everything*, I sometimes wanted to exclaim. 'But Ma, you write about teenagers,' you would say. 'You have to know.'

I suppose it's better to hear too much than too little, right?

In my final school year in Nelspruit, I also started to disentangle myself from the ties of the Dutch Reformed Church, which had wound around me quite tightly since my childhood. Not only because my questions about the hypocrisy of many of its members were becoming increasingly urgent. Or because I found it increasingly difficult to reconcile the New Testament message to love thy neighbour with the church's intolerance towards neighbours who weren't white. Maybe more than anything else it was the result of the forced church attendance imposed on us boarders.

Whenever I had to spend weekends in the hostel for a sports meeting or a cultural event, or more often because I had been gated as punishment for some or other sin, I had to go to church twice on a Sunday. The hostel girls had to attend both the morning service and the evening service, in the most uncomfortable clothing imaginable. I had to wear a pure white church dress of synthetic fabric with sleeves and a high neck and a hem that wasn't too high above the knee, along with flesh-toned nylon pantihose and patent leather shoes with heels that weren't too high, just like the hem of the dress.

Pantihose were a severe punishment in the Lowveld summer heat.

Even in winter they often felt uncomfortably hot and sticky. Twice on a Sunday our bunch of girls had to walk to church and back, in neat lines, like the little convent-school girls in Ludwig Bemelmans's *Madeline* books. Of course there were many more of us in Nelspruit than of Madeline and her friends in Paris. (And we were often dripping with sweat and weak from the heat by the time we reached the church, whereas Madeline and her friends always looked immaculate.) Between the morning service and the evening service you were supposed to stay in your prissy white dress and your pantihose and your high-heeled shoes – truly more than flesh and blood could endure.

Enough, at any rate, to make me shy away from any sort of regular church attendance for life. Just as the boys couldn't wait to grow their hair as long as possible the minute they were done with school (before the army got hold of them) and the girls couldn't wait to wear as much make-up as possible, so the rules and regulations regarding Sundays' double dose of enforced church attendance made me yearn to break with the church altogether as soon as I could.

Had I been able to choose whether I wanted to go to church, and above all what I could wear to church, I would likely have gone to at least one service most Sundays. Even if it was only to escape from the hostel for a while and exchange scribbled notes with the hostel boys, who were always seated as far away from the girls as possible, at the opposite end of the church.

But as with so many things in my youth, I was never allowed to choose.

The biggest news story of the year broke late in my matric year, an irresistible concoction of art and politics and espionage, a compelling courtroom drama with an attractive bearded poet and artist as the central character. I knew about Breyten Breytenbach, who had to live in exile in Paris because his Vietnamese wife was not considered white. I knew that he had violated the Immorality Act by falling in love with her. Even back then it barely made sense.

And when I tell you about it now, my darling child, it makes no sense whatsoever.

On 19 August 1975 one of the few Afrikaans poets I truly admired – whose words made me realise that not all Afrikaans poetry was written by dead white men on farms, and often about farms – was arrested and charged with a whole string of crimes. Among others, that he was an active member of the banned ANC, a founding member of other banned organisations, and several more 'acts of terrorism'.

In November, when I was supposed to be studying for my matric exams, I was aware of Breyten Breytenbach's sensational court case in Pretoria, which all the Afrikaans newspapers were covering in detail. Because Nelspruit High didn't offer French as subject, I had been struggling along for two years, entirely on my own, with French as an optional seventh matric subject. It was madness, stubbornness, whatever you want to call it, but I absolutely wanted to learn to speak French. And one of the reasons why I wanted to speak French and hopefully live for a while in Paris one day was that Breytenbach lived in Paris. While continuing to write in Afrikaans.

It was particularly ironic, then, that Breytenbach was found guilty on the day I wrote my French matric exam – and baffling to this day that I passed French with good marks. There were no French-speaking adults in Nelspruit who could help me, but there was a girl in the hostel with me whose father had been a diplomat in France. She was as Afrikaans as I was, but because she had lived in France for a while she could speak French a thousand times better than me. Her name was Carla and she was the only person I could ask when I wasn't sure about the pronunciation of a word –

and I was uncertain about the pronunciation of every single word.

Remember, Mia, there was no internet. Carla was the closest to the internet I could get. I remain convinced to this day that it was thanks to Carla that I passed French as a seventh subject.

Just before Breytenbach was sentenced to nine years' imprisonment, he delivered a moving plea in court. It made a deep impression on me when I read it in the newspaper, and two decades later it yielded the title of that bildungsroman about white teenagers in the seventies who gradually awake from the fool's paradise in which they've been living in such bliss.

'My lord, allow me to end by quoting from a poem,' Pa was still reading enthusiastically, 'wonderful, flaming words which were ignited ages ago but will always remain burning because they come from the depths of a human being's experience and compassion – and therefore they belong to all of us . . .'

Outside, behind the open glass sliding door, the sky was an unnatural blue, like a picture which a child had coloured too brightly. Next to the veranda a bunch of poinsettias hung from a tree like scandalous red underwear on a circular drying line. Further back were the bare trunks of pawpaw trees, the bare branches and the blush-pink flowers of frangipani trees, and the banana plantations shamelessly exposed to the sun. This was a wild, lascivious world, I realised again that morning.

'When I was a child, I spoke as a child, I understood as a child, I thought as a child,' Pa read with a beaming face as if he himself had conjured up the words in a packed court. 'When I became a man, I put away childish things . . .'

In the same week as Breytenbach was sentenced, I received the news that I had won a study bursary to Stellenbosch University with three poems I had written because I had wanted to emulate him.

The other poet who helped shaped my teenage mind, even more than Breyten Breytenbach, was Antjie Krog. Mainly because, just like me at that stage, she had been a schoolgirl in the platteland when her first collection, *Dogter van Jefta*, was published in 1970. Under the direction of an inspired Afrikaans teacher, I delivered an over-the-top eisteddfod performance of the famous 'barefoot poem' that Krog had written for her mother. (As did more than one generation of Afrikaans schoolchildren after me, though hopefully less dramatically.) But it was my first encounter with a poem that was written in the language my teenage friends and I spoke to one another, 'without fancy punctuation' indeed, delightfully unlike the 'heavy dull thud like bullets in mud' conjured up by Jan FE Celliers and all the other dead male poets that were prescribed for us at school.

And once I discovered the other poems in Krog's debut collection, they found their target not with a heavy, dull thud but with the crack of a bull's eye. I realised with amazement that Afrikaans poems didn't have to be written by old men about ox wagons and droughts. That a teenage girl could actually write a verse about how stupid she felt in the maths class, or about breaktime at school (*I look for you among the blue cadets / I look for you in every desk and blazer*) or even about dancing and kissing at a party (*we circle in the dark / in a garage on some street / our school rules and our duty / beneath our dancing feet*).

It was like a shuddering awakening from a deep dream.

It spurred me on to try my own hand at poetry.

Fortunately I never tried to publish my teenage poems, because I was certainly no Antjie (or Breyten). And in my matric year I could never have dreamt that I would meet these heroes in the flesh one day and call them by their first names. But when my sister posted that blue notebook with my handwritten poems to me in France a decade or so ago, I could see that at least not all of it was irredeemably bad.

Most of the poems were like a vaguely recognisable object that a clumsy schoolboy had knocked together in a woodwork class. There were parts that needed smoothing or sanding, and protrusions that ought to be summarily removed, but it could nevertheless be turned into a fairly original little jewellery box.

By way of explanation, my girl, in my school days boys, and only boys, were forced to do woodwork. Girls, and only girls, had to do domestic science. Some of the boys in my class may have fared better at domestic science, and some of the girls would definitely have preferred woodwork. But as I've said, we didn't have many choices.

And I suspect I would have done just as badly at woodwork as at needlework.

My poems needed editing, and because I was hopelessly too uncertain about my poetic ability to show them to anyone, no one could edit them. I would never have dared to exhibit my fragile creations in a school yearbook and risk being mocked by the other children.

That is why everyone, including the Afrikaans teacher and my best friends, was astonished when, during assembly on my last day at school, the principal announced that my poems had won me a very desirable study bursary.

It was certainly a strange confluence of events that lead to this bursary. My last year at school was declared the Afrikaans Centenary Year by political leaders who apparently held the sincere belief that Afrikaans was the white man's language, that the first Afrikaans words had been written down by white people, and that the language 'originated' in 1875 when a small group of men (nearly all of them related) founded the Society of True Afrikaners in the Paarl region.

I would only learn much later that an early version of Afrikaans had been in use since 1815 to replace Malay at Muslim schools in the Cape and that these schools were responsible for the first printed Afrikaans texts – in the Arabic alphabet.

In my youth, however, our national leaders succeeded in marketing Afrikaans as a purely white language – and in the process caused incalculable damage to the reputation of the language among South Africans of other races. A few months after I'd left school and started studying – with my Afrikaans bursary for Afrikaans poems – the policy of compulsory education in Afrikaans, 'the language of the oppressor', lead to the bloody Soweto uprising. The protest movement was begun by black teenagers of my own age, and quickly spread throughout the country.

After 16 June 1976 my white contemporaries and I would never again be able to say that we hadn't known. The Soweto uprising finally tore my eyes open – and made my complex love–hate relationship with my native tongue even more complicated.

Until here in France, at last, when you were already a teenager yourself, I wrote a young-adult novel about a teenage boy who uses spoken word poetry to express his love for his mother tongue. He calls his verse 'My traitor's tongue' and this is how it sounds when he recites it (because remember, spoken word poetry is meant to be heard rather than read):

Oh, mother tongue! Oh, sweetest song ever sung! You think so too?
Well, it's a lie, not one word of that is true, I am telling you
My mother tongue tastes like coffee, bitter and black
It's not white or sweet, it's like my mom, it gives you flack
My mother's tongue's as potent as homebrewed beer
My mother's tongue's as tough as a tsotsi with a sneer
My mother's language is lean and mean, no useless conjugations
I is, you is, he is, they is, we tolerate no complications
If you want to yap in English, it's I am, he is, we are
You have to know the rules, otherwise you won't get very far

My mother's tongue doesn't bother with such rules,
And it has the coolest swear words, some real jewels
It's my mother tongue and it's not as sweet as they say
But I'm no longer gonna pay for it, no bloody way
It's my traitor's tongue with a bitter history
Of apartheid and hate as its legacy
It's my traitor's tongue, my bra, it's a real whore's language
Bastard language, slave language, messed-up kitchen language
Oh, mother tongue! Oh, sweetest song ever sung! That's so lame,
so not true
Oh, traitor's tongue! Oh crudest language! Above all I love you!
That's more like it.

In this book, *All I Know*, I wrote verse for the first time since my youth – and the only reason I had the courage to do it, was that I could do it as a fictional teenage boy. It was a way of returning to my own teenage verse without making a complete fool of myself in the eyes of the poets I admire.

Because after school my veneration for poets kept growing, and the more good poetry I read the less I felt equal to the task of writing poetry myself. That is probably why poetry is the only genre in which I have never even tried to publish. Anything else I tackled in good faith, from children's books to short stories and even food books, from novels to radio dramas and screenplays for movies, but poetry will always remain for me the cherry on the literary cake. The most difficult and most magnificent word craft to master.

Maybe I should be grateful that my irrational fear of dying young drove me to publish my first young-adult novel when I was barely twenty-three. Had I waited until I was wiser, until I had read more novels by great writers, I may never have had the courage to take on a novel myself. The road I walked with poetry may also have become my road with prose.

But I rushed in like a fool where angels feared to tread, too young to know better, too ignorant, really, to be afraid.

I could still stop publishing – authors like JD Salinger have made this stubborn decision and stuck with it – but I will never be able to stop writing. Writing and reading are as necessary to me as eating and sleeping. You know this, my girl, just like your father and your brothers also know it. You don't love me because I write, you love me despite the fact that I cannot stop writing. For that I will always be grateful.

In my matric year the centenary of our 'sweetest language' was celebrated in various ways, such as the inauguration of a language monument in Paarl, where the language had originated according to the national myth. My mother's unforgettable words when she heard about this monument, were: 'So does this mean the language is dead?' Because monuments are built for dead people and things of the past, aren't they?

Perhaps your grandmother's words were prophetic, Mia. In those days Afrikaans was alive and kicking, but forcefully imposing it on so many people may have sealed its fate. Today Afrikaans doesn't look all that healthy, because there isn't a single public Afrikaans university left. And when a language is no longer an academic language, if no dictionaries are being created to disseminate new words, technological words, scientific words, it can get stuck in the past.

And yet.

I cannot predict the future of my beloved language. Yes, these days I can declare unambiguously that Afrikaans is the language of my heart. But this COVID-19 virus that continues to stalk me as I reach the beginning of the end of a very long letter, proves once again that no one can ever really predict the future. Just when we thought we had become so clever that we could control everything, out of the blue all of humanity came under attack from a contagious virus that changed our everyday lives dramatically.

Say what you like, but the future has a way of putting us in our place.

The future will continue to surprise us, of that I am certain.

And who knows, Afrikaans may also have a few surprises up its sleeve.

One day, in the distant future, this letter will perhaps be read as a 'witness document', an affidavit describing someone's hopeless love for a dying language. Or perhaps the language will endure after all, but in a different form, freer than before, so that people will struggle to decipher my words. More or less the way I had to decipher Chaucer's *The Canterbury Tales* at university. Perhaps my words will be regarded as an archaic form of the only African language that aspired to being white, but for obvious reasons couldn't manage it.

In the meantime, I continue to write and speak and live in Afrikaans, at least some of the time. Because although 'the future' surprised me two decades ago by washing me ashore in France, and although these days I speak three languages every day, Afrikaans remains the one I speak the best. And because as a mother I believe that I should give my children the best, I still speak to you in Afrikaans. Even though you often answer me in a different language.

But let us return to my final school year one last time, my dearest girl. One of the ways in which the Afrikaans Centenary was celebrated was through a countrywide poetry contest for matric pupils in which the first prize was a generous bursary for at least three years of study at the university of your choice. The only condition was that you had to take Afrikaans as a major – which I was planning to do anyway, my head brimming with dreams of writing. And when I'd obtained my BA degree in Afrikaans, English and French, the bursary was extended for a fourth year so I could do an honours degree in journalism.

The most surprising fact about this bursary was that the sponsor was not, as one might expect, an important Afrikaans firm, a large publisher or a newspaper group. The Afrikaans poetry contest was sponsored by an English–Jewish enterprise named Simon Wainstein and Company, manufacturers of Tastic Rice. It's not to 'my people', then, that I owe my first two university degrees and perhaps my whole writing career, but to my Jewish compatriots. And to rice.

Strange but true.

Because I had no idea how badly I would need this bursary when I wrote those three little poems. Remember, in matric I believed that my father was quite rich. We owned a banana farm and he'd bought himself a brand-new red Mercedes. (Driving that fancy car was out of the question for me. Pa wrote it off on a mountain pass without any help from me. We really had no luck with cars while we were living on our farm in Africa.) All I wanted was a Plan B for my university studies, just in case Pa's finances collapsed again, like when we'd had to move to the Transvaal at the end of 1969. But I really didn't think my poetry would be good enough to earn me a bursary.

And then the worst happened – and the best – more or less simultaneously, and forgive me if I sound like Dickens now. But I sometimes think the opening sentence of *A Tale of Two Cities* is wholly applicable to my two years in the Lowveld:

It was the best of times, it was the worst of times, it was the age of wisdom, it was the age of foolishness, it was the epoch of belief, it was the epoch of incredulity, it was the season of light, it was the season of darkness, it was the spring of hope, it was the winter of despair.

The best was that I won the poetry contest, completely unexpectedly, and the Stellenbosch bursary. The worst was that my father went bankrupt soon after my matric exam and lost the farm.

No, even better than the best was that one of the Stellenbosch judges of my poetry efforts was none other than DJ Opperman. The very same poet I used to spy on through the milkwood trees in Franskraal, the first writer I ever saw in the flesh. And then, in my third year at Stellenbosch, I found myself in his sought-after Literary Laboratory, which was considered an incubator for many Afrikaans poets. Where I had more than enough time to watch him closely and listen carefully when he spoke.

It was another opportunity to connect the dots in my life, to draw a line between apparent coincidences until it formed a lop-sided circle.

Because I can build a story from every lopsided circle.

Had I not shut my eyes and jumped off a cliff at the age of seventeen – that was what it felt like, submitting three little poems in a contest I thought I hadn't the slightest chance of winning – I would not have been able to go to university the year after matric.

By now, my darling girl, you know the story about Mister Thought, who planted a feather, almost as well as your mother does. What I haven't told you yet is that sometimes, just sometimes, the feather *does* grow into a chicken, don't ask me how.

Those three little poems that won me a bursary became the first time I saved my own life by writing. It was certainly not the last time.

It was the end of the beginning of the rest of my life.

And now I am going to astonish you, Princess Patat, and let you read one of my teenage verses. Let us call it a parting gift, because we have reached the end of this letter. It is a poem I have never shown anyone else. It has been buried in the pages of that old blue Transvaal Education Department school notebook for almost half a century. It makes me feel like an Egyptologist fetching a mummy from deep inside a dark pyramid, bringing it up and taking it outside for the first time in thousands of years.

Please remember that these are the unedited words of a schoolchild from long ago. Its spontaneity and intensity of feeling, I hope, make up for where it's lacking in discipline and refinement. I will never be able to feel as intensely about anything again as I did in my final year at school when I wrote these words.

'Pardon me, sir?
What do I want to be one day, sir?'

I would love to be
a blue-bearded tramp
so I can see, sir

and a violinist's violin
so I can feel, sir

and a soldier on a battlefield
so I can smell, sir

and a prostitute so I can
spit out the sweet and
taste the bitter, sir

and a blind beggar
shaking an empty tin
so I can hear, sir

and a coloured in a park
on a whites-only bench
so I can know, sir

I long to be
someone who really knows
how to be, sir.

'*Guess I will see, sir.*
First finish studying, sir.'

I still recognise that teenage girl's desperate desire to know what to become and how to live, because I am still she.

Or in the words of one of my writing peers, Ryk Hattingh, when – shortly before his death – he came back to South Africa for the first time in many years: 'I have always been here. Only here.'

I have only ever been here, my darling daughter, inside this body, inside this head, where I have lived, now, for more than sixty years. And in my heart I will probably always feel seventeen, as if it is still the morning of my life.

This is what I wish for you in closing. That you, like Bob Dylan sang, will stay forever young, no matter how old you become. Because youth has nothing to do with what you look like, it is simply the power to keep dreaming. And as I contemplated early on in this letter, perhaps all courage and daring begin with the very impossibilities we dream about.

Love
Ma(rita) – as I have always called myself on the postcards I send you from faraway places, because I am your mother, but I am still Marita van der Vyver.

France, August 2020

REFERENCES AND ACKNOWLEDGEMENTS

It would be impractical to include every book mentioned in the text in this list. The books below are therefore those from which quotations have been drawn in the text or which had a defining influence on my life as a writer. In addition, I wish to acknowledge the publications *Vrye Weekblad, Taalgenoot* and *Vrouekeur*, because some paragraphs in the text are borrowed from columns or articles I wrote for them.

Albertyn, CF & Spies, JJ (eds.). 1964. *Kinders van die wêreld,* South Africa: Albertyn Publishers.

Atwood, M. 2017. *The Handmaid's Tale.* London: Vintage (first published in 1985).

Barnes, J. 2019. *The Man in the Red Coat.* London: Jonathan Cape.

Berger, J. 1972. *Ways of Seeing.* London: Penguin Books.

Beukes, D. 1954. *Gebarste mure.* Pretoria: Voortrekker Press.

Blakemore, S. 2004. *Die meisies van Maasdorp.* Cape Town: Human & Rousseau (first published in 1932).

Blignault, A. 1969. *Die verlange loop ver.* Cape Town: Nasionale Boekhandel.

Blixen, K. 1989. *Out of Africa*. London: Penguin Books (first published in England and Denmark in 1937).

Bouwer, A. 1955. *Stories van Rivierplaas*. Cape Town: Nasionale Boekhandel.

Breytenbach, B. 1969. *Kouevuur*. South Africa: Van Buren Publishers.

Brink, AP (translator). 1968. *Alice deur die spieël* (Lewis Carroll). Cape Town: Human & Rousseau.

Brink, AP. 1985. *The Ambassador*. London: Faber & Faber (originally published in Afrikaans in 1963).

Brink, AP. 1974. *Looking on Darkness*. London: W.H. Allen & Co.

Burgess, A. 1988. *Little Wilson and Big God*. London: Penguin Books.

Camus, A. 1971. *The Outsider*. London: Penguin Modern Classics (originally published in French as *L'Étranger* in 1942).

Carroll, L. 2012. *Alice's Adventures in Wonderland*. London: Penguin Classics (first published in 1865).

Chekhov, A. 2004. In R. Bartlett (ed.). *A Life in Letters*. London: Penguin Books.

Choderlos de Laclos, P. 1975. *Les liaisons dangereuses*. Paris: Le Livre de Poche (first published in 1782).

Coetzee, A. 2019. *In my vel*. Cape Town: Tafelberg.

Coetzee, JM. 1981. *Waiting for the Barbarians*. Johannesburg: Ravan Press (first published in Britain in 1980).

Conrad, J. 1973. *Heart of Darkness*. London: Penguin Classics (first published in 1902).

De Beauvoir, S. 1979. *The Second Sex*. London: Penguin Books (originally published in French as *Le deuxième sexe* in 1949).

Dickens, C. 1985. *A Tale of Two Cities*. London: Penguin Classics (first published in 1859).

Dostoyevsky, F. 1971. *Crime and Punishment*. London: Penguin Classics (originally published in Russian in 1866).

Elkin, L. 2017. *Flâneuse: Women Walk the City in Paris, New York, Tokyo, Venice and London*. London: Vintage.

Fairweather, M. 2006. *Madame de Staël*. London: Constable & Robinson.

Flaubert, G. 1972. *Madame Bovary*. Paris: Le Livre de Poche (first published in 1856).

Gay, R. 2014. *Bad Feminist*. New York, NY: Harper Perennial.

Glendinning, V. 1988. *Rebecca West: A Life*. New York: Macmillan.

Goosen, J. 2007. *We're Not All Like That*. Cape Town: Kwela (originally published in Afrikaans in 1990).

Greene, G. 1962. *The Lost Childhood and Other Essays*. London: Penguin Books (first published in 1951).

Hattingh, R. 2016. *Huilboek*. Cape Town: Human & Rousseau.

Hawthorne, N. 1970. *The Scarlet Letter and Selected Tales*. London: Penguin Classics (first published in 1850).

Head, B. 1990. In C. MacKenzie (ed.). *A Woman Alone: Autobiographical Writings*. London: Heinemann.

Ibsen, H. 1990. *Hedda Gabler*. Mineola, NY: Dover Thrift Editions (originally published in Denmark in 1890).

Irving, J. 1982. *The World According to Garp*. London: Corgi (first published in the USA in 1978).

Jansen, E. 2019. *Like Family: Domestic Workers in South African History and Literature*. Johannesburg: Wits University Press (originally published in Afrikaans in 2015).

Joseph, J. 1992. *Selected Poems*. London: Bloodaxe Books.

Joyce, J. 2000. *A Portrait of the Artist as a Young Man*. London: Penguin Classics (first published in Ireland in 1916).

Kalmer, H. 1989. *Die waarheid en ander stories*. Johannesburg: Taurus.

Krige, U. 1960. *Ballade van die groot begeer*. Cape Town: A.A. Balkema.

Krog, A. 1970. *Dogter van Jefta*. Cape Town: Human & Rousseau.

Kühne, WO. 1958. *Huppelkind*. Cape Town: Tafelberg.

Larkin, P. 1974. *High Windows*. London: Faber & Faber.

Lefteri, C. 2010. *A Watermelon, a Fish and a Bible*. London: Quercus Books.

Levy, D. 2019. *Swallowing Geography*. London: Penguin Books (first published in 1993).

Levy, D. 2018. *Things I Don't Want to Know*. London: Penguin Books (first published in 2013).

Matthee, D. 2012. *Pieternella, Daughter of Eva*. Cape Town: Penguin Random House (originally published in Afrikaans in 2000).

Montgomery, LM. 1937. *Jane of Lantern Hill*. Toronto: McClelland & Stewart.

Nabokov, V. 2000. *Lolita*. London: Penguin Classics (first published in France in 1955).

Nabokov, V. 1989. In D. Nabokov & MJ Bruccoli (eds.). *Selected Letters*. San Diego, CA: Harcourt Brace Jovanovich.

Odendaal, P. 2018. *Asof geen berge ooit hier gewoon het*. Cape Town: Tafelberg.

Pistorius, M. 2012. *Fatal Females: Women Who Kill*. Johannesburg: Penguin Books.

Roth, P. 2016. *The Facts: A Novelist's Autobiography*. London: Vintage (first published in the USA in 1988).

Salter, J. 2007. *Light Years*. London: Penguin Books (first published in the USA in 1975).

Shakespeare, W. 1993. *The Complete Works*. London: Ramboro Books.

Smith, A. 2016. *Public Library and Other Stories*. London: Penguin Books.

Smith, S. 1957. *Not Waving but Drowning*. London: André Deutsch.

Sontag, S. 2003. *Where the Stress Falls*. London: Vintage.

Sontag, S. 2001. *Against Interpretation*. London: Picador (first published in 1966).

Spence, E. 1956. *Goudgeel kappertjies*. Pretoria: Die Keurbiblioteek.

Spender, D. (ed.). 1983. *Feminist Theorists: Three Centuries of Women's Intellectual Traditions*. London: The Women's Press.

Steinem, G. 1985. *Outrageous Acts and Everyday Rebellions*. London: Flamingo (first published in the USA in 1983).

Sterne, L. 1967. *The Life and Opinions of Tristram Shandy, Gentleman*. London: Penguin Classics (first published in 1759).

Thompson, K. 1955. *Eloise: A Book for Precocious Grown-ups*. New York, NY: Simon & Schuster.

Tolkien, JRR. 2012. *The Lord of the Rings*. Boston, MA: Mariner Books (first published in Britain in 1954).

Van der Vyver, M. 1994. *Entertaining Angels*. London: Michael Joseph (first published in Afrikaans in 1992).

Van der Vyver, M. 1996. *Childish Things*. London: Michael Joseph (first published in Afrikaans in 1994).

Van der Vyver, M. 2005. *Short Circuits*. Cape Town: Tafelberg.

Van der Vyver, M. 2007. *There is a Season*. Cape Town: Double Storey (first published in Afrikaans in 2003).

Van der Vyver, M. 2008. *Franse briewe: Pos uit Provence*. Cape Town: Tafelberg.

Van der Vyver, M. 2010. *Just Dessert, Dear*. Cape Town: Tafelberg.

Van der Vyver, M. 2012. *Forget-me-not Blues*. Cape Town: Tafelberg.

Van der Vyver, M. 2015. *Swemlesse vir 'n meermin*. Cape Town: Tafelberg.

Van der Vyver, M. 2017. *You Lost Me*. Johannesburg: Penguin Random House.

Van der Vyver, M. 2018. *Retoer: Pretoria – Provence*. Pretoria: Lapa.

Van der Vyver, M. 2019. *All I Know*. Pretoria: Lapa (first published in Afrikaans in 2016)

Van der Vyver, M. 2019. *Borderline*. Johannesburg: Penguin Random House.

Van Melle, J. 1962. *Bart Nel*. Pretoria: Van Schaik (originally published in Dutch as *Bart Nel, de opstandeling* in 1936).

Welty, E. 2001. *One Writer's Beginnings*. New York, NY: Warner Books (first published in 1984).

Wolfe, T. 1989. *You Can't Go Home Again*. New York, NY: Harper Perennial (first published in 1940).

Woolf, V. 1953. In L. Woolf (ed.). *A Writer's Diary*. London: The Hogarth Press.

Woolf, V. 1945. *A Room of One's Own*. London: Penguin Books (first published in 1928).

Yourcenar, M. 1951. *Mémoires d'Hadrien*. Paris: Plon.